D1171031

helping
children
overcome
learning
difficulties

helping
children
overcome
learning
difficulties

A STEP-BY-STEP GUIDE FOR PARENTS AND TEACHERS

JEROME ROSNER

WALKER AND COMPANY • NEW YORK

XAVIER UNIVERSITY LIBRARY
NEW ORLEANS. LA. 70125

Copyright © 1975 by Jerome Rosner

All rights reserved.
No part of this book may be reproduced
or transmitted in any form or by any means,
electronic or mechanical, including photocopying,
recording, or by any information storage
and retrieval system, without permission
in writing from the Publisher.

First published in the United States of America
in 1975 by the Walker Publishing Company, Inc.

Published simultaneously in Canada
by Fitzhenry & Whiteside, Limited, Toronto.

ISBN: 0-8027-0462-x

Library of Congress Catalog Card Number: 74-16083

Printed in the United States of America.

10 9 8 7 6 5 4 3 2 1

371.9
R822L

CONTENTS

CONTENTS

CONTENTS

helping
children
overcome
learning
difficulties

ACKNOWLEDGMENTS

HOW CAN YOU thank everyone who has influenced your professional thinking over the course of thirty years? Obviously, you cannot. I know that I will omit some names that should not be omitted—not because I do not recognize their contribution to this book, but simply because of the fallibility of human memory and the practical limitations of space. I apologize to them in advance.

In addition, all of the thousands of children, and parents, and teachers I have worked with merit a "thank you" from me. I am grateful to them even though I do not list their names.

Specifically, major recognition must go to the staff at Pace School—to Emy Lou Lower, its co-founder and first Academic Director, now retired, and to Eugenia Donatelli, Pace's current head. Most of the suggested activities described in the last half of this book are standard procedures at Pace. In addition, special thanks is given to my various colleagues at the University of Pittsburgh—to Joanne Cass, Jim DiCostanzo, Terry Dombrowicki, Billie Slaughter, Larry Vaughan, and Phyllis Weaver, all of whom work with me daily on various aspects of my research; to John Bolvin, Bill Cooley, Bob Glaser, and Lauren Resnick, all of whom have helped me administratively as well as intellectually; to Dorothy Walsh and Ruth Stone at Oakleaf School, who provided both practical guidance and needed encouragement; to Karen Block and her research assistant, Dorothea

Simon, whose ideas about spelling have had a mighty influence on mine; to Bernard Mallinger, my optometric associate, who provided many practical suggestions; and to countless others who should be mentioned but are not.

Finally, much more than tradition leads me to thank my wife, Florence, and my two daughters, Carolyn and Joyce, for their substantive contributions to this book, as well as for their support. Many of the ideas proposed in this book are the outcome of family discussions, and the shapes of those ideas reflect their thinking as well as my own.

PREFACE

A SURPRISINGLY LARGE number of children have difficulty in school. Some have trouble in one subject area only—reading or arithmetic, for example. Others have trouble in more than one subject area. Their learning problems are often hard to explain. They appear to be sufficiently intelligent and motivated, yet they do not seem to be able to catch on.

Many of these children have perceptual problems—a term I will define fully later on. In simple language, it means that they are not as capable as they should be in analyzing and organizing some of the details of what they see and what they hear in various instructional situations.

This book is concerned with ways to help those children. Although it is addressed to their parents, I hope that it will also be read by their teachers and all the other professionals who treat them because of their learning problems: psychologists, optometrists, physicians.

I started working with such children more than twenty-five years ago. Many were referred to me, a practicing optometrist, because they did such things as confuse *b* and *d*, and read *was* for *saw*. In some cases, my efforts seemed to help; in others, they did not, and for a long time I could not explain why. But I was not the only one who was stumped in those early days. Just about everyone was groping for answers.

In 1961, in search of those answers, I enrolled in an external studies program conducted at the Gesell Institute of Child Development, entitled "Vision—The School-Aged Child." The experience had significant impact on my professional development. Not that my questions were answered—they were not. But, it did help me start to formulate my questions a little better. And even more important, it helped me recognize the obvious: that a child is more than the sum of his parts; that it is not sufficient to examine one aspect of his make-up—vision, for example—and ignore the rest of him. This was made particularly apparent as I watched Dr. Frances Ilg evaluate children and discuss with us the outcomes of those evaluations from a frame of reference that reflected her broad knowledge of child development and her deep understanding of the child as a totality—a person.

Around that same time I met a teacher who was really worthy of the designation *teacher*—Emy Lou Lower. Mrs. Lower was teaching a Special Education Class—"educable mentally retarded," in school jargon—in the Oakmont, Pennsylvania, school system. I was conducting my practice in the same small community. We worked together on many children, and I started to get a real sense of what teaching is about when it is done as it should be. Emy Lou Lower is the kind of teacher all children should have. She is intelligent, motivated, and understanding. She accepts the responsibilities of being a teacher as a professional should. Her students do not fail; if they do not learn, she sees it as her failure for not being able to find a better way to teach them.

During the mid-1960s, I started more and more to shift my place of work to school buildings, working first with the Oakmont public schools and later with the Pittsburgh schools. In this latter situation, I worked in the Mental Health Services Division, focusing primarily on the learning problems of emotionally disturbed children.

All the while, I continued to maintain a private practice, although a greatly reduced one. Working with the same type of child in both places—office and school—was enlightening. It takes a long time to help some children, and longer still when you have to coordinate your efforts closely with others who have daily contact with those children—particularly their teachers. It became apparent to me that much of what I was doing could and should be done at home and in school; that the solution lay in moving my work out of the doctor's office and into the domain of education—making it available and understandable to teachers and parents, so that direct and immediate impact on the children could be accomplished effectively and inexpensively.

In 1968, a group of us—Mrs. Lower, Dr. Harvey Lacey (a clinical psychologist then working at the University of Pittsburgh), and I, in conjunction with a few other professionals and some interested and committed parents—founded Pace School, a private school that was intended to provide for these children what the public schools seemed unable to provide at that time: effective instruction in how to read, write, spell, and calculate.

Our goal was to teach them, not cure them. The school has thrived, thanks to the dedication of its staff, board, and the community at large. It has helped many children and, perhaps even more important, its staff has helped some public schools initiate similar programs of their own. I do not work at Pace any longer, but I continue to be a member of its Board of Directors and an active participant in many of the research efforts that are conducted there.

About the same time that Pace was founded, the Learning Research and Development Center (LRDC) at the University of Pittsburgh started to develop a program for preschool children. The Center invited me to participate as a consultant. About a year later I accepted a full-time appointment as a Research Associate in LRDC and a faculty member in the School of Education.

I welcomed the opportunity. As a faculty member I could influence future teachers. As a researcher, I would be able

to test out many of the clinical ideas I had been using, de,
termine which were truly important, which were superflu,
ous, and why.

My research group, called the Perceptual Skills Project,
had four goals:

- 1. Identify the perceptual skills that are closely related to
  school achievement.
- 2. Determine whether these skills can be taught and, if
  so, how.
- 3. Determine whether learning these skills affects children's schoolwork—their ability to learn.
- 4. If the first three goals are achieved, design a curriculum to teach these skills; a curriculum that can be used
  by a typical teacher in a regular everyday classroom.

All four goals were accomplished. The Perceptual Skills
Curriculum was published during the summer of 1973 and
is now being used in more than 2,000 schools throughout the
country.

But there are still unsolved problems. What about the
child who is now in school and experiencing significant
learning difficulties; the child who does not have adequate
basic skills, either because he was not exposed to the Perceptual Skills Curriculum or because, for some reason, the
Curriculum was not completely effective with him.

This child *can* be helped. Stated too simply, perhaps,
there must be a change in the way he is taught. We must
find out his strengths and weaknesses—the skills he has
and the skills he lacks—and then relate these to his daily
learning activities so that he can start to succeed rather
than flounder in school.

I have been working on this problem since my days of
private practice. Despite its importance, I know of no adequate single written source on the topic—nothing that provides adequate direction for a teacher when he or she is
confronted with a child who requires this kind of assistance.

Hence this book—but with one modification. I address it

to parents rather than teachers. Not because I think parents are better suited to do the job, but rather because I know that in most instances, parents have more time to spend with their child than does his teacher, and a stronger reason for doing so.

I do not underestimate the importance of good teachers and what they can accomplish. On the contrary, I value them greatly. When there are enough of them, and when school administrators and school boards finally recognize that some children need not only good teachers but also small classes and individualized instruction, then there will be no need for parents to supplement teachers. Until that time, however, the parent's participation is essential.

This book is meant to be a practical resource. It tells, in some detail, what to do and when to do it. I have not tried to answer the question, "What's wrong with my child?" Rather, I have dealt with the question, "What can I do to help my child do better in school?"

I have included some theory about *why* my suggestions are designed as they are. I have done this for two reasons. First, it will help parents use the procedures more effectively and adapt my ideas to their child's specific needs, rather than blindly following an inflexible formula. Second, I *do* hope to influence teachers; to show them how they can recognize and respond to the unique characteristics of all their students, and do so in their own classroom—with the help of their students' parents.

I do not have all the answers. But what I present is not based on speculation. Everything I suggest has been tried in Pace School and elsewhere, and shown to be effective.

Too many parents and teachers have been convinced that children with severe learning difficulties cannot be helped; that they must accept their fate and learn to cope with it. That is not correct. These children can be helped—they can learn. *But they surely must be taught.*

7

INTRODUCTION

"YOUR CHILD is not making satisfactory progress in school. He may have a learning disability." Many parents have heard this crushing statement and gone off in search of help. Anywhere. From anyone who appeared to have something to offer.

All too often their efforts led to nothing but frustration and anxiety. Their questions were answered in obscure, technical-sounding language—if answered at all. They talked to teachers, principals, psychologists, doctors; sat in countless waiting rooms; paid lots of bills for lots of tests; and ended up knowing no more about their child's learning difficulties, and how to help him, than they knew when they started out. And their child continued to struggle with his problem!

Sometimes it was called something different. *Dyslexia.* "What is that? Is it worse than having a learning disability?" Sometimes they were told that a series of treatments were necessary: vitamin therapy; eye training; motor training. Costly. Time consuming. "But what difference does that make, if it will help?" And the treatments often did help—at least they helped in terms of what they were designed to treat. The trouble was that the treatments were generally for some supposed cause of the learning problem rather than the learning problem itself. And somehow, even though the treatments seemed to have a beneficial effect on the designated cause, the learning problem persisted. Another case, figuratively, of "the operation was a success, but the patient died." Literally, of course, the patient did not die; he merely continued to fail in school.

Other times there were only opinions, no treatments. But even these differed widely, ranging from "Stop being an overanxious parent; there's nothing wrong with the child," to "Give him time; he's young; he'll grow out of it," to "You had better accept the fact that he's never going to be much of a learner; some children just aren't."

The result of all this? A pair of confused, unhappy parents who never expected their child to have trouble in school. "He always seemed bright and interested in everything around him. Oh, he may not have had the patience to sit in one place for very long, but there is no doubt that he is capable of learning. Just listen to the conversations he has with his friends and family. We didn't think he had a problem until he entered school and was expected to learn to read, and write, and do arithmetic. That is when this problem showed up."

This is the kind of child we will be talking about; the child who is able to communicate intelligently with his friends and family, but becomes confused when he has to deal with the symbols of the classroom—letters and numerals—and use them as a code in reading, arithmetic, spelling, and writing.

Why this book is for parents

The purpose of this book is to help the parents of children with learning problems by laying out a practical and effective plan of action; a plan that they can follow, step-by-step, in making decisions about what should be done, when it should be done, and who should do it. I offer no magic cures nor simple solutions. But the situation is far from hopeless.

Approximately three hours of a child's school day in the primary grades is assigned to instruction in the basic skills —reading, writing, spelling, and arithmetic. If your child's class consists of twenty-five children, it means that, on the average, his teacher can give each student approximately seven minutes of individual attention—that is, if no time at all is spent on group instruction. However, practically all teachers teach to groups; individualized instruction of any kind is still a rarity in our schools. As such, she* has even less than seven minutes per day for each child. Of course, children are supposed to learn from group instruction—and they do. At least, most do. Unfortunately, the child we are talking about does not. He needs something different.

Now, how about your (the parent's) time? It is a rare parent who cannot find at least thirty minutes a day to work with his or her child individually. By spending that thirty minutes each day with your child, you give him more than six or seven times the individual attention he can get from his teacher in a regular classroom. It is bound to be helpful, if you do the right things at the right times.

This does not mean that you will take over his teacher's role. Your program is not going to replace hers. Rather, it will supplement her program, but not in the usual way— not by helping the child with his homework.

You will work toward two goals: first to improve the child's basic abilities to learn from regular classroom instruction. These are the skills that underlie learning—"how to" skills, not facts. You will teach him how to analyze, organize, and associate information more efficiently than he does now.

Your second goal is to help the child learn better in reading, arithmetic, spelling, and handwriting by modifying his lessons in a way that takes into account his basic abilities— the strengths and weaknesses of his "how to" skills.

The two goals are obviously interrelated. The first aims at changing him by improving his learning skills. The sec-

---

*At the risk of being marked a "sexist," I will consistently refer to the teacher as "her" and to the child as "he." I do not mean to offend anyone—neither the male teacher nor the liberated female. I do it for practical reasons; it is simpler than using "(s)he" or any of the other devices that attempt to merge the two sexes into a single word.

ond focuses on changing his lessons in recognition of the fact that his skills are not yet adequate. If you achieve either goal, he will do better in school. If you achieve both, he will do *much* better in school.

Working with the teacher

Will his teacher be annoyed that you are getting into the act? No, certainly not most, at any rate. She, too, is concerned about "her children"; she welcomes any help she can get. And, if you fill your role properly, you will be helping in a way that does not interfere at all with her day-to-day teaching efforts.

This book will not make you into a teacher. It concentrates exclusively on skills—basic abilities that some children (good learners) have and other children (poor learners) do not have. What these skills are, why they are important, and how to teach them, is discussed in nonprofessional terms; language that the parent without a degree in education can understand. As such, I may be criticized for oversimplifying a complicated subject. I would accept that criticism, but I would not agree that it is a fault. The procedures will be no less effective because they are described in everyday language. But, on the other hand, it should not be assumed that this is all there is to being a teacher. Teaching is complex; both a science and an art. It cannot be reduced to a collection of procedures in a book.

What is a learning disability?

There are many official definitions (I will cite some shortly), but in practice the term is used to describe any child who does not make normal progress in school, even though he appears to be sufficiently intelligent and properly motivated. He may have trouble in one subject, or in more than one; his problem may be in reading, or in arithmetic, or in both. He is distinguished from the "slow" child by his apparent ability to learn outside the classroom; away from information that is represented by symbols. The slow child, in contrast, is slow outside the classroom as well as in.

Is the term *minimal brain dysfunction* something different from a learning disability? Generally speaking, no. In 1966 the United States Department of Health, Education and Welfare organized a task force to investigate this newly recognized and widespread problem. In their first report,* they listed well over twenty different labels that could be applied. These included (along with *learning disability, minimal brain dysfunction,* and *dyslexia*), *educationally handicapped; educationally maladjusted; special learning disorder; emotionally handicapped; educationally maladjusted; special learning disorder; socially and emotionally maladjusted; neurologically handicapped; perceptually handicapped; extreme language disorder; specific language disability.* (Formidable! Enough to strike terror into the heart of any parent.)

Why so many different names? There are perhaps two reasons.

First, many different professionals from different disciplines seemed to recognize this pervasive problem at about the same time. If they were in education, they favored an educational label, such as learning disability. If they were in the health professions, their inclination was to use a medical-sounding term, such as neurologically handicapped.

Second (and this is not the case in every school, but it is certainly true in some), high-sounding labels are comforting to some educators because they provide an excuse to the educator for not succeeding at a primary responsibility: teaching children. I have heard more than one educator assert: "How can I teach this child? He's neurologically handicapped!" Once that attitude is taken, little teaching is likely to take place.

---

*Clements, S.D. "Minimal brain dysfunction in children; terminology and identification," Washington, D.C.: U.S. Department of Health, Education and Welfare, 1966. (NINDB Monograph No. 3)

Official definitions

Along with the variety of official labels, a number of official definitions have been proposed over the past ten years. One states: "A child with learning disabilities is one with adequate mental ability, sensory processes, and emotional stability, who has specific deficits in perceptual, integrative, or expressive processes which severely impair learning efficiency. This includes children who have central nervous system dysfunction which is expressed primarily in impaired learning efficiency."*

Here is another one: "A learning disability refers to a specific retardation or disorder in one or more of the processes of speech, language, perception, behavior, reading, spelling, writing or arithmetic."** Try one more; this one from the United States task force itself: "Children with learning disabilities are those (1) who have educationally significant discrepancies among their sensory-motor, perceptual, cognitive, academic, or related developmental levels which interfere with the performance of educational tasks; (2) who may or may not show demonstrable deviation in central nervous system functioning; and (3) whose disabilities are not secondary to general mental retardation, sensory deprivation or serious emotional disturbance."†

Although these definitions differ, they all seem to agree on the basic point I mentioned earlier—that the term *"learning disability," or any of its counterparts, applies to those children whose poor achievement record in school cannot be explained in terms of impaired intelligence, emo-*

---

*Barsch, R. "Working definition," Council for Exceptional Children, Division for Children with Learning Disabilities.

**Kirk, S.A. "The ITPA: Its origins and applications, in Hellmuthm J (ED.)." *Learning Disorders*, Vol. III, Seattle, Washington, Special Child Publications, 1967.

†Haring, N.G. & Bateman, B.D. "Minimal Brain dysfunction in children, Phase II," Washington, D.C.: U.S. Department of Health, Education and Welfare, 1969 (NESDCP Monograph).

*tional disturbance, or lack of motivation.** The key phrase in that sentence is "cannot be explained," an important thing to remember when we consider what tests should be given and how to interpret their results.

Signs of a learning disability

How can you tell if your child has a learning disorder? A number of characteristics have been linked with the condition. These include inattentiveness, confused hand dominance, printing letters backward, reading certain words in reverse, poor handwriting, and general awkwardness. The list could be extended, but I question the value of doing that since so many of these characteristics can also be found among children who are *not* failing in school. At the risk of seeming facetious, which is not my intent, the most reliable sign of a learning disability is the child's unsatisfactory, and unexpected, school record—the learning problem itself. Why look for circumstantial evidence when the hard facts are so very apparent.**

A psychological problem, a medical problem, or an educational problem?

Should a learning disorder be seen as a psychological or a medical problem that, in turn, causes an educational problem? Or should it be thought of as primarily an educational problem?

A little history would be helpful here. During the 1950s, educators and parents started to place great emphasis on children's academic achievement, even in the very early grades. It soon became apparent that a significant percent-

---

*This is the working definition I will use in this book. In addition, I will use the terms "learning disability," "learning difficulty," "learning problem," and "learning disorder," interchangeably. The same definition fits them all.

**Signs that can be seen *before* the child starts school are worth noting. These are discussed in the final section of this book: PREVENTION.

age of students were not learning as well as would normally be expected.*

EMOTIONALLY DISTURBED?

For a while, most learning difficulties were attributed to "emotional blocks" and with good reason. Most children with learning problems do show signs of emotional disturbance. But then, how long would you remain calm if, no matter how hard you tried, you continued to fail daily in your job and, on top of that, had your failure widely advertised? You would be very upset! You would quit—if, indeed, you were not fired first! Children cannot quit elementary school—at least, not literally. And they do not get fired. They merely get shamed in public, as their failure is made known to their classmates and their parents. Then we urge them to try again and to try harder, and to stop being so lazy.

Only a fool would simulate the behavior of a squirrel in a wheel cage for very long. It should come as no surprise, therefore, when this child starts to act up during class. He is upset and angry! But unfortunately, this disruptive behavior—though understandable—in combination with his unsatisfactory achievement record, is bound to annoy his teacher. She punishes him and that only makes him angrier. His behavior deteriorates further and, ultimately, there he is—another child who cannot meet the standards of the classroom, becomes frustrated, misbehaves, forces his teacher to a negative conclusion about his long-term prospects as a student, and—in a sense—he *is* fired: he is referred to someone. During the late 1950s and early 1960s this "someone" was most likely to be a psychologist, or a counselor, or a psychiatrist.

Although there certainly are some successful psychotherapy cases around, the results of this approach were gen-

---

*There is no reason to believe that the learning disability is a new phenomenon. It has probably always been with us and it is certainly not limited to the United States. Mass education, widespread testing, and, above all, close monitoring of student learning from kindergarten on, have made us more aware. What, at one time, did not cause concern became a national issue, practically overnight!

16

erally disappointing in terms of effects on the child's classroom performance. Worse yet, with each step of this referral process, the child was removed further from the one place, and the one person, where he could be helped more directly—his classroom and his teacher.

BRAIN-INJURED?

In time, the emphasis on emotional blocks started to diminish. Professionals began to talk more about the fact that many of these children showed characteristics very similar to those commonly found among individuals with some central nervous system problem. They were distractible, hyperactive, confused by symbols. Perhaps here was the real cause—the place to look for answers? *Brain-injured* became the popular term and with it, more confusion.

DYSLEXIA?

The term *dyslexia* is a good case in point. At one time that term had a specific meaning. It described a condition where a person literally could not read, and where the cause of the impairment could be traced directly to a damaged brain; the outcome of a penetrating wound, a blow to the head, or a stroke that affected a specific site in the brain. Today, however, the term has no precise meaning. It no longer refers to a specific condition with a clearly identifiable cause. Many people now use the term *dyslexia* simply as a synonym for a reading problem, regardless of the cause or severity of the problem. There is nothing wrong with that; word meanings often change over time. The trouble arises when the two meanings are confused; when, by using the term to describe a reading problem, the impression is given that the child is, in fact, brain-injured.

HYPERACTIVE? DISTRACTIBLE?

With the brain-injured notion in mind, the child's distractibility and hyperactivity were, for a while, seen as possible causes of learning problems—the thing to work on. "After all," it was reasoned, "how is the child going to learn when he can't sit still long enough to find out what his teacher is saying and doing?" The idea sounded reasonable. Many classrooms were converted into monochromatic cells —gray ceilings, gray walls, gray floors. In some places even the windows were painted over with gray paint. Children were placed in carrels—small enclosures, about the size of telephone booths. All this in an effort to get rid of extraneous stimuli, distractions that diverted the child from his learning tasks.

The approach seemed to help some children, but it certainly did not cure them. Their learning problems persisted. As this became apparent, investigators started once again to look for clues that might help solve the problem.

MINIMALLY BRAIN-INJURED?

During this same period, educators began using a variety of tests that had been developed to identify *minimally brain-injured* children. (The word *minimal* is misleading in this phrase; it really means that the child *acts as though* he is brain injured, even though no hard evidence of that damage can be found.) Screening examinations were conducted in schools all over the country. The results were astonishing and overwhelming. Conservative figures estimated that somewhere around 15 percent of all elementary school children would fail the screening tests. Sometimes these estimates rose to 25 percent, depending upon where the testing was done.*

All over the country, children with learning problems

---

*The percentages are even higher in the neighborhoods of certain minority groups and the poor. But these children are not ordinarily called "learning disabilities." They are more often called "culturally deprived." The fact of the matter, however, seems to be that many poor children encounter the same confusion and frustration in the classroom as do their middle-class counterparts. Conceivably the cause for their school failure is different from what it is for the middle-class child; but not only is that a moot question, it is also irrelevant. There is every reason to believe, and several educational research projects support the idea, that the poor children of this country would benefit from the educational approach described in this book.

were being identified as having something wrong with their brains—clearly not a matter for an educator to deal with! The children had to be referred. But to whom? Most physicians did not see where they fitted in. Brain injuries, if they really were that, are permanent. There is no known method for repairing damaged brain tissue.

DRUG THERAPY?

At about this same time, however, some physicians observed that certain drugs helped at least some of these children control their behavior better; that, under the influence of a particular drug, they could sit still and be attentive for much longer periods of time, even without the assistance of a carrel. As the word spread, thousands of children started to take drugs prescribed for this purpose. And in many cases the drug did work—the child did quiet down—but he continued to display a learning problem despite the fact that he was responding well, in medical terms, to the treatment.

PERCEPTUALLY HANDICAPPED?

Perceptual skills became another topic of interest during that same period.* These have been studied before, primarily by researchers investigating child development, and psychologists interested in measuring intelligence.

Now, however, perceptual skills were seen as a way of explaining learning disabilities. Children's perceptual deficits—their disorganized ways of looking, listening, writing and speaking; their difficulty in using symbols in reading and arithmetic—were interpreted as indicators of a central nervous system problem. But they were not seen to be permanent conditions. Some clinicians—optometrists, primarily—were convinced that children with substandard

---

*Perceptual skills will be thoroughly discussed later on. For the present, consider them simply as the capacity to interpret patterns of sensations—light (printed letters and numerals; geometric designs) and sound (spoken language)—in a detailed, organized way.

skills could be helped by putting them into training programs that taught them the skills they lacked.

Many children were entered into such programs and, in numerous cases, they were, in fact, helped. The training programs varied extensively. Each clinician tended to do "his own thing," ranging from having children bounce up and down on trampolines, to creeping about on hands and knees, to tracing geometric shapes with one eye covered.

A certain number of miracle cures were reported; but they could not be replicated with any degree of reliability. In other words, what seemed to work in one case did not work at all in the next, even though both cases seemed to be much the same. Sometimes the child's perceptual skills improved, sometimes they did not; sometimes his schoolwork improved, sometimes it did not—even when his perceptual skills did. It was the era of the bold innovator who proclaimed new theories daily and discarded them when a more appealing one came along. He knew he was doing something right—sometimes. But precisely what that something was, he could not say. He was a hero to some, a charlatan to others.

To the parents of a child with a learning disorder, it presented a dilemma. What to believe and who? Some experts urged that the children be referred to optometrists and psychologists who could give them perceptual training. Others, equally expert, said, "That's nonsense; training doesn't work. Send the child to a neurologist who will give him a drug." To this, yet others responded, "I took my child off drugs. He walked around looking as though he had been doped. I didn't like it at all. It frightened me."

An educational problem

Slowly the truth has become apparent. Learning problems should be treated in an educational setting, ideally by good teachers. Yes, these children often do display symptoms that are of clinical interest to neurologists, psychologists, optometrists, pediatricians, and heaven knows who else, but that is exactly what they are—symptoms, not causes. *Just as the learning problem itself is a symptom of some basic, but as yet unspecified, condition.*

Many of the symptoms can be treated, often successfully; but the learning problem tends to persist unless it is treated directly. It is the child's primary problem; all his other symptoms are of secondary importance.*

Although we do not know what causes learning disorders (and it seems highly likely that there is more than one cause), it is obvious that in many cases the cause disappears as the child matures. He grows out of it. But the learning problem, originally a symptom of that cause, hangs on. It becomes firmly established, having gotten worse each year the child attended school and failed to make normal progress. Worse yet, the child often develops more than a learning problem. The trauma of failure takes its toll. Realizing the gap between where he is—what he knows, what he can do—and where his classmates are, overwhelms him and destroys his motivation.

The child with a learning problem needs help. What should be done? Ideally, of course, the problem should be recognized long before the child begins his pattern of failure. But what about the child who was not identified early? All his symptoms should be treated. If he is hyperactive and drugs help him control it, then they should be used— under proper medical supervision, of course. If he has a perceptual problem, that too should be dealt with—in school, where understanding his perceptual skills will help his teacher better understand how to teach him. But most im-

*Not all professionals have accepted this fact. There is still a fair amount of talk in some sections of the country about the "team" approach—about how the best way to help the child with a learning problem is by mounting a multidisciplinary attack on his problems, the team usually being heavily loaded with medically oriented specialists. There is emphasis placed on "staffing" the child; having the team convene around a large table to discuss the case and decide what to do. The fallacy in the approach becomes apparent when the maneuvering starts over who will sit at the head of the table; who will captain the team. Who do you think gets the worst seat and is generally ignored? Correct—the educator; the person who has the potential for doing the most for the child in question; the person who is able to treat the child's most important symptom—his learning problem.

portant, he should be taught in a way that recognizes his learning difficulty. Whatever benefit he derives from the other treatments is a bonus.

Said another way, the purpose of treating the other symptoms is to help the child achieve the ability to learn from regular teaching in regular classrooms. Treating the educational problem should involve a different approach: changing the instructional materials and conditions to accommodate the child the way he is. In the first instance, it is the child who is to change; in the second, it is the school. In the best of situations, both approaches will be taken. In neither instance should lower academic goals be set for the child. These should remain the same as they are for all other children. Adapting means, simply, an acceptance of the fact that achieving those goals—learning to read, write, calculate and spell—will necessitate certain teaching strategies that most children do not need.

Although this way of thinking may be relatively new for children with learning disabilities, it is hardly new to the field of Special Education; to teachers of the blind, for example. The completely blind child cannot see, no matter how much his teacher urges him to try harder, no matter how large the print, no matter what medicine or eyeglasses are supplied. He cannot be cured of his blindness. Does that mean that we should not try to teach him to read, to write, to calculate? Of course not. We do teach him, but we take his blindness into consideration; we have him use his fingers in place of his eyes.

The child with a learning disability also has a handicap. Obviously, he is more fortunate than a blind child in many ways; his handicap is not so debilitating. Yet, in another way he is worse off because he looks normal. No one has to urge a teacher to provide special teaching conditions for a blind child. The same can hardly be said for the child we are concerned about here, despite the fact that he will learn only if he is taught in specific ways—ways that often require specially planned, individualized instruction.

Again, then, we see why some of the responsibility for teaching the child with a learning disability must be borne by the parents, at least until such time as more properly trained teachers become available and school boards are willing to provide the funds needed to keep classes very small. It is just too much for a teacher in today's regular classroom to handle. Parents are the only resource currently available. This book is for those parents—to help them help their child succeed in school.

DEVELOP A PLAN OF ACTION

You will have to deal with the child's problem in an organized way, step by step. A haphazard approach will, at best, add to his confusion, and yours as well.

First, design a very simple plan of action. Write it down, and check off the steps as they are accomplished.

Start off by stating a final goal. This is a crucial point. It is easy to forget a long-term goal when you get caught up in worrying about day-to-day problems. What is that goal? It is for the child to be able to perform in school in a way that does not earn him the label "learning problem." Stated positively, your goal is: "*My child will be able to read, write, spell, and do arithmetic as well as the other children in his class. His progress in school will be equal to the progress shown by the majority of his classmates.*"

Now that you have the goal identified, memorize it. Keep it in mind as you decide on the actions you will take to achieve it. Check every decision you make against that goal, and avoid decisions that divert you from it.

What next? Working backward from the goal, it is obvious that something will have to be done to help the child perform better in school. What is that something? Is it medical treatment, special tutoring, or what? You will not be able to answer that question until a certain amount of testing has been done. Thus, in broad terms, your plan of action should show two steps en route to the goal:

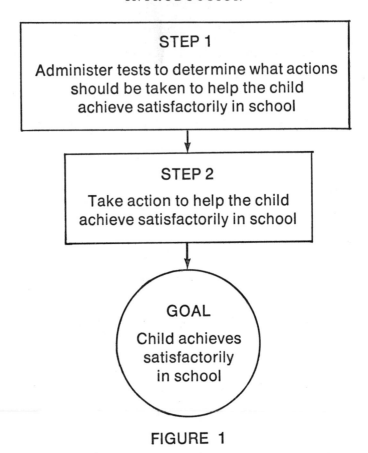

FIGURE 1

Embedded in this diagram is a basic principle. Testing should be done *only* when it might provide information that will help you make decisions concerning actions you should take. Actions should be taken *only* if they appear to be justified; only when they are based on reason rather than wishful thinking.

ORGANIZATION OF THIS BOOK

This book is organized around that plan of action. As such, it is divided into two major sections: *Testing, Teaching,* and then a follow-up section devoted to the *Prevention* of learning problems through proper preschool actions.

24

In the section *Testing*, we will consider:

- 1. What tests are essential? Health-related and education-related?
- 2. Who should administer them? A doctor, teacher, parent?
- 3. What other tests might be called for, and who should make that decision?
- 4. In what way do the tests relate to the child's learning problem? What can they tell you that will enable you to *help* him?

In the section *Teaching*, we will discuss procedures for helping the child acquire better:

> Perceptual Skills
> Reading Skills
> Arithmetic Skills
> Spelling Skills
> Writing (printing) Skills

In the final section, *Prevention*, we will deal with early recognition of learning difficulties and what to do to spare children from the trauma of school failure.

PART I
TEACHING
the Child

REMEMBER, THE REASON the child is to be tested is because you are seeking information that will help you decide what actions to take to help you achieve your goal. It is essential that this be made clear to everyone who will be doing testing. Their goals may not be the same as yours.

The tests listed below are important. None should be omitted. Some of them can be administered only by highly trained professionals. Some can be given, and interpreted, by you.

The tests are organized into two categories: health-related and education-related. The health-related tests should be administered first. It would be foolish to search for better teaching methods without first making sure that the child's learning difficulties do not stem from a health-related problem that could be successfully treated. Unfortunately, it rarely is that simple, but the possibility does exist and should be dealt with at the start.

HEALTH-RELATED TESTS

Medical

"Is there some medical problem that is causing, or contributing to my child's learning problem?" You will need a physician to answer this one. Who? A specialist? If so, what kind? That depends. I think you will do well to call upon the physician who has been looking after the medical needs of the child up until this time. However, if your past experiences with this physician have convinced you that he will not look at the child with a fresh eye—that he does not recognize the seriousness of a learning problem and will tend to view it as inconsequential—then have someone else do it. In any instance, the physician need not be a specialist; your family doctor is well suited to carry out this task.

State the purpose of your visit to his office at the very beginning: *"My child is having trouble learning in school. I am assured that he is smart enough; I know he is trying to succeed. I want to know whether you, in your examination, observe any medical problems that could help explain his learning disability."* In other words, "Can I rule out a medical factor as a potential cause of his learning problem?"

Be careful not to state the question this way: "Why is my child having a learning problem?" That only sets the stage for speculation that could distract you from your mission. The doctor, after all, has had lots of schooling and may, therefore, consider himself knowledgeable in the field of education as well as medicine. He might be tempted to offer an opinion, even though that opinion is based on intuition. Obviously, if it is offered, even though you have not asked for it, listen to his opinion and assess its value. But remember that it is probably based on uninformed hunches rather than specific knowledge.

A decade or so ago very few physicians were aware of the possible relationship between certain medical conditions and learning problems. As I noted earlier, in those days the characteristic reaction was to assume that the child had a mental block and refer him to a psychiatrist. Today, most physicians are more likely to be aware of the potential link between their field and education, and will have informed opinions regarding the use of drugs that tend to lessen a child's hyperactivity, the use of certain vitamin therapies, and so forth.

Unless you are unfortunate enough to choose a physician who has not kept informed (and, if you have, find another), accept his conclusions and recommendations at face value. If he says, "There is nothing wrong with your child," he means *medically*, and is not arguing with the education diagnosis that caused you to go to him in the first place. As such, be grateful that the youngster is healthy, check that potential factor off your list, and move on. For your own mental (and economic) health, do not insist upon calling on a progression of physicians until you find one that tells you what you might want to hear—that he has an easy medical cure for your child's educational problem.

If, in contrast, your physician concludes that ·the child does have a medical condition that *could*, at least in part, be related to his learning difficulties, follow whatever recommendations he makes, but do not stop there. The child will almost invariably also need educational help—special instructional assistance. Accept the physician's prescriptions and apply them, but continue with your plan of action. If your physician recommends that the child be seen by certain specialists, such as a neurologist or a psychiatrist, follow that recommendation if you can. If you cannot, because of the realities of economics, tell this to the physician and ask for his advice—"Is it essential to see this specialist?" "What should I do if I can't afford it?" Do not be ashamed to talk honestly regarding costs.

If you are referred to a specialist, approach him with the same set of questions. This is vital if you want to avoid a veritable merry-go-round of professional visits.

Vision

All right. You have received medical clearance. Your child is healthy. Now what? Are there others who should examine him? How about his eyes? Are they functioning properly? The answer to this last question is important. A child with a visual problem is apt to have trouble in school. Where can you find the answer? This one is sticky. Some will argue that the school nurse can supply it. "After all," you may be told, "she examines their eyes regularly, and if the child passes that test it means his eyes are okay; he doesn't need to be examined by an eye doctor." That is not really accurate.

SCHOOL VISION SCREENINGS

It is true that in many schools, some sort of vision exam is conducted regularly and routinely. Unfortunately, these so-called examinations are usually superficial and inadequate. Ordinarily, the vision test is limited to checking how clearly the child can see a chart of letters from a distance of 20 feet. If he can see the "20/20" letters, or close to that, his eyes are judged to be normal and he is dismissed. The fact is, however, that 20/20 visual acuity (eyesight) is not sufficient evidence of adequate visual abilities, in terms of the visual demands of a classroom. To do well in the classroom, the child must see clearly close up as well as at a distance. Clear eyesight at one distance does not necessarily guarantee clear eyesight at another. In addition, the child should be able to use his two eyes together efficiently, coordinating —aiming—them without undue strain. He should be able to shift his focus, from a distance to close up, and back again, with relative ease—from the chalkboard, to his desk, to the chalkboard.

Well then, what if the school examination is more thorough? Is it still necessary to have a professional examination? Perhaps; perhaps not. Some school systems (too few, unfortunately) bring in a professional who, in conjunction with school nurses and volunteers, provides "visual screenings" that test much more than how clearly a child sees at 20 feet. Find out if your school does this. If so, fine. Accept the results of that screening and, if your child passes it, assume that his learning problem does not stem from an eye problem. If he fails that screening, then a visit to the eye doctor is essential. Screening examinations, even the better ones, never do more than "pass" or "fail." They do not, nor can they, take the place of a professional evaluation. They merely identify those who should have that professional evaluation.

Who do you call upon, if you have to take your child to an eye doctor? Many parents continue to be confused by the available options and what they really are. There are two general categories of eye doctors. One group is medically oriented and, in the main, are currently identified as ophthalmologists, although there are still some who are called oculists and even eye-ear-nose-and-throat doctors. The others are called optometrists. Both groups are adequately trained to answer your questions, *if* they will take the time to look for the answers. Both groups have their share of dedicated practitioners. Sometimes your child's teacher (or some other school person) will be able to help you make the choice, based upon their knowledge of the past experiences of other children with similar problems.

At any rate, it is not so important which kind of eye doctor you take your child to, so long as wherever you go, you make certain to ask the proper questions and to not settle for less than full answers. Do not allow yourself to be intimidated by the busy office, bustling office assistants, and elusive doctor. You have brought your child there to get answers to the following questions. Let the doctor know this and that you will not be satisfied with less: *"Does my child have a vision problem that could be causing, or contributing to his learning problem? Does he see well up close as well as at a distance? Can he shift focus easily? Do his eyes work together properly? Can he do all this without undue strain?"* Again, I caution you, do not get sidetracked by asking, "Why does my child have a learning problem?" Try to keep the issues clear.

Once you are satisfied that the eye doctor has taken your questions seriously, accept his conclusions and recommendations at face value. If he says, "There is nothing wrong with your child's eyes," be grateful. If he recommends glasses, procure them—after you have again asked the doctor if he thinks the need for glasses is relevant to the child's learning problems. If he cannot support that relationship, then question why the glasses are called for. Glasses are

33

often prescribed for extensive reading. That is fine, if the child reads extensively. It is silly and wasteful for the child who can hardly read at all, and never does so voluntarily. There is time for him to obtain glasses for extensive reading once he starts to overcome his reading problem.

If the eye doctor recommends a series of treatments to improve your child's perceptual skills, show him this book and ask him whether what he has in mind goes beyond what I am suggesting. And, if it does, find out why he thinks this is warranted, what the extra benefits will be, and what the professional fees will amount to. Make your decision based upon that information. I do not argue against the relative value of a private practitioner over a book such as this one that is written for nonprofessionals. Obviously, the private practitioner's judgment should be better in individual cases. However, I do caution you to avoid committing yourself and your child to a series of treatments that may aim for skills he really does not need, at the expense of neglecting skills that he needs desperately. This point will become clearer when we discuss perceptual skills in detail.

Hearing

This is another important consideration, often overlooked. If the child has a reading problem, make certain that his hearing is unimpaired. Once again, the school nurse often investigates this ability, but you had better inquire as to whether it has been checked lately. If it has, and you are satisfied that the examination was adequate, leave it at that. If you are not convinced, then arrange for a professional evaluation.

Most reading problems are not caused by hearing problems. However, if the child does have a hearing problem, it will significantly affect his classroom performance, especially his ability to learn to read. Therefore it should be determined at the outset.

Who should do this, if you are not willing to accept the school nurse's opinion? Ask your family doctor or pediatrician. His opinion will be helpful here. Obviously, if a hearing problem is discovered, follow professional advice. If no problem is found, be grateful and proceed about the business of completing the first phase of your plan of action.

EDUCATION-RELATED TESTS

The tests discussed so far were all concerned with health-related matters: the child's general physical condition, his vision, and his hearing. Certainly, all of these can affect how well a child will perform in the classroom, but other abilities should also be examined. Specifically, the following:

- 1. *Visual perceptual skills*—his ability to interpret patterns of light (printed letters and numerals; geometric designs) in a detailed, organized way.
- 2. *Auditory perceptual skills*—his ability to interpret patterns of sound (spoken language) in a detailed, organized way.
- 3. *General-motor skills*—his ability to manage his own body movements in a detailed, organized way.

I will discuss all of these thoroughly, but before I do, we should consider the question of who will conduct the examinations.

It is only in recent years that the close relationship between a child's perceptual skills and his ability to learn in school has been clearly recognized. When this occurred, many different disciplines became interested in perceptual skills at virtually the same time. These included, among others, optometry, psychology, education, and even occupational therapy. Each group developed its own tests. To some extent, all of the tests are similar but, in other ways, they do differ. Many of them are exceedingly complex; too much so, in terms of what we are concerned about—the

child's school performance. In my judgment, extensive testing is not called for. It is essential to test the three skills I
listed above; nothing more.

Who should do the testing?

A decade or so ago, perceptual testing required a professional—an optometrist, psychologist, or occupational therapist who had become expert in the field of perceptual testing. And there were not too many who had. More recently,
some educators have begun testing perceptual skills, thus
widening the range of professionals from which to choose.

Today you need not be limited. You no longer have to
search for a specially trained person. You can do it yourself.
Further along in this section I will describe some perceptual
tests that you can use. And I will tell you how to apply the
information you acquire from them.

Well then, given this choice, who *should* do the testing—
a private practitioner, an educator, or you? That depends
on your individual situation. Certainly, the private practitioner who specializes in this field should be able to do the
most thorough job. The question, however, is whether such
an in-depth investigation is warranted. If you have reason
to think that it is—or if you feel too insecure to do the testing yourself—then by all means seek the services of a competent private practitioner. But, if you have no reason to
believe that you need professional involvement at this
point, then do the testing yourself.

Before we turn our attention to the specific tests, how to
administer them, and what they tell us, there should be
some general discussion about perception, what perceptual
skills are, and why they are important.

Perception

To perceive, according to my dictionary, is "to become
aware of directly through the senses." To perceive is more
than to see, or hear, or smell, or feel, or taste. To perceive is
to interpret whatever information is being received, regard-

less of which senses are involved. To do this, the perceiver:

- 1. pays particular attention to certain features of that information; features that he considers to be distinctive in that situation.
- 2. attaches to those distinctive features his own personal emotional, physical, and intellectual values.
- 3. comes to some conclusion; that is, interprets the information.

For example, when I am shown a photograph of a person, I focus on certain features of that photograph, depending upon whatever is important to me at that time, under those circumstances. If it is a photograph of a person I know, I will probably look at it differently than if I do not know the person. If it is a person I like, I will undoubtedly look at it differently than if it is a person I dislike. My perception is colored by past experiences that have shaped my personal values.

Suppose it is a photograph of someone I like and who you, in contrast, dislike. Will we see the same thing? Literally, yes. But in terms of our examination of that photograph, no—we will *perceive* differently. I will pay particular attention to certain features and make my judgment primarily from those. You may perhaps look at the same details or, more likely, at other aspects of the photograph, and come to a different judgment. Do you want to test this? Examine a photograph of your mother-in-law and compare what you perceive to what your spouse perceives.

Perceptual skills

Now, to get a little closer to the classroom, picture in your mind's eye two individuals walking in a forest. Imagine that one of these persons is a bird-watcher. He has spent years looking at and listening to birds. He is very familiar with the characteristics of a great many species. Imagine that his companion is a lifelong city dweller who rarely gets out to the countryside. He can tell the difference between a pigeon and a canary, but beyond that he is lost.

Suppose, further, that before this outing both men had eye examinations and hearing examinations. It was established that both have equally excellent sight and hearing. Do you think they both hear and see the same in this forest? Literally, yes; but in terms of what they perceive, of course not. The bird-watcher is aware of many distinctly different bird songs; his companion is aware of birdlike noises—their songs all sound the same to him. The bird-watcher is aware of many different birds all around him. His companion manages to notice a bird only when it flies across his path.

The bird-watcher can describe the birds verbally—use words to define their distinctive visual and acoustical characteristics. His companion cannot, even though he knows all the words that the bird-watcher uses. He knows the verbal code, but is not sufficiently familiar with the bird's physical characteristics to use the code effectively.

Why the differences, since we know they both have the same excellent visual and auditory abilities? The answer is obvious. The bird-watcher knows *what to look for* and *what to listen for*. He is familiar with the acoustical features that distinguish the various bird songs, and the visual features that distinguish the various bird forms. *He has acquired the perceptual skills needed to be a good bird-watcher.* His companion is not at all familiar with those distinguishing features. To him, birds are simply birds; they all look and sound alike to him. He does not have the perceptual skills needed to be a good bird-watcher.

Could this city dweller become a better bird-watcher? Sure. He merely has to acquire the necessary visual and auditory perceptual skills; to be told—taught—what to look and listen for, and then to use what he has been taught. In fact, he need not even be taught, if he will devote the necessary time and effort to learning on his own, but this will take longer and demand more effort on his part. But what should we call him if, even after much effort, he continues to have trouble identifying, and keeping straight in his head, the distinctive acoustical and visual features of the various birds and the words that define these features? A learning problem—for that is what he would be in this situation.

Classrooms are not forests, and recognizing the distinctive physical features of birds, or their songs, is not the equivalent of recognizing the distinctive features of a reading, spelling, or arithmetic lesson. But there are some general principles that apply to both settings. If you are to use information, you must know how to get at that information —that is, what details to look for and to listen for—as well as how to define them verbally.

Can you see how this fits into our concerns about the child in the classroom? Does a teacher ever point out— teach—*all* the details she wants the child to see or hear? Does a child literally have to be taught all that he is to learn? No, there is not enough time in a school day for that. Rather, the teacher usually points out some details, expects the child to see, or understand, how those pertain to other details that are not pointed out, and to learn much on his own.

For example, in teaching a child how to read, the teacher may very well point out that a certain letter has a certain sound, and follow that up with a list of words that illustrate the point. But the teacher will not illustrate it with every word in the language that contains that letter and sound. She will reasonably expect the child to see that letter, and hear that sound, in an unfamiliar word—a word that has not been used in prior instruction—and read the word by applying what she has taught him.

Can you imagine how impossibly tedious school would be if every word containing that letter-sound combination had to be taught? However, some children do require this—at least to some extent in some subjects. (Keep in mind that some children have trouble only in arithmetic; some only in reading; some in both.) They are among the children we are concerned with in this book.

39

Perceptual skills and classroom performance

The perceptual skills that concern us are those that enable the child to identify pertinent visual and acoustical details; the details he will be taught to represent—to code—with letters and numerals, the symbols of the classroom. In order for him to see and hear those important details, he must be able to find them—isolate them from the surroundings in which they are embedded. (This is not unlike identifying the birds in the forest.)

To accomplish this, he must be able to see that visual patterns (designs, letters, numerals) are made up of a finite number of parts (lines, shapes) that fit together in a certain way. That final phrase is important. Just seeing all the parts of a *b* and a *d*—or all the parts of a cardboard pie that has been cut into three equal sections—is not enough. The child must also recognize how those parts interrelate, if he is to make sense out of reading, spelling, and arithmetic. How well the child can do all this depends upon his *visual perceptual skills.*

In addition, he must be able to "hear" that acoustical patterns (spoken words) are made up of a finite number of parts (sounds) that fit together in a certain way. Again, this latter ability is crucial. Identifying the individual sounds in the spoken words *cat, tack,* and *act* is not enough. He must also recognize that these three spoken words comprise the same sounds, but that they differ in how those sounds fit together—their sequence. How well a child can do all this depends upon his *auditory perceptual skills.*

Visual perceptual skills

To give you a better idea, try the following. Look at the upper pattern of the two shown in Figure 2 and copy it on a separate piece of paper. Is it a difficult task? Hardly. If someone was to check the accuracy of your work, there would probably be total agreement that you had done what you were asked to do. Does your printing exactly match the printing shown in the book? No, but who cares? The task is

FIGURE 2

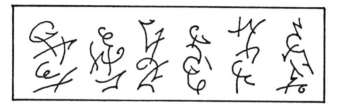

a straightforward one of copying a word and, as such, so long as you spelled it correctly, it would be senseless to worry about whether your printing was an exact match. You were operating at a *symbolic level* of information processing. You were paying attention to a word—a meaningful unit made up of symbols—not the shape of the lines that form the letters that spell the word. You were not drawing shapes; you were reading and writing language. The skills you used to perform this task were high-level ones, but they were built on a base of adequate, lower-level perceptual skills.

Now copy the lower pattern. That is a very different task. Will one look be enough? That is, can you read it, then write it, as you did with the top pattern? Of course not.

Then what do you do in copying it, if you are convinced that the task is an important one and really worth a try? You choose a place to start—a single line in the pattern. It is unimportant whether the line is at the left end, the right end, or, for that matter, somewhere in the middle. You study that line, figure out its shape, and attempt to draw it. You then focus on another line. Almost invariably, this second line is one that is closely related to the first; probably one that intersects it. You then copy that second line, and so on, working your way through the pattern. Each component part, each line, has to be dealt with separately; each one requires separate study and drawing. It is impossible for you to take one look, as you did with the upper pattern, and produce the copy.

This copying task calls for visual perceptual skills, forerunner to information processing skills that are fundamental in the classroom. You concentrate on the elements of the pattern—its parts—one at a time, figuring out as you proceed how those elements interrelate. This is not greatly different from the way many young children perform when they enter first grade and are asked to recognize and print letters and numerals. If they are not already familiar with these symbols, they will be looking at designs, and when they copy them, they will be drawing the parts, one at a time.

What are the chances that you will omit one or more elements in that lower pattern when you copy it, or misplace an element so that it ends up in a wrong position? It certainly is not unlikely, simply because of the many times you will have to look at the pattern, find your place, copy a line, look back at the pattern, and so on. It would not be surprising if you misplaced one of the lines, putting it on the left of another line when it really belonged on the right. What could cause this? Mirror vision? Is it possible that you literally saw the two lines in reverse? Of course not; you merely got lost in the detail. It would be silly to argue that this was evidence that you saw the world backward. No one does! Yet, this is precisely what is often suggested when people examine and discuss the paper work of a child with a learning problem. Many children do confuse *b*'s and *d*'s, but not because they literally see them backward. Rather, it is because they do not accurately interpret the interrelationships of the parts that form the letters.

Pretend that the lower pattern in Figure 2, instead of being nonsense, is really a foreign language, and that each separate cluster of lines represents a letter. If you were to enroll in a class that taught this language, your teacher

42

would start to teach you to recognize these as *letters*—not as designs, but as organized arrangements of lines that can be given letter names. The teacher would point out some of the distinctive features of each letter, you would observe others, and in time you would learn the letter names. No longer would you take notice of each squiggly line in each letter.

These individual lines could now vary quite a bit, yet the letters would still be recognizable—just as you can look at various English typefaces and never take notice of their differences. You would then be dealing with larger chunks of visual information; symbols, not designs that must be analyzed element by element. The difference, then, between perceptual and symbolic processing appears to be, at least in part, the nature of the features that are considered to be important. Perceptual processes focus on concrete sensory details—lines and the way they fit together. Symbolic processes focus on abstract information that is represented by those sensations. The latter is built on the former. Competent symbolic processes are based on competent perceptual skills.

One more step. Suppose you continue to study this foreign language. You learn to read it. You reach a point where you can read the pattern in Figure 2 as a word. You learn that it says *perception.* You continue to study. You read that word in a variety of contexts. It becomes a familiar word. Once this happens, do you really look at each letter, let alone each element within each letter, as you read? No—nor should you. It would slow you down too much. Rather, you now read it as a *word*; even the precise spelling is not very important. Only when you come across a new word do you revert to paying attention to the individual letters. In fact, in time finding misspelled words becomes a demanding job. To illustrate this, try proofreading something you have typed. Try to find errors. It is not easy to do; you have become too good a reader to focus on smaller units under normal circumstances.

The visual perceptual skills that you originally used, in

order to look at the pattern in some organized way, have been replaced by symbolic processing skills. These enable you to function much more efficiently; to focus on larger and more complex units of information that consist of a collection of less complex details, each of which once required your individual attention and, in fact, may again under conditions where a lower-level analysis—attention to less complex features—is called for. Your perceptual skills, though no longer employed, are still available. They can be called upon when necessary—when your symbolic processing skills are inadequate to the task. Then the less efficient, lower-order perceptual skills will be put to use.

Auditory perceptual skills ·

These same concepts apply in auditory tasks. For example, say aloud the word *Massachusetts*. Difficult? Not for an average American adult who speaks the English language. You do not have to think very hard to produce the correct sounds in proper sequence. This, then, is like copying the printed word *perception*. You operate at a symbolic level in processing the information—listening to it being pronounced, recognizing it as a familiar word, and then saying it. You do not pay attention to the separate sounds. Surely, you would interpret the word correctly even if it was pronounced by someone with a southern drawl, a western twang, or a heavy French accent. Its perceptual characteristics—the sounds themselves—would no longer be important.

Now think of a listening task that is analogous to copying the lower word shown in Figure 2. Suppose I ask you to repeat accurately what a tobacco auctioneer says as he chants during an auction. Can you do it? Perhaps, but it is very difficult to do, even if you have excellent hearing. Why? Again, simply because the stream of sounds in that chant is too complicated—too full of details for the uninitiated. The only way you can begin to accomplish this task is by dealing with the chant one sound at a time, by analyzing the chant into its parts, and figuring out how those parts—those separate sounds—are sequenced. In other words, by processing the information at a perceptual level; by using your auditory perceptual skills.

Once you have done this, repeating the auctioneer's chant will not be overly demanding and, indeed, after some practice, you will no longer be hearing or speaking his chant as segmented seminonsensical sounds. You will now be dealing with spoken language consisting of sounds that, in themselves, are not important and do not require close attention.

Testing perceptual skills

Some children have inadequate visual perceptual skills and adequate auditory skills, or vice versa. Some have trouble with both. It is important, therefore, to test both sets of skills. Then, based on the outcomes of these tests, you may or may not test certain general-motor skills.

In addition to describing the tests you are to use with your child, I will discuss one standardized visual and one standardized auditory perceptual test which are fairly commonly used by professionals. I have two reasons for doing this. First, to explain away some of the misconceptions—even mystery—that pervades this topic; to add to your understanding of what perceptual skills are and why they are important. This will help you understand his classroom difficulties. Second, to help you see the similarity between the tests you will use and the ones that many professionals and schools use. This will help you understand your child's test scores.

VISUAL PERCEPTUAL SKILLS TESTS

Generally speaking, the best way to investigate a child's visual perceptual skills is with a copying test. There are other kinds of tests available—discrimination tests, for example—but they are not as useful to us.*

The Gesell Copy Form Test and what it tells us

One of the better-known visual perceptual tests is the Gesell Copy Form Test. It was developed many years ago by Arnold Gesell and his co-workers at the Yale University Child Development Clinic. Gesell did not investigate school learning problems as such. He was interested in describing the way children change as they grow and develop from birth onward. With his Copy Form Test, he showed that children are able to copy more complex designs as they mature.

The test uses the seven designs shown in Figure 3. Each one is presented to the child on a separate card that measures approximately 5″ x 7″.

To administer the test, the child is given an 8½″ x 11″ sheet of unlined paper and a pencil. He is then shown the first design, the circle, and asked to "make one like this on your paper." After he has done that, he is shown the second design, the plus sign, and asked to copy it. The designs are shown to the child one at a time until all seven have been copied.

I will not try to describe all of the things that a professional looks at in assessing the quality of the child's responses; this information is available elsewhere.**

It is sufficient, for our purposes, to know what Gesell found to be normal in terms of copying skills. His research

---

*Discrimination tests usually ask the child to match patterns, given an assortment from which to choose—"find the two that are the same" or "find the one that is different." In such tests, the child only needs to see differences in the patterns; he does not have to demonstrate that he understands how a specific pattern is constructed—how to break it down into its parts and figure out the interrelationships of those parts. Certainly you had no trouble recognizing that the two patterns in Figure 2 were different. That does not mean, however, that you could copy the lower one accurately.

**A full description of this and other tests from the Gesell battery can be found in *School Readiness*, by F. Ilg and L.B. Ames (Harper & Row, 1964).

FIGURE 3

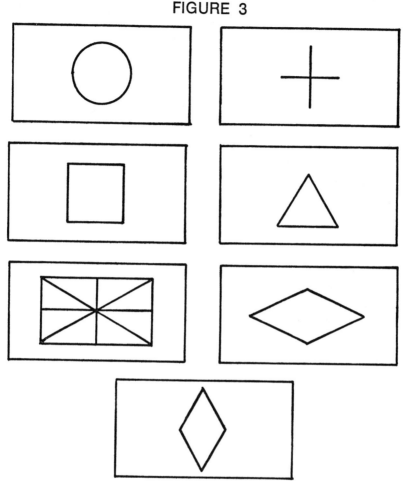

showed that most children are able to copy a circle fairly accurately when they are about three years old. They are able to copy the plus sign somewhere between the ages of three and one-half to four; the square at about the age of four; the triangle somewhere around the fifth birthday; the divided rectangle at about age six; and the diamonds when they are about seven years old.

All these ages are approximate; a few months variation is not significant. But the interesting fact is that most children do achieve these developmental milestones on sched-

47

ule. As such, the test is a valid way of assessing a child's visual perceptual skills—for comparing what he can do with what is normal for his age; that is, with what can be done by the majority of children of about the same age.

It will help to look at some examples. The four sets of drawings shown in Figure 4 (reduced in size so that they all fit on the same page) were done by four different children, all about six years old. For discussion purposes, we will identify them as Johnny, Jimmy, Mary, and Sue.

FIGURE 4

| SUE | MARY |
| JIMMY | JOHNNY |

The drawings differ markedly. Johnny's drawings appear to be the poorest; then Jimmy's; then Mary's. Sue's are the best. What do these differences tell us? Let us study one design, the divided rectangle, and see how this varies among the four first-grade children. Figure 5 shows all four copies of the divided rectangle.

FIGURE 5

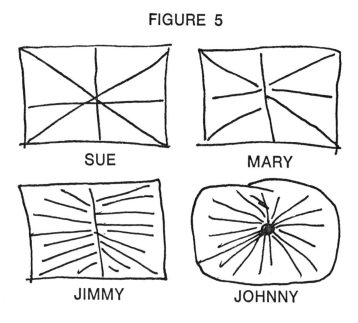

SUE   MARY

JIMMY   JOHNNY

A logical first reaction could be that perhaps Johnny does not see the designs clearly enough, and that Jimmy is not too much better off. Maybe this is so, but it is extremely unlikely that their very poor copying skills can be attributed to poor eyesight. However, as I pointed out earlier, this possibility should be investigated—just to be safe.

Well, then, if it is not Johnny's eyesight, what is it? As noted, all four children are about six years old. All four have normal intelligence, which means that all four scored at least average or above in an I.Q. test. Maybe Johnny, despite his clear eyesight, literally sees the pattern in a distorted way? We can investigate that by showing Johnny all four patterns—his, Jimmy's, Mary's, and Sue's—along with the test pattern itself, and asking him which one of the four drawings looks most like the test pattern. Almost invariably Johnny will choose Sue's—the one that *is* the best copy—not his own. (That is why discrimination tests are so much less useful to us.) If this happens, then he really does not see a distorted pattern, even though the one he drew was quite distorted.

What else could be causing his trouble? Maybe it is because of his poor motor skills; maybe he cannot control a pencil adequately? We can reject that idea, since he satisfactorily drew the plus sign which contains a vertical and a horizontal line, and he drew the diagonals of the triangle fairly accurately. Hence, he was able to draw all the lines of this design when they occurred in simpler designs. No, poor motor control does not explain his problem either.

In order to help you understand Johnny's inadequate responses, imagine the following task: "Go into the park on a pleasant day in June and find a section of healthy lawn. Mark off one square foot of that thriving lawn and *copy* it, showing each blade of grass as it actually appears in its correct position and exact size."

Could you do it? No, there are just too many blades of grass. You are bound to omit some, misplace some, draw some too large or too small. The fact that you cannot accomplish this task is not surprising; no one could. And since no one can do it, no one else will design a lesson based on the assumption that you can deal with that much detail. Thus, it is not a problem.

But most of Johnny's classmates, if they are in the first grade or higher, *can* copy the divided rectangle fairly accurately, which means that they can analyze it into its separate parts and recognize the interrelationships of those parts. That is, they can see it as a rectangle containing a vertical, a horizontal, and two diagonal lines; and they can also see how these parts fit together.

What can we say about the other three children? Jimmy's drawing shows that he is starting to analyze the pattern into its parts, but he is doing it rather poorly. He gets the rectangle and the vertical line, but that is about it for him. Mary is analyzing the parts accurately. That is, she draws the correct number of lines, but she is having trouble with the interrelationships. Sue is doing both tasks accurately—analyzing the parts and organizing them accurately. Hence, hers is the best.

Skills for learning letters and numerals

Since most of Johnny's classmates can manage that amount and type of detail and he cannot, he has a problem. They will be able to meet the demands of certain classroom tasks; he will not. For example, look at these letters:

m   n

How do they differ? Only in that the *m* has one more hump than the *n*. To recognize this difference, so obvious to anyone who is already familiar with the lowercase letters, you have to be able to analyze both letters into their separate parts. As you identify and compare the parts, the difference between the letters is apparent. If you were unable to isolate these individual parts—as is probably the case with Johnny—the differences would not be very evident. The humps would not be quantifiable. It is very difficult to count what you cannot sort out.

But breaking patterns down into their parts is only part of the picture How about the additional task of recognizing the way those parts fit together? Consider these letters:

b   d   p   q

How do they differ? In each case, there are the same number of parts and the parts are identical. It is only in how the parts are combined—their organization—that makes the difference. Again, then, visual perceptual skills of a certain level are required.

Look at yet another example:

a   d

Here, one of the two component parts of each of the letters differs, while the other one does not. Both letters contain a circle. However, the vertical line of the *a* is appreciably shorter than the vertical line of the *d*. Once more, it is the child's visual perceptual skills that enable him to see this difference.

Recognizing the letters is important, but there are other reasons why visual perceptual skills are important to the elementary-aged school child. After all, the letters of the alphabet are not that complex; they do not contain a great number of parts nor are the interrelationships of the parts that unique. True, there are certain pairs of letters that mirror each other, thus adding a confusing dimension. But there are not very many of these, and straightforward instruction and practice can usually get the child past this point of confusion.

Skills for arithmetic

It is in arithmetic that visual perceptual skills are truly fundamental. I already made the point that if the child has trouble analyzing a visual pattern into its separate parts, he will also have trouble counting those parts accurately. To learn arithmetic, a child must be able to count objects accurately. Beginning counting skills are based on first being able to count aloud in correct sequence, starting with 1, and second, being able to coordinate that oral counting with whatever is being counted. Thus, if the child is shown four objects and asked to count them, he characteristically touches each object in some order while reciting the sequence of numbers from 1 to 4. His understanding of the total quantity will be based on the last number he says aloud as he touches the final object. If his visual perceptual skills are poor—if he does not view the collection of objects as finite—he cannot view them as organized. Counting them, then, will be a random activity, where some objects may be counted more than once while others may be completely overlooked. That is one reason why visual perceptual skills are important to learning arithmetic.

There is yet one more way that visual perceptual skills relate to arithmetic. Numerals are used not only to represent quantity; they also are used to represent relationships. Not only must the child learn very early in his school career that the 1 stands for one object, the 2 for two objects, and so forth, he must also quickly catch on to the fact that certain quantities are both a *specific* and a *relative* amount larger or smaller than other quantities. Look at Figure 6.

FIGURE 6

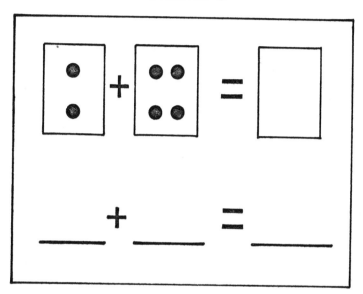

This is a typical first-grade arithmetic problem. What must the child do to complete this task? He must count the objects in the first box and record that amount (print 2) on the line below the first box. He repeats this activity with the second box, recording a 4 on the appropriate line. Now he must draw the correct number of circles in the right-hand answer box and write the appropriate numeral 6 below it. We have already discussed the importance of adequate visual perceptual skills for this task.

But there is something else he should see. Namely, that there is a fixed *relationship* between the number of objects in each of the boxes. Thus, if he is now asked to solve the problem 4+4=? he will not have to start counting from 1 again. He will be able to reason that since 4 is two more than 2, then 4+4 must equal 8, two more than 6. In time he will see another relationship between these quantities; that 4 is *two* times (2×) 2, and 8 is two times (2×) 4. Then multiplication and division will start to make sense.

Recognizing the dual function of numerals—that they may be used to represent both quantity and relationships—is very confusing to the child whose visual perceptual skills are less than satisfactory. In time he will learn to count accurately. But recognizing relationships? That is something else again. It is an elusive concept, yet one that is critical to understanding arithmetic as an orderly, systematic approach to describing absolute and relative quantity. Until the child acquires this ability, each arithmetic problem will be a new one. The fact that after much effort he has just solved 7×7 = ? will not facilitate his solving 8×7 = ? The only way he will be able to solve the second problem is by starting over again from the very beginning. He will not recognize its relationship to the first problem. You can imagine what a burden this gets to be around the fourth grade, when most of his classmates have come to see these relationships among numbers, and are able to apply the concepts in their daily arithmetic class.

Skills for reading comprehension

There is yet one more reason why visual perceptual skills are important in school. This one is general, relating to all subject areas, although it probably is more closely linked to reading comprehension than to anything else. Reading for meaning requires the child to translate the letters on the printed page into language that has meaning, not just words. To gain meaning from that language, he has to organize the information he reads so that he can remember it long enough to associate it with other information. Remembering and associating information is exceptionally difficult unless it is properly organized. The child who reads words and tries to remember the text verbatim, so that he can repeat it upon request, is not likely to remember very much after a single reading, nor will he understand very much beyond the actual facts that are specifically stated in the text.

In other words, when the child reads a story that, say, involves people, animals, objects, and events, he is more likely to remember the central theme of that story if he classifies the information—sorts it out and organizes it—as he reads it. This classification strategy may simply be according to who or what in the story is a person, animal, object, event, and what they encounter. Or it may be according to a time sequence—what happened first, what happened next, and so on. Or it may be according to certain relationships—a boy and his pet, another boy and his pet, and so on. The point is that the strategy will vary from situation to situation, and the child, as he reads, must be able to classify the information in a variety of ways in order to meet those varying conditions.

One way of describing the child with inadequate visual perceptual skills is in terms of his substandard ability to classify information. Since he does not sort out and relate concrete information as readily as most of his classmates, he will not comprehend as well, even if he does know how to read all the words in the text.

The Test of Visual Analysis Skills (TVAS)— A test you can administer

There are, as I mentioned, a number of visual perceptual tests on the market. Most of them are easy to administer. However, I am going to describe only one—the Test of Visual Analysis Skills (TVAS). This is a new test that will work well for you.

The TVAS is, in fact, more than a test. If you find that the child's visual perceptual skills are inadequate, it will also serve to define the goals for his instructional program. You will teach him to "pass the test."

That is a unique feature of the TVAS. Virtually every standardized test becomes invalid if you set about teaching the child to pass it. For example, if you intentionally set out to teach the child to copy a diamond, you will probably succeed. He will learn how to copy a diamond. But you certainly cannot infer from that accomplishment that he has also learned the underlying processes called for in copying all shapes of that complexity. Just because a child learns to copy a diamond, and copying a diamond is something expected of seven-year-olds, does not indicate that he has acquired the visual perceptual skills of the average seven-year-old.

The opposite is true with the TVAS. As you teach the child to pass the test you will be teaching him underlying processes—perceptual skills. But more about that later on. Right now, let us look at how you can test your child's visual perceptual skills.

Preparing materials for the TVAS

First you must construct the test materials. Here is how:

- 1. Make *two copies* of the 5-dot, the 9-dot, and the 25-dot maps shown in Figures 7, 8, and 9. Your maps should be the same size as the ones shown here. This is easily done by placing a sheet of unlined 8½"×11" writing paper directly over a map and tracing it; or you may photocopy them.
- 2. Insert each of the six maps in a separate transparent plastic page protector, which you can purchase at most office supply stores. The page protectors will enable you to reuse the maps indefinitely.
- 3. Obtain two dark-colored wax crayons. You and the child will use these to draw on the plastic page protectors that are covering the maps. These lines are easily erased with facial tissue.

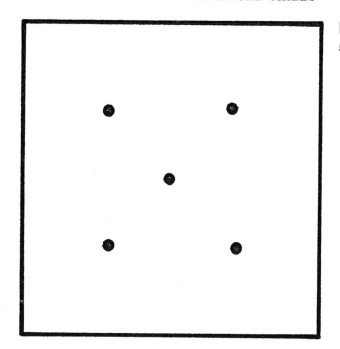

FIGURE 7
5-dot map

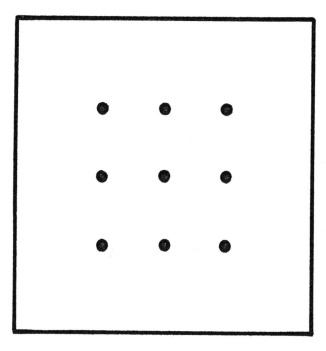

FIGURE 8
9-dot map

57

FIGURE 9
25-dot map

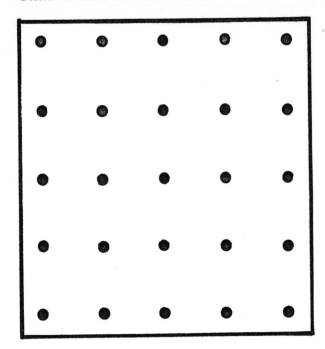

FIGURE 10
17-dot map

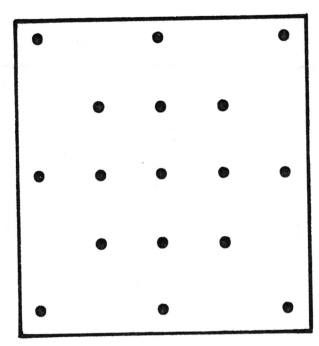

FIGURE 11
0-dot map

- 4. You are almost ready. You still need two more maps; a 17-dot one and a 0-dot one. Both are shown here, in Figures 10 and 11.

Trace or photocopy these just as you did the others, each one on a separate 8½"×11" sheet of paper, and place both of these maps in plastic page protectors.

Giving the TVAS

Now you are ready to start testing. The test involves copying designs. You draw test patterns neatly on one map; the child must copy them on his map. Once a design is completed, erase the crayon lines with a facial tissue and proceed to the next pattern. The patterns are relatively easy at the start and become progressively more difficult. *Stop testing when the child makes errors on two successive patterns.*

The test items are shown in the pages that follow. Look at item 1. This test item shows a design drawn on one 5-dot map and another 5-dot map on which no lines have been drawn. You copy the test design neatly on one of your plastic-covered 5-dot maps—*out of the child's sight.* Then give the child the other plastic-covered 5-dot map and a crayon, and ask him to "Make your map look like mine. Draw the lines on your map so that it looks just like mine."

To be scored as correct, his drawing must have the right number of lines *and* they must be located on the proper dots. If he omits or adds a line, or if he locates a line on the wrong dots, score the item as incorrect. Although he should be encouraged to draw his lines neatly, that is not a critical factor. Accuracy is what counts. However, if one or more of his lines miss the dots, and you cannot tell whether he copied inaccurately or was merely being sloppy, have him do it over again, instructing him to "Make sure you connect your lines to the correct dots."

Do not coach him. This is a test and, although you want him to do well, it is essential that he be able to copy the designs without assistance. Remember, you are testing him to find out if he has learned the skills he needs in order to succeed in school. You will use this test information when you set about teaching him the skills he does not know. Hence, you want accurate information. You will not be doing him a favor if you help him, or if you overlook his errors. You will be fooling yourself and denying him the important knowledge that he can acquire from being taught the skills he currently lacks.

ITEM 1

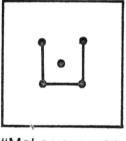

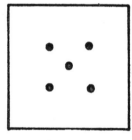

"Make your map look like this"

Child's map

Item 1 gives the first test design. Remember, you are to copy the test design on your map, out of the child's view. Then have him copy your drawing on his map.

Now check his work. Did he draw the correct number of lines? Are the lines positioned on the proper dots? Make a note of whether his copy was correct or incorrect, erase both your design and his, and go on to the test design in item 2. Be noncommittal with the child about his performance. Say such things as "okay" rather than "right" or "wrong."

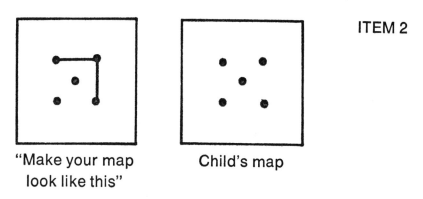

ITEM 2

"Make your map look like this"

Child's map

Score this one as either correct or incorrect and go on to item 3.

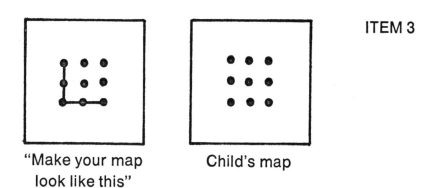

ITEM 3

"Make your map look like this"

Child's map

In the item 3 test, you are to use a 9-dot map, but the instructions and scoring procedure are exactly the same as before. Once you have scored it, go on to the test designs in items 4 and 5. Remember, stop testing when the child is incorrect on *two successive* patterns—and when you end the testing, do it with some kindly remark, such as "That's enough *for now*." Do not fail him with your words or your actions.

ITEM 4

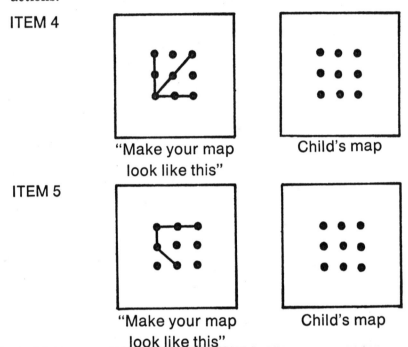

"Make your map
look like this"

Child's map

ITEM 5

"Make your map
look like this"

Child's map

Now you are to start using the 25-dot maps (see items 6 through 9), unless the child has already committed two successive errors, in which case you are done testing. Again, the instructions to the child and the scoring procedure remain the same.

ITEM 6

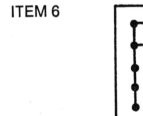

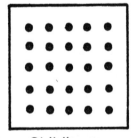

"Make your map
look like this"

Child's map

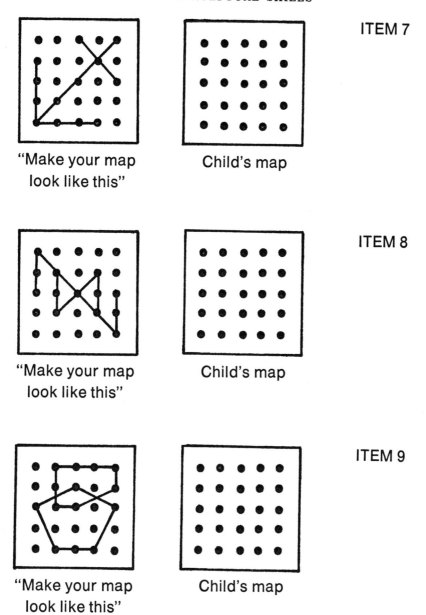

ITEM 7

"Make your map
look like this"

Child's map

ITEM 8

"Make your map
look like this"

Child's map

ITEM 9

"Make your map
look like this"

Child's map

Now a small change is necessary in the instructions you give the child. Look at item 10.

ITEM 10

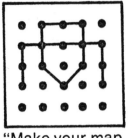

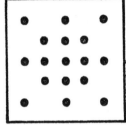

"Make your map
look like this"

"Some of the dots
are missing"

With this item, say to the child, "*Some* of the dots are missing on your map. Don't draw in the dots. Just pretend they are there. Draw the lines on your map *as though* the dots were there." To score this, you too must pretend the dots are there and determine whether the child drew the correct number of lines and whether he positioned them in their proper places. If he did, fine. Give him credit for being correct. If he did not, note it as incorrect and move on to item 11—unless this is his second consecutive error, in which case, of course, you should stop testing.

ITEM 11

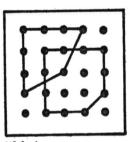

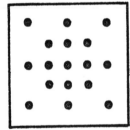

"Make your map
look like this"

"Some of the dots
are missing"

The instructions to the child for items 11 through 16 are the same as for item 10. Notice that more of the dots are missing. Score them as described in item 10.

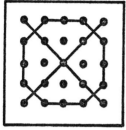

"Make your map
look like this"

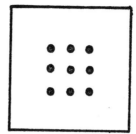

"Some of the dots
are missing"

ITEM 12

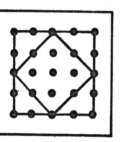

"Make your map
look like this"

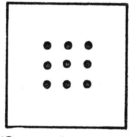

"Some of the dots
are missing"

ITEM 13

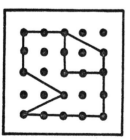

"Make your map
look like this"

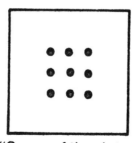

"Some of the dots
are missing"

ITEM 14

ITEM 15

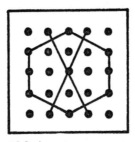

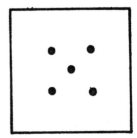

"Make your map
look like this"

"Some of the dots
are missing"

ITEM 16

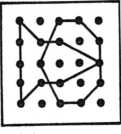

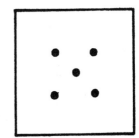

"Make your map
look like this"

"Some of the dots
are missing"

The instructions again change slightly for the last two items of the test, items 17 and 18. Now you say to the child, "*All* of the dots are missing on your map. Don't draw the dots. Just pretend they are there. Draw the lines *as though* the dots were there." Scoring is the same. If all the lines are copied and if they are positioned correctly (as though the

ITEM 17

"Make your map
look like this"

"All of the dots
are missing"

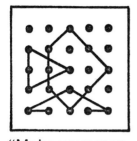

ITEM 18

"Make your map
look like this"

"All of the dots
are missing"

dots were there), give him credit for a correct. If he leaves out one or more lines, or if he places any of the lines in the wrong position, score it as incorrect.

That is the end of the test if, indeed, he has lasted this long. Before I tell you how to interpret his performance, I will show you some examples of test responses and how they were scored. It might help prevent some confusion.

Shown on the pattern maps below are four responses, labeled A, B, C, and D.

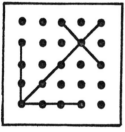

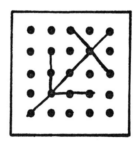

ITEM 7

A

Incorrect

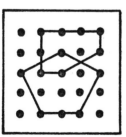

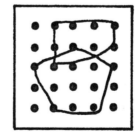

ITEM 9

B

Correct

ITEM 12
C

ITEM 18
D

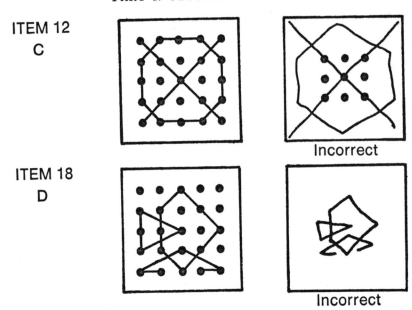

Incorrect

Incorrect

"A" shows a child's incorrect response to test item 7. Can you see why it is incorrect? All of the lines are there, but some are positioned on the wrong dots. "B" is a correct response to item 9. All the lines are there and, even though they are not drawn precisely, it is obvious that the child was able to identify all the lines and their proper positions on the map. "C" is an incorrect response to item 12. Although all the lines are there, some are positioned incorrectly—you have to pretend the dots are there when you assess the child's performance. Finally, look at "D". It is an incorrect response to item 18 because it, too, is not positioned properly—even though all the lines are there and the shape is drawn correctly.

Interpreting the test results

Scoring these items is not that confusing if you will keep in mind what is being tested—the child's ability to analyze a pattern into its separate parts and show that he recognizes how these parts fit together; and the border is one of the parts in these test items.

Now you have to determine whether the child's performance is adequate for his grade level. What is the last item he copied correctly before he produced two incorrects in succession? That is his score on the TVAS. For example, suppose he copied items 1, 2, 3, and 4 correctly, but was incorrect on items 5 and 6. His TVAS score would be 4. Try another; suppose he copied items 1, 2, and 3 correctly, was incorrect on 4, correct again on 5 and 6, and incorrect on items 7 and 8. The test ends here (2 incorrects in a row). His TVAS score would be 6.

Relate his TVAS score to this chart:

TVAS SCORE	EXPECTED FOR CHILDREN IN:
1	Preschool
2	Preschool
3	Kindergarten
4	Kindergarten
5	Kindergarten
6	Kindergarten
7	Kindergarten
8	Grade 1
9	Grade 1
10	Grade 1
11	Grade 1
12	Grade 2
13	Grade 2
14	Grade 2
15	Grade 2
16	Grade 2
17	Grade 3
18	Grade 3

To read the chart, find the child's score in the left-hand column. Opposite that number is the grade level of children who customarily earn this score on the TVAS. For example, if the child's score is 5, we would expect him to be in kindergarten. If, in fact, he is in kindergarten, you can assume that his visual perceptual skills are normal. If he is only in preschool, he is probably precocious. If, on the other hand, he is in first grade or beyond, you can assume that his visual perceptual skills are below the expected level and are contributing to his school learning problem.

A score of 11 would be satisfactory for a child in the first grade or below. If he is in a higher grade, his performance on the TVAS would be considered substandard.

As you can see from the chart, no item in the TVAS—not even the final two—should be too difficult for a child in the third grade or above. If it is, it again indicates inadequate visual perceptual skills.

Many people ask whether there should not be some more difficult items—items that would challenge sixth and seventh graders, for example. The answer is no, it is not called for. Once a child can respond accurately to the final items on this test, his visual perceptual skills are as good as they need be. That does not mean that a child who completed all the items of the TVAS could not be having difficulty in analyzing and organizing relatively complex spatial patterns. He could, indeed. But such a child will be better served if you deal with his problem in the subject areas themselves reading, spelling, arithmetic, and writing—rather than by trying to teach him more elaborate perceptual skills. I will tell you how to do that later on.

What next? If the child's performance with the TVAS is not at an expected level, make a note of what he did score. We will discuss what to do about it in the next section. Right now, move on to testing auditory skills.

AUDITORY PERCEPTUAL SKILLS TESTS

There are a variety of ways to test auditory perceptual skills, just as there are for testing visual perceptual skills. Most of these are auditory discrimination tests. In an auditory discrimination test the child is told to listen to a pair of spoken words that may or may not be identical, and asked to say whether they are the same or different. For example, the pair "win-when" is stated by the examiner, and the child is expected to say "different." If the pair is "win-win," the correct answer is "same."

Auditory discrimination tests have been used extensively with children from about five years of age and up, and some relationship has been shown between children's performance on this test and their reading achievement. I have two complaints about such tests. One, they require *only* a discrimination response; once the child recognizes that the two words differ, he need not analyze them further. He does not have to show that he knows how to analyze the whole spoken word down into its separate parts—individual sounds known as phonemes—and that he recognizes how those phonemes fit together, their sequence. Second, teaching a child to pass an auditory discrimination test does not appear to have any great value in helping him learn to read.

The Test of Auditory Analysis Skills (TAAS)— A test you can administer

The Test of Auditory Analysis Skills (TAAS) is a mate to the TVAS. In fact, it was designed with the same general goals in mind—that is, not only to provide a way for testing a child's auditory perceptual skills, but also to identify goals for teaching these skills. The child can be taught to pass the test and the effects of the teaching will be apparent elsewhere—most important to us, in his reading and spelling.

First, I will give you a general description of what the test is about. Then I will describe the test itself. Later on I will tell you how you can teach the child the skills he needs to pass the test.

The TAAS starts at a relatively simple level; it can be used with kindergarten children. For example, the child is asked to analyze a two-syllable, compound word into syllables. He is told, "Say *baseball*." Then, "Now say it again, but don't say *ball*" or, "don't say *base*." He is to say only what remains, once he has located and deleted the part of the word designated by the tester. Then three-syllable words are used. For example, the child is asked to "Say *cucumber*." Then, "Now say it again, but don't say *cue*."

Once the child shows that he can deal with this task at the syllable level, he is confronted with a more refined unit of analysis—the phoneme—the single sound. For example, he may be asked to "Say *meat*; now say it again, but don't say the /m/ sound."* To respond correctly, he must search for the /m/ sound in the word *meat*, delete it, and say what is left (*eat*). The position of the sound is controlled, starting with the easiest—the beginning sound as in the above example; then the final sound ("Say *wrote*; now say it again without the /t/ sound"); then part of a consonant blend ("Say *play*; now say it again, but don't say the /p/ sound"; or "Say *stale*; now say it again, but don't say the /t/ sound"). Fuller details will be given after the complete test is described. Before I do that, I want to give you some insights into what an auditory perceptual problem means to a school-aged child.

Skills for reading

What does the child with inadequate auditory perceptual skills experience in the classroom? It is analogous, in a way, to a task I described earlier—copying a square foot of grass lawn. Consider the following (imagine that I am speaking to you orally, rather than through the medium of this printed page): "Please listen to this phrase and write it down *exactly* the way I say it. In other words, show me how you heard what I said, and do it in a way that represents my spoken message exactly. The phrase is '*I like you.*' I'll repeat it; '*I like you.*' Write that down exactly the way I said it."

Whenever I use this illustration, I invariably get the writ-

---

*When a letter is shown between slashes /m/, you are to say the letter *sound* "mmm," not the letter name "em"; for /s/ say "sss," not "ess"; for /r/ say "rrr," not "are."

ten answer "I like you." But what I literally said was *"ilikeyou,"* not pausing at all between the words. Was the conventional answer wrong? No. We all follow these rules when we put spoken language on paper. The rules say—and you were taught them so long ago that you no longer think about them—that when we represent speech with print, we must use certain organizational devices: small spaces to separate the individual letters within a word, and larger spaces to separate the words; capital letters to indicate the start of a sentence, a period to signal its end, and a comma or some other punctuation device to separate clauses. A second line of print ordinarily parallels the first and is positioned a certain distance below; all lines of print start at the same place on the left side of the page—in other words, there is a margin. All these rules help the reader obtain information efficiently from the printed page. They are important rules. Imagine how difficult itwouldbetoreadfrompagesthatlookedlikethis.

We do not apply the same rules when we speak. Although we will pause between certain clusters of words (if only to breathe), we do not pause between each word. Indeed, who could tolerate us, let alone pay attention, if we did. It would be extremely dull and, worse yet, the listener would be very likely to forget the first part of the sentence before the last part was spoken. This point is important. Visual information is relatively permanent. It stays visible as long as whoever is in charge allows it to remain in view. Acoustical information—spoken words—becomes inaudible immediately. There is no time to waste; if the listener cannot organize the information rapidly, he is bound to encounter difficulty.

To make matters worse, we all tend to use different speaking styles. Some of us talk fast, some drawl, some speak in long sentences, some in short sentences; all of which serves to place additional burdens on the listener. We assume that the listener will be able to deal with the job of organizing the sounds into proper clusters—a reasonable assumption if the listener not only knows all the words, but knows them well enough to sort them out and keep them ordered as they are spoken in a continuous stream.

If you studied a foreign language for a few years while in school, try to imagine what this would be like: Say your foreign language was French and that you have a fair background in the language. Imagine that you are tuned to a French language radio station, and that you are trying to translate what the speaker is saying. It is challenging, to say the least, even though you may know every word that is being said. Being able to translate individual words is not equivalent to dealing with them in the context of oral language. When someone speaks rapidly, the task of translating becomes exceedingly demanding. Think, for example, of the old song "mareseatoatsanddoeseatoats, etc."; a long string of nonsense sounds until the sounds are sorted out and organized into meaningful words. Find someone who is unfamiliar with that song and ask him to memorize the first few lines. Difficult, to be sure. There are a lot of sounds to memorize. Now, speak the phrase, "mares-eat-oats, etc." so that each word is stated separately rather than run together. Memorizing would now be much easier. There are far fewer words than sounds, and to help matters, the words are meaningful.

Now back to the child with an auditory perceptual problem. He listens to spoken instructions and tries to remember all that is being said, but he runs out of space in his memory—particularly if the instructions are at all lengthy and complicated. He then tends to stop paying attention. (How long will you pay attention to the French radio announcer when you cannot keep up with the task of translation?) Yet, when the child's hearing is checked (and it should be), there is usually nothing wrong. That is, he can hear as well as anyone else. It ordinarily is not the child's hearing that is inadequate—it is his capacity to organize what he hears as quickly as the situation demands.

Visualize this situation: A teacher tells her class, "Everyone open their desk, take out the blue workbook, open it to page 23, and start to answer the questions. I'll be around to see each of you in a moment." There are five separate directions in that statement. How many of those will the child with substandard auditory perceptual skills recall? We cannot say for sure, but we can take a fairly good guess at what he is apt to forget.

Memory studies have shown that the best-remembered part, in a string of spoken parts, is usually the final one; then the first; then what is in-between. So the child will probably best remember that his teacher said she would "be around to see him" soon. There is no comfort in that! Then he will probably remember that he is to "open his desk." But the rest, the part that was in-between? Maybe he recalls it, maybe he does not. Chances are that he does not; and, if he has any practical intelligence, he knows that asking the teacher to repeat herself will usually just cause him more trouble. So he tries to figure out what his neighbors are up to, and crosses his fingers in the hope that the teacher will not get to him.

There is another even more important level of concern. That is, the fine-grained analysis of spoken words into phonemes—sorting out the individual sounds within a spoken word. It is not difficult to see how this relates to reading. After all, what is involved in learning to read? Certainly the child must learn to discriminate the letters of the alphabet, to recognize them as distinctly different symbols, and to remember their individual identities. But he must do more. He must learn to "map" sounds onto these letters; that is, to attach certain specific spoken sounds to certain specific printed letters or combinations of letters.

It is true that some children learn to read by remembering whole words as "pictures" of a sort, rather than by "sounding them out." Such words are called "sight words," and they are usually learned as units—memorized—since they cannot be sounded out. For example, the words "said" and "the." But there is a limit to how many sight words a child can remember. One cannot memorize the entire printed language.

This, of course, was the basis for the old, and now discarded, "Look—Say" method of teaching reading. Indeed, a lot of children did learn to read with that method, but they certainly did not memorize all of the words. They had capable perceptual skills. They learned to sound out words by figuring out for themselves the phonic rules of reading (or a good teacher taught them some of the sounding-out rules as a fringe benefit). How? Well, each child who did accomplish the transition from "Look-Say" to "sounding out" probably arrived at it somewhat differently, but consider this as a possibility: The child first learned the following sight words—*mother, something,* and *jump.* (Many of you must recall how Spot was forever jumping!) His visual and auditory perceptual skills were good. He recognized certain visual and acoustical features· that showed up in each of those three words—specifically, that in each word there was a letter *m* and a /m/ sound that were obviously related. ("Obviously" to him, that is—not to his classmates with less competent perceptual skills.) Having observed this, when he came across the printed word *me,* for example, he applied what he had discovered—and it worked! He could read the word by sounding it out! Pretty soon, he was discovering more letter-sound relationships. And his teacher, if she was a good one, was helping him discover them by pointing out the relevant visual and acoustical features when he did not discover them on his own.

Could the child have done this if he was not able to analyze spoken words into their individual sounds? Hardly! You have to recognize the elements that are to be coded before you can start to use the code. This, then, is why capable auditory perceptual skills are vital to beginning readers. No teacher managing a classroom of twenty-five or more children can take the time to teach every letter-sound rule to every child, no matter how well trained and motivated the teacher might be. The children must discover some of the rules on their own, or at least understand the concept —"get it"—the first time it is presented to them. If their auditory skills are such that they cannot readily isolate the individual sounds *within a spoken word,* the probability of their understanding the concept of letters standing for sounds is quite low.

Thus, auditory perceptual skills are important for at least two reasons. First, they enable the child to receive and recall oral communication effectively—an absolute must for satisfactory classroom performance; second, they make it possible for the child to be aware of the individual sounds that will be represented by letters when he starts to learn to read and spell.

Giving the TAAS

The test starts off with two demonstration items that are intended to show the child what he is expected to do. The first (item A) goes like this: "Say *cowboy.*" (Now pause and allow him to respond. This lets you know that he heard the word.) Then say: "Now say it again but don't say *boy.*" Give him time to respond. (The correct answer, of course, is *cow.*)

If he gets this one correct, move on to the second demonstration item. If he does not get item A correct, see if you can explain it to him. But if it requires more than a simple explanation, stop testing.

The second demonstration item (item B) is "Say *steamboat.*" (Pause—wait for his response.) "Now say it again, but don't say *steam.*"

If he answers both demonstration items correctly, start the test with Item 1. If he does not answer both demonstration items correctly, do not administer any more items.

NOTE:

• 1. Do not give him hints with your lips. Speak distinctly, but do not stress any particular sounds. In other words, do not give him any additional information that might make the task easier. Sure, you want him to do well, but not at the expense of looking better on the test than he really is. The results would be misleading and deprive him of the chance to learn the skills needed for reading and spelling. Just as with the TVAS, this test gives you a way to determine if the child's auditory skills are up to the demands of his classroom instructional program, what skills he already knows, and which ones he should learn next.

2. Remember, when you get to the items that ask the child to "Say the word, but don't say /. . ./. [a single sound]" you are to say the sound of the letter, *not the letter name.*

3. Stop testing after two successive errors—*two incorrects in a row*—and record the number of the last correct item before those two errors. That is his TAAS score. For example, if he was correct with items 1, 2, 3, 4, and 5, then incorrect on items 6 and 7, his TAAS score would be 5. If he was correct on 1, 2, and 3, incorrect on 4, correct on 5 and 6, then incorrect on 7 and 8, his TAAS score would be 6.

FIGURE 31

A	Say **cowboy**	Now say it again, but don't say **boy**	**cow**
B	Say **steamboat**	Now say it again, but don't say **steam**	**boat**
1	Say **sunshine**	Now say it again, but don't say **shine**	**sun**
2	Say **picnic**	Now say it again, but don't say **pic**	**nic**
3	Say **cucumber**	Now say it again, but don't say **cu (q)**	**cumber**
4	Say **coat**	Now say it again, but don't say /**k**/ (the **k** sound)	**oat**
5	Say **meat**	Now say it again, but don't say /**m**/ (the **m** sound)	**eat**
6	Say **take**	Now say it again, but don't say /**t**/ (the **t** sound)	**ache**
7	Say **game**	Now say it again, but don't say /**m**/	**gay**
8	Say **wrote**	Now say it again, but don't say /**t**/	**row**
9	Say **please**	Now say it again, but don't say /**z**/	**plea**
10	Say **clap**	Now say it again, but don't say /**k**/	**lap**
11	Say **play**	Now say it again, but don't say /**p**/	**lay**
12	Say **stale**	Now say it again, but don't say /**t**/	**sale**
13	Say **smack**	Now say it again, but don't say /**m**/	**sack**

XAVIER UNIVERSITY LIBRARY
NEW ORLEANS, LA. 70125

AUDITORY PERCEPTUAL SKILLS

Interpreting the test results

That is the end of the test—if he has lasted this long.

Now you have to determine whether the child's performance was adequate for his grade level. Make note of his score—the last item he answered correctly before he produced two wrong answers in succession—and relate it to the following chart.

TAAS SCORE	EXPECTED FOR CHILDREN IN:
1	Kindergarten
2	Kindergarten
3	Kindergarten
4	Grade 1
5	Grade 1
6	Grade 1
7	Grade 1
8	Grade 1
9	Grade 1
10	Grade 2
11	Grade 2
12	Grade 3
13	Grade 3

To read the chart, locate the child's score in the left-hand column. Opposite that number is the grade level of children who customarily earn this score. For example, if the child's score is 3, we would expect him to be in kindergarten. If he is in kindergarten, you can assume that his auditory perceptual skills are normal. If he is in preschool, he is probably precocious. If, on the other hand, he is in first grade or beyond, you can assume that his auditory perceptual skills are inadequate and, as such, are contributing to his school learning problem.

What if his score is 9? Then his auditory perceptual skills

79

can be considered satisfactory if he is in the first grade or below. If he is in a higher grade, his performance on the TAAS is to be considered substandard.

As you can see from the chart, no item in the TAAS—not even the final ones—should be too difficult for a child in the third grade or above. If it is, it again indicates inadequate auditory perceptual skills.

Just as with visual perceptual skills, many people are interested in finding auditory perceptual skills tests that are difficult enough to challenge older children—fifth and sixth graders, for example. In my judgment, this is not worthwhile. It would be possible to construct such a test, but there would be little of practical value in it. Children who can pass all the items on the TAAS could, perhaps, still have some discrete auditory perceptual problem. But such children will be better served if you deal with their problem as it is revealed in the subject areas—reading and spelling —rather than by teaching elaborate auditory perceptual skills. After all, your goal is satisfactory classroom achievement—not superior perceptual skills.

Now what? If the child's performance with the TAAS is not at an expected level, make a note of what he scores. We will discuss what to do about it in the next section. Right now, move on to testing general-motor skills.

GENERAL-MOTOR SKILLS

So far, very little mention has been made of general-motor skills. What are they? Are they important? Should they be tested? By whom? How do they fit into what has already been discussed?

General-motor skills have been associated with learning problems for some time. In fact, when professionals first became aware of the child with a learning disability, the major treatment methods emphasized general-motor training—activities that helped the child become better coordinated. As time passed, it became clear that good motor skills, in themselves, were not the answer. We all know too many beautifully coordinated illiterates and too many clumsy geniuses to support that position.

It is true that many children with learning problems do display poor motor coordination, but there is little evidence that the one is the direct cause of the other. In a way then, emphasizing motor skills is much the same as centering on such symptoms as distractibility and hyperactivity. Helping a child improve his motor skills, and doing nothing else for him, will not solve his learning problems.

Then why test motor skills? Earlier in this book, I observed that testing is justified only when it provides information that will help you make better decisions about how to help your child. We test general-motor skills because, although they are not *directly* linked to school achievement, they are related to the higher level perceptual skills just discussed—visual and auditory analysis and organization abilities.

To explain that relationship appropriately, we will now look at how all these skills develop. This is of more than theoretical interest, for you will be identifying certain basic principles that can be applied in all of your subsequent work with the child. Then I will describe the general-motor tests that he should take.

Perceptual skills development

No child is born with the skills that he will ultimately need in order to succeed in school. If he is lucky, he is born with the proper equipment—eyes, ears, hands, voice, and an intact nervous system that, in time, will be able to control that equipment efficiently. It is predictable that if these two conditions are met, and nothing else occurs to interrupt normal development, he will acquire the skills necessary for school success. He is human, and therefore genetically programmed to develop much the same as the rest of the members of the species. The big question, however, is will he acquire the skills on schedule, in accord with society's expectations. In other words, we know that he will enter the first grade sometime near his sixth birthday. Will his skills be ready for the task? How ready they will be is a function of his growth and development. It is an interaction between what he was endowed with at conception, and the environment in which he spends his early years; the condition of his equipment at birth, and how well he learns to use that equipment.

There are two general rules of development that apply throughout this discussion. The first is that all developed abilities are quite global—inseparable—when the child is very young and, after a period of time, become increasingly differentiated—sorted out. The second rule to bear in mind is that as children develop, they require less tangible confirmation of what they see and hear in order to analyze and organize it. That is, as they grow and accumulate experiences, it is not as important for them to touch what they see in order to be certain about the construction of what they are seeing, nor to repeat what they hear in order to confirm the construction of the sounds they are hearing.

Gross-motor development

I will illustrate what is meant by the first rule: that all developed abilities are global at first, and get more differentiated as the child matures. Think of the gross-motor actions of the newborn. He responds reflexively to stimuli in the environment; that is, he does not voluntarily control his actions. If you lie him on his back with his head turned to one side, he will assume a position called the tonic-neck reflex. The arm and leg on the side toward which his head is turned will be extended; the opposite arm and leg will be flexed.

If the child's head turns, or is turned, to the other side, both arms and legs will shift position accordingly. The arm and leg that were extended will flex. The arm and leg on the opposite side will extend. It is evidence of the global nature of the infant's motor system; he does not move one part of himself without making some compensatory or balancing movements in the rest of his body. He has yet to

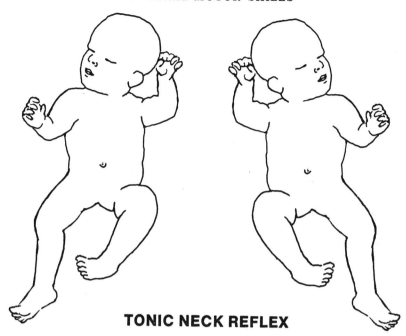

TONIC NECK REFLEX

learn that he is made up of a number of movable parts, many of which he will ultimately be able to control separately and precisely.

Sometime around his sixteenth week of life, this reflexive posture disappears, replaced by another that allows him a little more freedom of movement. Now he is able to move certain parts of himself—his arms, for instance—without moving all of himself. As time passes he continues to develop, learning to roll over at will, to sit up, creep, and stand with some support.

At his first birthday party, he displays greater differentiation of his general-motor skills. He is able to reorganize his body parts in a broader variety of ways. He is probably able to walk, with some support. In some cases, he might even be able to walk without support, although this is not necessarily expected at this time in his life.

He has made obvious progress along the pathway of growth and development—learning differentiated control of his own body movements. But he has not yet reached the point where he can balance on one foot, hop on one foot, or skip. These will occur somewhere between his third and sixth birthday; he will learn to balance on one foot; a while after that he will learn to hop on one foot and, ordinarily, he will learn to skip during his kindergarten year.

What is so important about all this? First-grade teachers are concerned about teaching children to read, print, count; yet a knowledgeable first-grade teacher is not pleased when she observes that a child is poorly coordinated—that he cannot hop on each foot, for instance. The awkward child, the one who is poorly coordinated, is immature. Intuitively or otherwise, his teacher recognizes this and knows that it is not a good sign.

Most teachers know that if a child is immature in one aspect of his behavior, he is probably immature in others as well. Each of the behaviors I mentioned—early reflexive postures, sitting up, standing, walking, balancing on one foot, hopping on one foot, skipping, and others—show that the child is learning to understand his own body construction as a collection of separate parts that work together in a variety of ways. They are milestones in his development.

MOTOR DEVELOPMENT MILESTONES

APPROXIMATE AGE	MOTOR ACTION
60 months	Skips
50 months	Hops on one foot
32 months	Balances on one foot
15 months	Walks unaided
14 months	Stands unaided
7 months	Sits up unaided
4 months	Rolls over unaided
0-4 months	Tonic neck reflex

There is an expected date when most children achieve these milestones, and although a certain amount of variance is acceptable, significant lags in reaching these stages signal immaturity and all that it implies. Each milestone is another sign of general maturation and a major factor in predicting classroom performance. Indeed, it is not by coincidence that most I.Q. tests for infants focus heavily on various motor skills.

Fine-motor development

How about the finer motor skills—especially those called upon in the classroom? These, too, progress along similar pathways. For example, the newborn does not use his hands in a very precise way. Yes, he will momentarily grasp a rattle when it is placed in his palm, but he will just as readily let it go. It is not a voluntary behavior. He has not yet gained any real control over his hands.

As he grows, he shows changes. At his first birthday, he can intentionally pick up a block, although it is with his whole hand, in what is called a palmar grasp. He holds his spoon in his fist, a normal behavior. He manages to get food into his mouth, but not without a certain number of near misses that necessitate a general clean-up operation after each meal. Picking up small objects, such as raisins, is no small feat. He has not yet achieved the developmental stage where he can use one finger and the thumb together in a precise manner. But it will come.

By the time he enters the first grade, he should have gained precise control over the separate parts of his hand— his fingers—and learned how they can operate together in a variety of ways, depending on the task. If he still clutches a pencil with his whole fist, or if he still has to hold it with four or five fingers, it will signal something to his teacher. It will not necessarily be seen as a sign of low intelligence, but it certainly will be considered a sign of immaturity.

An experienced teacher will know that in many instances it predicts trouble. Why? Surely a child's ability to read, spell, and calculate should, to a large degree, be independent of the way he holds a pencil; and it is. But his pencil grip, his ability to tie his shoelaces into a bow, his ability to manipulate a scissors, are all important indicators of his general development. Again, they are milestones that enable us to chart the child's maturation. As such, lags in the development of certain fine-motor skills may predict similar lags in other processes—processes that, when joined together, form the basis for the remarkably complex set of learning and thinking abilities that are called for in school.

Similar observations can be made of the infant's control over his speech production mechanism. He can make vocal noises at birth—undifferentiated cries that vary only in volume. As the infant grows, some mothers insist that their baby has more than one cry; that they can tell when he is crying from hunger in contrast to when he cries from pain—evidence of some sorting-out process, but still quite gross. As he continues to develop, the baby starts to experiment with his vocal mechanism—cooing, babbling, and making all those marvelous sounds that babies make when they are content. Finally, he learns a word or two, and is strongly applauded for the accomplishment. He learns more words, but his words are not clearly articulated. He talks baby talk —a totally acceptable behavior from a two- or three-year-old. But if he arrives in the first grade still talking baby talk—still unable to demonstrate that he has learned how the various components of his speech production mechanism work together—his teachers will be concerned. He will be showing that he is immature—not unintelligent but, rather, someone who has not achieved certain developmental milestones on schedule. Again, not a shameful state, but one that tends to foretell less-than-satisfactory classroom learning performance.

We can discuss the child's ability to control his eye movements from this same aspect. It has been shown that the very young infant will, for very brief periods of time, look at and even follow a visual target that is unusually bright or otherwise interesting, *if* the target is placed squarely before his eyes and then not moved too far away from the central zone of his vision. These are fairly elaborate abilities, but hardly up to the level called for in a first-grade classroom. By that time, the child should be able to control his eye movements both accurately and easily. He should be able to shift his gaze from the blackboard, to his desk, to his teacher, and wherever else, with facility. He should be able to move his eyes across a line of print without losing his place and without devoting a great deal of mental energy to the task.

By the time the child enters the first grade, these should all be virtually automatic actions; he should not have to think about them, nor should they require a lot of physical effort. When he starts to learn to read, he should be moving his eyes, not his head, as he proceeds along a line of print. Is it bad to move the whole head rather than just the eyes? No, it is not bad, but it is inefficient. It is once again an indicator of immaturity, a sign that the child has not learned to use his oculomotor mechanism—the muscles that control his eye movements—in a precise way.

The relationship of motor skills development to perceptual skills

What does all this have to do with the visual and auditory analysis skills discussed earlier—skills that are so very important to school learning? This brings us to the second general rule relevant to developed functions. The first (the one we have been discussing for the past few pages) is that all these developed abilities are unsorted at first and get more differentiated over time. The second rule, you will recall, is that as children mature they require less tangible contact with sensory information in order to understand it effectively.

What does that mean in practical terms? Simply, that young children tend to confirm what they see by touching or tasting, or otherwise making physical contact. As they mature, this need diminishes. Most first graders do not have to come into direct contact with everything they want to locate and examine. They can do it visually, from a distance.

For example, as a child develops, he is less likely to bump into doorways and furniture as he walks about. He reaches for his glass of milk with more precision. He places his feet more accurately as he goes up and down stairs. In part, of course, this can be attributed to the fact that his motor skills are becoming more differentiated. But it also is due to the fact that each physical contact with a visible object has helped teach the eyes to control the motor action a trifle more precisely. It is evidence that vision has slowly taken over the dominant role in guiding the child's actions; that he has learned to look, then act, and then learn from what happens.

In a sense, it is as though the child has grown imaginary hands that extend from his eyes. He can grasp and explore with his eyes; certainly a more efficient process than literally needing to grasp and explore with his hands. His ability to investigate his visual world expands greatly and becomes more efficient. Said another way, by physically exploring the visual world and coming into contact with objects in that world with various parts of the body—particularly his hands—the child learns how the visual world is constructed; that it comprises many different elements that relate to each other in a variety of ways.

Eventually, physical contact becomes relatively unimportant. Visual examination will do for most situations; that is, unless a sufficiently demanding or novel situation arises. Then the child, and indeed the adult, will behave in a less mature fashion and display the need for physical contact once again.

For example, suppose you found yourself perched on a narrow plank, high in the air. Which would you trust most —your eyes or your feet? What you saw or what you felt? Undoubtedly, you would use both sources of information, but there is little question that you would explore that plank very carefully with your feet. Tangible information is highly important in such circumstances.

Here is another example, more familiar to many adults. Have you ever had the experience of getting new eyeglasses and noticing that, despite the fact that you saw more clearly, things were not in their proper location? The floor looked too close, perhaps, or too far away, or distorted? What did you do about it? In the vast majority of cases, you got used to the glasses. That does not mean you accepted the fact that the floor *should* look distorted. Not at all. You walked around with your new glasses on, you touched the floor with your feet, it *felt* level, and gradually the distortions disappeared. Your body actions and contacts taught your eyes. In a way, this was a reliving of the kinds of experiences you had as a very young child when the world around you was completely unfamiliar and had to be explored physically in order to be understood.

The need to touch, to explore physically, persists with some children. Some enter the first grade showing this very clearly. They seem unable to walk through a corridor or a classroom without touching walls, desks, other classmates. They have trouble discriminating between the *b* and *d* unless they go through the physical act of exploring, tracing over, the letter. In a primary arithmetic class, their need to touch when counting objects continues far longer than it does for most of their classmates. Bad behaviors? No, merely inefficient—and, once more, a signal that there is some lag in maturation.

A similar kind of relationship exists between the speech mechanism and the ears. Again, in a sense, one teaches the other. As the child learns to speak, he hears what he says, matches that with what he hears others say, speaks again— a trifle more distinctly—and so on. Gradually his auditory perceptual skills become more precise, which facilitates his acquisition of articulate speech, which, in turn, tends to make his auditory skills more differentiated. Again it is a looplike hook-up, with each function assisting the performance of the other.

Just as the hands enable the child to get tangible information about what he is seeing, so too does the speech production mechanism provide tangible information about sounds that are heard. It is the only way you can get your "hands" on vocal sounds. The /m/ sound and /n/ sound "feel" obviously different to the speaker—more different, actually, than how they sound to the ear.

But, once the child enters first grade, it should no longer be necessary for him to repeat all that he hears in order to analyze and organize it. His ears should be able to function independently—and certainly more efficiently. Repeating words—making tangible contact with the sounds—should be unnecessary, except when a new and complex word is introduced. What if this behavior persists? Bad? No—just one more indicator of delayed maturation.

Now let us see if we can put all this information into some organized framework that will help us decide which of his general-motor skills we want to test. The diagram shown in Figure 34 illustrates the relationship between general-motor skills, auditory and visual perceptual skills, and school learning—reading, spelling, arithmetic, and writing.

FIGURE 34

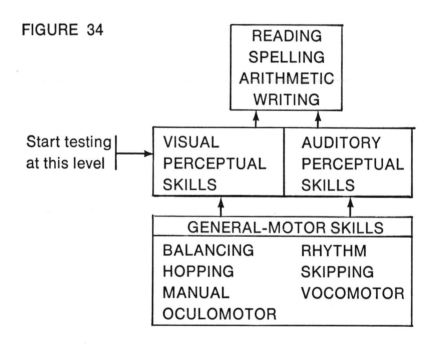

Note that the lower level general-motor skills are directly connected, as supports, to the auditory and visual perceptual skills. Also note that the general-motor skills are shown as two clusters rather than as one general set of abilities.

On the left-hand side, shown as being more directly related to visual perceptual abilities, are those skills that indicate how refined a body concept the child has developed; how aware he is of his body parts and the way those parts can work together. These include such gross-motor actions as balancing and hopping on each foot, and fine-motor manual skills such as cutting with a scissors, controlling a crayon or a pencil, and tying a bow. Oculomotor skills—the ability to control eye movements—also fall into this category. Certainly, if the child is to learn by looking, then how well he can control where his eyes are aimed is pertinent.

On the right-hand side, more closely related to the auditory perceptual abilities, are those gross-motor skills that are essentially rhythmic in nature, involving a synchronized coordination of the two body sides. Skipping and tapping rhythmically are representative. One fine-motor skill belongs in this cluster. This is the ability to control tongue, teeth, and lip movements—the vocomotor skills that are closely connected to speech production which, in turn, is related to auditory perception.

As the diagram indicates, testing should start at the middle level—with the auditory and visual skills. If these appear to be adequate, there is no need to test the lower-level abilities unless you have a separate interest in that information. If the middle level (visual and auditory) skills are not adequate, then you should test the general-motor skills.

There is a second reason for testing general-motor skills, namely, when you observe that the child's school performance is being directly affected by certain inadequate motor abilities—such as an inability to speak clearly or write legibly. Children are judged in schools not by what they know but by what they can demonstrate that they know. There are children who have trouble with the motor act of writing or, for that matter, speaking clearly—the two ways that are almost invariably called upon when the child is asked to show what he knows. It therefore makes sense to take a careful look at the child's fine-motor skills simply because of this efficiency factor. The harder the child has to work at writing legibly or speaking distinctly, the less opportunity he will have to devote attention to more abstract matters— the information he is trying to think about and communicate.

Who should test the child's general-motor skills?

Manual skills are easy to assess; their investigation does not ordinarily require a trained professional. You are probably not as certain about your ability to test the child's speech production and eye-movement skills. These two do warrant the involvement of trained professionals, if such persons are available, and if you observe evidence that suggests the need for their participation. However, do not ignore these speech production and oculomotor skills if professionals are unavailable. You will not do the job as well as a professional, but some help for the child in these areas is far better than no help at all.

Which skills should be tested?

Testing general-motor skills is simple—that is, the general-motor skills we are concerned about. Standardized tests are available, but, in my opinion, these are not necessary. Simply go through the following procedures.

If the child did not do as well as he should have on the TVAS (visual), see if he can:

- 1. Balance on one foot for about ten seconds; then on the other for ten seconds.
- 2. Hop a distance of about 15 feet on one foot; then on the other.
- 3. Draw a pencil line connecting two dots situated four inches apart horizontally, then vertically, then diagonally.

- 4. Cut along a line with scissors.
- 5. Tie a shoelace into a bow.
- 6. Stretch his hands out in front of himself, thumbs held upright and about 16 inches apart. Then, as you say "left," "right," etc., he is to *look at* his left thumb, his right thumb, and so forth, making five or six cycles. (This is not a test of his knowledge of left and right. Show him which is which.) Call out "left," "right," in a regular tempo, with the shifts occurring about every two seconds. (You do not need a stopwatch. The time is not that critical. Just do it at a moderate and regular pace.) Watch the child's eyes. Do they move together? Can he find the target quickly and stay on it until told to shift?
7. Follow a visual target with both eyes as it is brought toward his nose. He should be able to keep *both eyes* on that target, at least until it is within a couple of inches of his nose. His eyes should then appear to be crossed. Watch his eyes as you do this test.

If the child did not do as well as he should have on the TAAS (auditory), see if he can:

- 1. Skip, and maintain that pattern over a distance of about 15 feet.
- 2. Tap rhythmically, as follows: you (the examiner) demonstrate. Tap two times with your right hand, then two times with your left, then two times again with your right hand, and so forth, saying to the child as you tap, "Watch me, then tap this way . . . two times with this hand [R], then two times with this one [L], then two times with this [R]. Don't stop between any of the taps. Keep it up until I tell you to stop." The child is to tap at a steady, rhythmic pace. The taps should be spaced at about two per second. There should be no disruption in tempo when he shifts from one hand to the other, nor should he lose the right-left tapping sequence. Stop him at the end of five complete cycles if he gets that far.

If he is eight years old, or older, introduce a more complex rhythm after you have tested him with the simpler one. This more complex one goes as follows: you (the examiner) demonstrate. Tap one time with your right hand, then two times with your left, then one time again with your right, and so forth, saying as you tap, "Watch me, then tap this way . . . one time with this hand [R], then two times with this [L], then one time with this [R], and so forth. Don't stop between any of the taps. Keep it up until I tell you to stop." The child is to tap at a steady, rhythmic pace—about two taps per second. There should be no break in tempo when he shifts from one hand to the other, nor should he lose the right-left tapping sequence. Stop him at the end of five complete cycles, if he gets that far. Then, repeat the test, this time with the right hand tapping twice and the left hand once.

- 3. Control his tongue movements to the extent that he can puff out his right cheek with his tongue, then his left cheek, then his right, and so forth, at a steady tempo. Show him what he is to do and set the pace by calling "right," "left," "right," "left," and so forth, at about a one-per-second pace. Stop at the end of six complete cycles, if he has not lost the rhythm before that.

If the child is old enough to be in the first grade, he is old enough to be expected to perform all of the motor acts described above, with the exception of the 1-2-1-2 rhythmic tapping task (this is quite difficult for children younger than eight). Take note of the ones that he fails. We will discuss what to do about it in the next section.

This testing sequence could be extended further and made more elaborate, but what I have described is sufficient to get the basic information you need. Namely, to find out whether you should have the child spend some time improving his motor skills, the justification being that the effort will pay off in the classroom. Once you have the answer to that question, additional tests are not necessary. There is no need to turn the affair into an exhibition, especially if the child is poorly coordinated. The repeated tests will merely ask him to display his inadequacies repeatedly.

I.Q. TESTING

I.Q. testing is a well-established institution in our schools, yet rarely have I seen it used to the child's advantage.

What is an Intelligence Quotient (I.Q.)? It is easier to tell you what it is not. It is *not* a measure of a child's intellectual or learning potential. It is *not* a stable index—it can vary a great deal with individual children. Hence, it is *not* a foolproof predictor of how well a child will do in school.

A child's I.Q. is a number that tells you how well he did on an I.Q. test. That circular definition just about sums it up. If a child has the problem-solving skills and the general information necessary to answer the I.Q. test questions in the allotted time—and if he is motivated to perform well— he will earn a high score and have a better-than-average I.Q. If, on the other hand, the child is not motivated, or if he does not have the skills and information necessary to answer the I.Q. test questions in the allotted time, he will do poorly on the test and have a lower-than-average I.Q.

The rationale behind I.Q. testing is that if you measure what problem-solving skills and general (factual) information a child has learned up to some time in his life, and compare it to other children of the same age, you can predict fairly accurately how well he will learn in the future. On the average, this rationale works quite well; but it is not infallible, particularly when applied to individual children. Nor does it take into account that the child may very well perform differently tomorrow than he did yesterday—particularly if he is treated differently, or if he learns a set of problem-solving skills he never knew before, or if he acquires some new factual information.

What does all this mean in practical terms? Should your child have an I.Q. test? I see no value in it, *unless* the information derived from the test is going to be used clinically for the child's benefit. If the psychologist who administers the test is going to interpret the child's performance in terms of how he can be helped—then fine, I have no reservations about having the child tested. If, however, the test is given to make certain about whether the child has the potential to do better in school, then I strongly object to its use. What nonsense! To determine whether it is worth working with a child who is doing very poorly in school, based on how well he has done in school in the past, defeats the child before he begins. And, sure enough, once his teachers find out that he has a low I.Q., he is not likely to evoke any inspired efforts from them. "After all, he is not too bright—he has a limited potential." So, the prediction will come true. This process—a self-fulfilling prophecy— has had a devastating effect on many children. This does not mean that I deny the fact that some children can learn more and faster than others. Some children are indeed retarded. However, I have seen many retarded children learn to read because some dedicated person knew how to teach, and took the time and the trouble to teach them. They were still retarded, in terms of their I.Q. score, but *they could read*—at least at a level where they could compete more effectively in the job market. Why predict? Why not try to help the child first. You will cause no harm, unless you treat him cruelly. And you might help a lot.

ACADEMIC TESTING

Should you test his reading, spelling, and arithmetic skills? Or have someone else test them? No. Accept the school's judgment. If his teacher says he is lagging behind in these skills, believe her. You do not need anything more specific than that. When you start helping him in those areas, you will be teaching him *how* to do better—general underlying skills, rather than specific facts—and you will coordinate your efforts with his teacher. She will continue to determine *what* he should learn. I will discuss this more thoroughly in each of the subject area sections. For the present, accept the fact that there is no value in having the child take any academic tests beyond what he has already taken in school.

SUMMARY

This is about all the testing you need before you get to work helping your child acquire better skills. To review, I recommend the following tests:

HEALTH-RELATED
>   General medical status
>   Vision
>   Hearing

EDUCATION-RELATED
>   Visual perceptual skills
>   Auditory perceptual skills
>   General-motor skills (where indicated)

That is not a great deal of testing. In most cases, one visit will suffice for each of the health-related tests. Unless you are extremely uncomfortable with the idea, test the child's perceptual skills yourself. The TVAS and the TAAS are simple to administer and easy to interpret—and in the next section I will tell you what to do with that information.

One final word about testing. All children are sensitive to being different; that includes your child. Avoid excessive testing. Not only is it expensive in terms of time and money, it may also be demoralizing for the child. Tell him why he is being tested: that it is not because you want to see if he is abnormal in some way but, rather, to find a way to help him do better in school. And assure him that he can be helped. It is essential that both he and you are convinced that this is really so. And it is.

PART II
TESTING
the Child

NOW WHAT? You have taken care of the testing described in the previous section; you have tested the child's perceptual skills and have had professionals check into the state of his health, vision, and hearing. You are following through on the various professional recommendations. What do you do next?

There are two approaches, and we will consider both of them in depth. Namely, given a child with a learning problem and certain perceptual skills deficits,* you can:

- 1. Teach the child better perceptual skills wherever the testing showed a need.
- 2. Help the child with his school subjects (reading, writing, arithmetic, and spelling) in a way that takes his perceptual skills deficits into account, thus making it easier for him to do what he cannot do well on his own: recognize distinctive features and how they interrelate.

---

*This does not imply that every child who is having trouble in a school subject must also have some perceptual skills deficit. Some children have difficulty with some school subjects simply because they did not learn certain basic concepts—*and would have had no trouble learning those concepts if someone had taught them.* That is precisely how they differ from the child with inadequate perceptual skills. *He has unexpected trouble learning those basic concepts even though someone has tried to teach them to him;* "unexpected" because he does not appear to have trouble learning in the real world outside the classroom—the world of real things rather than symbols. The procedures described in the school subjects section of this book will help both kinds of children, although there is little doubt that it will help the one—the child with adequate perceptual skills—much more rapidly than it will help the other.

Said another way, the first approach suggests that the child be taught whatever basic perceptual skills he may lack so that he can learn to read, write, spell, and calculate as efficiently as his classmates do, using the same instructional materials they use. The second suggests that, since his perceptual skills are substandard, he should be taught to read, spell, write, and calculate in special ways—ways that accommodate his inadequate perceptual skills and will help him catch up with his classmates.

Which approach is best? Or should you combine them? In what proportions? That depends upon the age of the child and the extent of his problem. The younger he is, the more I lean toward teaching him better perceptual skills. The older he is, the better it is to spend your time teaching him to read, spell, calculate, and write in ways that accommodate his needs. In any case, except for the very young, preschool child, you should not exclude one approach completely and concern yourself solely with the other. That would be foolish. Your central goal is to help the child succeed in school, and to achieve that goal it is important that you explore all possibilities.*

The importance of daily lessons

You will have to work with your child daily. If he is to succeed in the public school, he must acquire skills that are

---

*So far I have been assuming that you will be able to accept the role of "teacher-in-residence." I recognize, however, that some of you will be unable to do it—either because you literally do not have the time or because, in your particular case, the situation is so highly charged emotionally that the outcome might be catastrophic.

If you cannot take on the job, then by all means look for someone who can. Perhaps a friendly neighbor, a grandparent, a college student who is interested in education, or any other understanding adult who can spare the time and has the motivation and capacity to follow simple directions.

If you cannot find such a person, look beyond your personal sphere of relatives and friends to your child's school. Perhaps they have someone available. If so, lend them this book and offer them whatever support you can.

Or, look to the community-at-large. In some areas parents have joined together for this express purpose. The Association for Children with Learning Disabilities (ACLD) is such a group. You can get information about them from their national offices at 5225 Grace Street, Pittsburgh, PA., 15236.

truly skills—competencies that he can display effortlessly, almost automatically. If he has to think about each step of the underlying processes—how to—as he engages in reading, spelling, writing, and arithmetic, he will not be able to keep up.

This is a crucial point. Let me give you a practical illustration. If you can drive an automobile, think back to your first driving lesson. Suppose that during that first lesson your driving instructor asked you to pay special attention to something on the radio. Even though you heard as well as anyone, the task of listening to the radio for the purpose of really getting information would have been exceptionally difficult. Also, what about your peripheral, or side, vision? How good do you think that was during your first driving lesson? Not very, I bet. Yes, your straight-ahead vision, your eyesight, was probably very adequate. Most states test that even before they issue a learner's permit. But even though your sight was excellent, you probably had to pay such close attention to the road ahead—the central portion of your visual field—that straying very far from that central zone of vision was likely to be very frightening.

How would you have responded in that situation to oral arithmetic questions? How well do you think you would have done on an oral I.Q. test? I venture to say you would have done poorly; you might even have tested out as mentally deficient. Obviously, not because you were; rather, because you have only so much attention to devote to a task and cannot share it with too many other competing activities. Under the conditions we are discussing, there is no real problem making a choice. That is, do you take your mind off your driving and think about the test questions, or the other way around? The will to live is strong in all of us— you would have continued to pay attention to driving and not have devoted very much attention to the I.Q. test questions.

Add one more part to this illustration. As you drove that first time, you probably had to think about where your hands and feet were and what they were doing. You segmented your body into parts and thought about them separately. Doing otherwise would have increased the possibility of an accident.

In a relatively short time, you learned to drive well enough to be granted a license. You drove; and then really learned to drive. That is, you acquired experience and confidence. Now suppose that after a year or two of driving experience you were asked to answer I.Q. test questions, or keep a sharp ear on the radio, or be alert to your side vision, or talk, or whistle, or whatever, while you were driving? What would happen? Would you endanger your life by not devoting complete attention to controlling the car? No, within reasonable limits, you would be able to pay attention to your driving and still do those other things. How about the location of your feet and hands? Do you know where they are when you drive? I am sure you do not, under ordinary circumstances.

What has happened? Your driving teacher showed you (or you, yourself, identified) a cluster of individual operations that constitute driving a car. You learned these and, in time, assembled them into a single operation. As you did this, your driving became more efficient—you did not have to *think* so much about *how* to drive. Yet, if a dangerous situation arises, you are alerted and return to the less efficient level of operation. You again experience difficulty talking or thinking abstractly while driving. What was automatic again involves conscious thought. As that occurs, you have less time and energy available to think about other details that are trivial in contrast to avoiding an accident.

The same goal exists for a child in learning the skills basic to adequate school performance. At first he will have to think hard about how he uses his perceptual skills, how he sounds out words and interprets sentences, how he solves arithmetic problems. Then, with practice, he will get better at it, the skills will become more and more automatic, and he will be able to do these things without having to devote so much thought to the process.

The best rule-of-thumb is to schedule daily sessions and make every effort to maintain that schedule. Keep the sessions short enough to be interesting and long enough to be effective. The first can be determined by observing the child's attitude; the second, by looking at his progress. If progress is evident, if the child gets better at what he is working on, then the sessions are long enough. Generally speaking, twenty-minute sessions are effective at first. These can be extended when the child is able to see that he is making progress.*

Teaching him—general principles

Before we get into specific procedures, I want to define the guidelines that underlie any good instructional program. The goal of a teacher is to see to it that the student learns what he is supposed to learn. This can be accomplished in different ways.

First, the teacher can tell the student what it is he should know, and then have the student memorize and restate the information to demonstrate that he has, in fact, learned it. This approach works well in certain situations, but not for the child we are concerned about here.

A second way, also not so suitable for the children under discussion, is to motivate the student to such a degree that he persists at whatever task is presented until he, himself, discovers what it is that he is supposed to know. This method works well with children who have competent skills, but not so well with "our" child—he is not a good discoverer.

---

*Warning: Do not allow yourself to become impatient. That, of course, is easier to suggest than to live up to. But it is vital. One of the greatest problems that the child with a learning disability faces is the fact that he *learns slowly*, usually only after a substantial amount of drill and practice. To try to hasten that process unduly is to invite frustration, disappointment, and a marked lessening in the motivation that is so necessary both on the child's part and on yours. Take one step at a time, and keep records so that you can compare where he once was with where he is.

But do not look at the records too often. He will not show daily progress on the charts. There will be days when he will seem to be bogged down completely or even a little bit worse than he was the day before—as though he is never going to be any better. Nonsense! Delete the word *never* from your vocabulary when you work with him. He will progress, if you and he stay with it. On those really bad days (yours or his), cut the session short and allow yourself to say, "I can't teach him *today*. But I will, *tomorrow*." And then begin tomorrow's session with fresh vigor.

A third way is for the teacher to provide problem-solving situations which she knows are appropriate to the student's level of competence. She highlights what it is that the student is to pay special attention to, thus making it easier for him to see the information he needs to solve the problem. This can be done by eliminating as many distracting elements from the learning situation as is necessary;— simplifying it by organizing it in a way that increases the student's chances for success; or by specifically calling the student's attention to the relevant information—giving hints, which she will eliminate in later tasks. Further, she encourages the student to explore the concrete aspects of the task thoroughly, by handling it or otherwise making direct contact.

This last way is the most suitable of the three for teaching the child with a learning problem. It employs three basic principles that apply to all instructional situations, regardless of what is being taught:

- 1. Organize for success.
- 2. Provide whatever information—hints—are needed for the student to understand what he is to *do*; then gradually remove them. (Hints, in this instance, does not mean helping him produce the answer; it means helping him know what to do in order to arrive at the answer.)
- 3. Encourage the student to use all his senses—not just his eyes and ears—to explore the concrete aspects of the task.

These three principles form the basis of all the teaching activities defined in this book. Rather than illustrate them here, I will restate them in each section that follows and show how they apply in those particular contexts—teaching perceptual skills, reading, arithmetic, spelling, and writing.

TEACHING VISUAL PERCEPTUAL SKILLS

The central goal of a visual perceptual skills program should be to teach the child *how to* analyze relatively complex visual patterns into their separate parts and recognize the way those parts fit together. Each lesson in the program should be based on the basic principles just defined.

- 1. Organize for success. Avoid giving the child tasks that are too difficult for him. Start with relatively simple activities and move toward more complex ones only when the child shows that he is ready for them.
- 2. Provide the child with additional information when he needs it—hints that help him understand how to do the task. Then teach him how to do the task without those hints.

What does this mean? Do you recall the illustration I used earlier—the one that asked you to imagine the difficulty you would have copying a square foot of grass lawn, blade by blade? Suppose this task was really important; that it was really worth the effort. How can I modify the task so that you have a better chance of succeeding? How about placing, over that mass of detail, a wire grid that divides the square foot of space into 144 square inches. The illustration in Figure 35 shows a less complex visual pattern —a bouquet of flowers—handled that way.

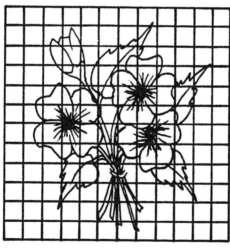

FIGURE 35

In addition to this, suppose I have you make your copy on graph paper, where the vertical and horizontal lines form one-inch squares. Now the task, still formidable, becomes a little more manageable. Given adequate time and proper encouragement, you can now choose any one of the one-inch spaces as a starting point and settle down to work. Once you have copied all the details in that square, you can move on to the next, and so on, until you are finished.

The grid provides additional information—a device that helped you deal with smaller portions of the task, one at a time, without getting lost. There is still the job of copying each detail, one at a time, but the total amount of detail that has to be dealt with in any given unit of work is greatly reduced—a 1/144th reduction, to be exact.

Let us apply this principle to a more reasonable task, one that is pertinent here, such as copying the diamond shown in Figure 36. Your task is to copy it on a blank sheet of paper.

FIGURE 36

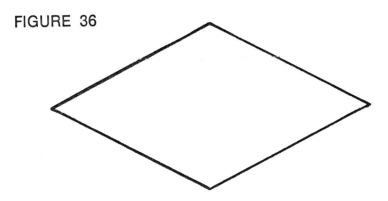

Now look at the same diamond—the same, that is, except that some lines have been drawn over it, as in Figure 37. Set below the diamond is a space containing similar lines; this is where your copy is to be drawn. Is copying the diamond now less difficult? Sure. There are now some reference points available—additional information—hints—that help you accomplish the task.

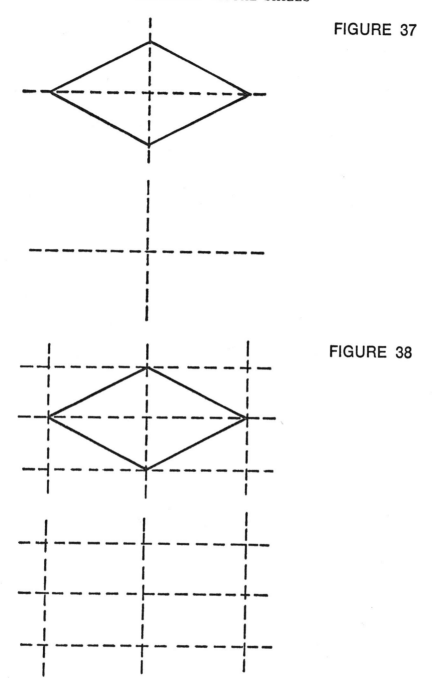

FIGURE 37

FIGURE 38

Now look at the next illustration, in Figure 38. Again we see the diamond, but this time there are even more reference points—more hints. These have also been added to the space where your copy is to be drawn. The task is now relatively simple. All you have to do is to perceive the diamond as four separate lines, and position your four lines in the same relative position in your space. If you can read the map, there is very little challenge.

FIGURE 39

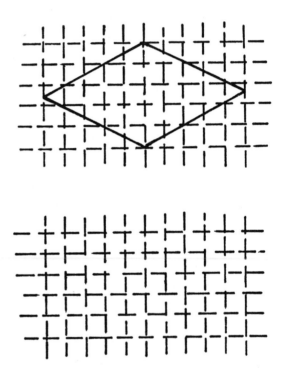

Look back at the original diamond in Figure 36. Would copying that diamond be easier, now that you have seen the two that followed it? I think so. Even though there are no dotted lines over that original diamond, you now will tend to imagine the dotted lines; you will map the space in your mind's eye. You have learned how to do the task better and no longer need the hints. You have learned how to imagine that information. It no longer has to be provided by some-one else; it no longer has to be embedded in the task.*

CAUTION: Do not supply too much additional information. Too many hints will confuse rather than help. There should be enough hints to make the task understandable, and no more. Figure 39 illustrates this point.

The additional lines in the grid are no help, are they? In fact, they only make the job of copying the diamond more difficult.

Now we can move on to the next principle. Assume that the child is to be taught to copy fairly complex designs, as represented by the asterisk shown in Figure 40.

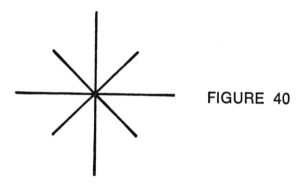

FIGURE 40

Suppose that when he was tested, his copy of the asterisk looked like the one shown in Figure 41.

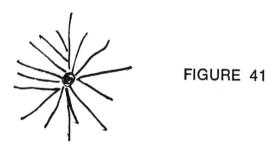

FIGURE 41

*In truth, there is still a lot of helpful information embedded in the original "copy the diamond" task, even though there are no dotted lines. The edges of the page and the lines of print help you map the space. Is it any wonder that some children position all their arithmetic problems along one edge of a page? They get lost when they stray from that reference point.

What can we infer from this? Simply, there are too many details in the design. What would help him respond more appropriately? Counting the lines, understanding that there are a finite number of elements in the design. But perhaps when he tries to count the elements, he gets lost in the de-tails. How about having him touch each line while counting? Better yet, how about having him trace over a line, then copying it before proceeding to the next line, which he will again trace, then draw, and so on. As he does this, he is matching what he sees with what his hands feel. He is ana-lyzing the design into its separate parts, and succeeding at that analysis by coming into tangible contact with each part, one at a time. This brings us to the final principle:

- 3. Encourage the child to use all his senses to obtain ad-ditional information about what he is seeing—by examin-ing it manually as well as visually. This does not mean that the child will always need this kind of support. In time, he will learn to analyze with his eyes alone, using imaginary hands. He will learn to point with his eyes in-stead of his hand (unless, of course, the pattern gets too busy; then real hands will again be needed).

This last point is important. Too often a child is pre-vented from using a crutch—a behavior or device that would help him—because "He has to learn to get along without a crutch and how will he so long as he uses one?" Well, we can also argue that to deny a crutch to a person with a broken leg does not hasten the healing process; it merely immobilizes him. What is the good of that? Allow the use of a crutch; indeed, encourage its use if it helps, because if it does help the chances are excellent that, in time, it will not be needed—he will learn to imagine he is using it. And if he does continue to need it, so what? Is it not better to learn, albeit with a dependency on a crutch, than to not learn and suffer all that that implies in this society?

112

*THE VISUAL PERCEPTUAL SKILLS PROGRAM**

Now we can turn our attention to instructional activities —what to do and when. Since you want to organize for success, you should avoid placing the child into situations that are much too difficult for him. You want to inspire motivation in him, not extinguish it with frustrating experiences. For this same reason, you should avoid placing the child into situations that are much too easy for him. At best, this would be a waste of time. At worst, he will view it as "baby stuff" and lose interest in the whole enterprise.

To determine where the youngster should begin his learning activities, take a look now at his performance on the Test of Visual Analysis Skills (TVAS). You will recall that one of the test's features was that it could serve to define the instructional goals for your teaching program. Well, you are now ready to teach. The question is "teach what?" The answer to that, stated simply, is to teach him the skills that are expected for his current grade placement, as measured by the TVAS.

Look back at the TVAS chart on page 69. The chart shows that if the child is currently in kindergarten, he is expected to score a 7 on the TVAS—to complete the seventh item on the TVAS before being incorrect on two successive items. If he is in first grade, he will be expected to score a 12. If he is in second grade—16, and third grade or beyond—18.

All right, now you know his instructional goal—what he is expected to be able to do, given his current grade place-

---

*The activities described here resemble those that appear in a formal program of instruction now being used in many schools throughout the United States and Canada—the Perceptual Skills Curriculum. Since I am its author, its similarity to the activities described in this book is not coincidence, in that they all derive from my more than twenty-five years of private practice. As a parent, you do not need the Curriculum. It was designed for classroom use. It is more extensive than is necessary for the purposes of one-to-one teaching. However, if your school is already using the Curriculum in some of its preschool and primary grade classes, the faculty may be willing to work with you. The Curriculum is published by Walker Educational Book Corporation, 720 Fifth Avenue, New York, N.Y. 10019.

ment. Where do you start? You start where he is. There is no justification for teaching him what he already can do, although a little overlap for review is not too bad a thing.

In Appendix A, you will find 200 patterns that resemble those in the TVAS. You will teach the child how to copy these, because in learning how to copy them he will be acquiring critical visual perceptual skills; and he will display his learning by being able to pass TVAS items that he originally failed. As you can see, the patterns range from simple to complex. He can probably do some of them already; some he cannot. Your next step, then, is to determine where he should begin and what he should do with each of the patterns.

Preparing materials

First, you will need some simple equipment. I may as well tell you about that now, before getting started with teaching procedures. You will need a geoboard. The geoboard is an educational device that can be found in many mathematics classrooms. It usually consists of a panel of wood or plastic containing 25 pins (or posts) that are arranged in 5 rows, 5 pins in each row. Children stretch rubber bands between the pins to explore principles of arithmetic and geometry. Your child will use the geoboard for a similar purpose, but in a much more organized way.

My visual perceptual skills program makes use of three different geoboard configurations—one with 5 pins, one with 9 pins, and one with 25 pins. These are shown in Figure 42. (You may not need to use all three pin arrangements. It depends on where your child starts in the program. You will find this out when you get to the Placement Table on page 117).

These three geoboards (5-pin, 9-pin, 25-pin) may be purchased* or you can make them yourself easily and inexpen-

*Available from Walker Educational Book Corporation, 720 Fifth Avenue, New York, N.Y. 10019.

FIGURE 42

GEOBOARD ARRANGEMENTS

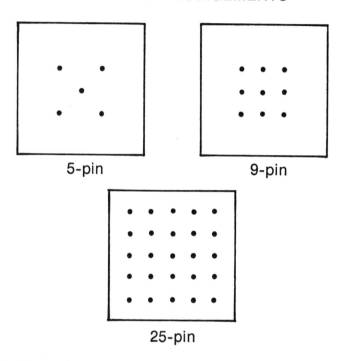

5-pin   9-pin

25-pin

sively. If you decide to make your own, obtain one square of perforated Masonite from your local lumberyard. The square should measure 10 inches on each side. The perforations should be spaced at 1-inch intervals. This will yield a board that contains 81 holes, arranged in 9 rows of 9 holes each. (One square is enough because you will be able to construct all three pin arrangements on the same square of perforated Masonite.) You will also need 25 bolts, approximately 1-inch long, and 25 nuts to secure the bolts to the board.

Starting in the corner hole of a board, insert a bolt in every other hole and secure it with a nut. When completed, the board will contain 25 bolts, arranged in a 5 x 5 pattern. This is shown in the sketch in Figure 43.

FIGURE 43

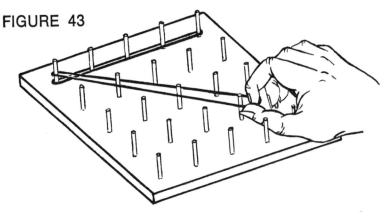

If you need a 9-pin geoboard, simply do not insert the 16 bolts along the outside borders. This leaves only the 9 center bolts arranged in a 3 x 3 pattern. Should you need a 5-pin geoboard, all you have to do is omit 4 more bolts—those positioned in the center of each of the remaining outside rows and lines. This will leave 5 bolts arranged as the corners of a 4-inch square with one additional peg in the center.

In addition, you will need the acetate-covered maps you made when you were preparing to test the child's visual perceptual skills with the TVAS.

Getting started

Now you are ready to start teaching. The following table will tell you which pattern to begin with, and which geoboard pin arrangement you will need.

To use the Placement Table:

- 1. In the left-hand column, locate the child's TVAS score.
- 2. The second column then shows you which teaching pattern to start with. (see Appendix A)
- 3. The third column specifies the *map* onto which *you* are to copy that pattern. (Do not ask the child to copy the patterns directly from the book. They are too small, and there are too many on each page.)
- 4. The fourth column specifies the *geoboard* onto which

VISUAL PROGRAM PLACEMENT TABLE

TVAS Score:	Begin with teaching pattern:	Parent copies teaching pattern from book onto a:	Child copies that teaching pattern onto the following	
			GEOBOARD	MAP
0	1	5-dot map	5-pin	5-dot
1	1	5-dot map	5-pin	5-dot
2	21	9-dot map	9-pin	9-dot
3	25	9-dot map	9-pin	9-dot
4	30	9-dot map	9-pin	9-dot
5	49	25-dot map	25-pin	25-dot
6	60	25-dot map	25-pin	25-dot
7	75	25-dot map	25-pin	25-dot
8	100	25-dot map	25-pin	25-dot
9	151	25-dot map	none	17-dot
10	160	25-dot map	none	17-dot
11	160	25-dot map	none	9-dot
12	165	25-dot map	none	9-dot
13	170	25-dot map	none	9-dot
14	175	25-dot map	none	5-dot
15	180	25-dot map	none	5-dot
16	180	25-dot map	none	0-dot
17	185	25-dot map	none	0-dot
18	190	25-dot map	none	0-dot

the child will copy this pattern, using rubber bands.
5. The fifth column specifies the map onto which the child will then copy the geoboard pattern.

For example, if the child's TVAS score is 2, he will start his instructional program by learning to copy pattern 21 (which you have copied onto a 9-dot map) with rubber bands on a 9-pin geoboard, and then with crayon on a 9-dot map. (There is one additional thing that you are to do just before the child starts this last step of copying from the geoboard onto a map. I will describe it in a moment.) That means you will need a 9-pin geoboard and two 9-dot maps. (You have already prepared these maps for testing. Remember? Why *two* 9-dot maps? One on to which you will copy the pattern from this book, the other for the child to copy the pattern from his geoboard.)

To continue with examples from the Placement Table, if the child's TVAS score is 7, he will start with pattern 75, copying it with rubber bands onto a 25-pin geoboard, and then with crayon onto a 25-dot map. Hence, you will need a 25-pin geoboard and two 25-dot maps.

What if his TVAS score is 9? Consulting the Placement Table, you will find that his first task is to start with teaching pattern 151. Notice that he bypasses the geoboard and moves directly to copying it with crayon on a 17-dot map. Here he will have to "pretend the rest of the dots are there and draw the lines *as though* the dots were there." As such, you will need one 25-dot map and one 17-dot map.

Having gone through the above, you should now be able to identify the pattern the child will start with, the geoboard he may or may not need, and the map on which he will ultimately copy the pattern. There are still a few details to be covered. We will do that now so that you can get started with the job of teaching these skills to your child.

Find your child's TVAS score on the Placement Table and identify the number of the pattern he should start with. Find that pattern (Appendix A) and copy it neatly with crayon on one of the maps. Make sure you use the correct map (one with the same number of dots). Place this before the child, alongside the appropriate geoboard or map, as indicated in the Placement Table. (As you can see from that Table, if his TVAS score was 8 or below, he starts with a geoboard; if it was 9 or higher, he skips that step and starts directly with a map.)

Assume that his score was 8 or below. You would give the child the correct geoboard and some rubber bands, and ask him to construct or "make" the pattern on his geoboard. He is to use one rubber band for each line in the pattern.

Do not help him except in the following ways: if he is unable to copy the pattern correctly, you have three options:

- 1. Have him place his rubber bands directly over yours, on your geoboard. (This way he is breaking the pattern down into its parts, but is avoiding completely the need to read the map.)
- 2. Make the task more concrete. You construct the pattern on a geoboard instead of a map, place it next to another, matching geoboard, and ask him to copy the pattern on his geoboard. (You will need a second geoboard to do this, but do not prepare one now. Wait until you see if it is necessary; it does not happen very often.)
- 3. Move back to an easier teaching pattern, consult the table regarding what materials you will need, and start working with him at that level.

Only rarely, if ever, will you have to exercise any of the above options. Ordinarily, the child will be placed properly and will be able to construct the pattern on his geoboard without any assistance.

There is more. After he has copied the pattern with rubber bands, rotate his geoboard 90° (1/4 turn), remove your drawing of the pattern, give him another acetate-covered map (the one shown in last column of the Placement Table) and a crayon, and ask him to copy the pattern onto his map as it *now* appears on his geoboard. (It is a new pattern because the geoboard has been rotated 90°.)

When this is done, and checked for accuracy, erase his drawing from his map, your drawing from your map, and remove the rubber bands from the geoboard. Then move on to the next teaching pattern and go through the same procedures. After the child has worked through ten teaching patterns in this fashion, go back to the first one and start over—except that this time, once you have copied the teaching pattern from the book onto your map, you are to rotate your map 90° (1/4 turn) *before* you give it to the child. It will then, in most cases, be a different pattern from what appears in the book. As before, he is to copy it on his geoboard, after which you will remove your map, rotate his geoboard another 90°, hand him the proper map (as shown on the table) and have him copy that rubber band construction on his map.

Repeat this entire procedure after the child has once more successfully completed these same ten teaching patterns—only this time you rotate your map 180° (1/2 turn) before you ask the child to copy it on his geoboard. Finally, after the child has successfully completed the same ten patterns under these new conditions, repeat the entire procedure once again, this time rotating your map 270° (3/4 turn) before giving it to him for copying on the geoboard.

In this way, each pattern will do the job of four—each can be used four times. Granted, some of them (a square, for instance) do not change when rotated, but most do. And there is something to be learned from those that do not change, by virtue of that fact alone.

Suppose we set up a hypothetical situation: The child's TVAS score was 6. The Placement Table indicates that he should start his program with teaching pattern number 60. You find this pattern in Appendix A, and, since it appears on a 25-dot map, you copy it onto an acetate-covered 25-dot map. Give this to the child along with a 25-pin geoboard and ask him to make one just like it on his geoboard. He does. You then remove the drawn pattern that he just copied (the one you drew), turn his geoboard 90°, give him a blank 25-dot map and a crayon, and ask him to draw *that* (rotated) geoboard pattern on his 25-dot map. If he is properly placed in the program, he will be able to do it.

Assume he is able to work through the nine subsequent teaching patterns (61-69) in the same way. When he completes pattern 69, you again copy teaching pattern 60 on a 25-dot map, but this time you rotate the map 90° before giving it to him for reproducing on the geoboard. Then, when he has done this, the geoboard is rotated 90° and that pattern is copied on a 25-dot map. In this way, he will work through teaching patterns 60-69 four times before he starts on teaching pattern 70.

Once the child has started to work through the sequence of teaching patterns, he need not stop unless he bogs down (remember, however, that each block of ten patterns is to be done four times—each time with the pattern oriented differently).

Continue this procedure until the child completes teaching pattern 150. Then two changes are introduced. First, he no longer uses a geoboard; he copies your pattern directly onto his map. Second, although you continue to use a 25-dot map, he now uses a 17-dot map and, thus, has to pretend the other dots are there.

He will follow this procedure through teaching pattern 160 at which time teaching pattern 151 is to be used again, this time rotated 90° *before* the child copies it on his 17-dot map. Just as with the lower-numbered patterns, when he has worked his way through ten patterns (151-160), he again returns to pattern 151, which now will be rotated a half-turn (180°) before it is presented to him for copying . . . and so on. So you see, the major difference, once teaching pattern 151 is reached, is the elimination of the geoboard.

The child continues in this fashion until he completes all patterns through number 200, copying each pattern four times (four different orientations) on his 17-dot map. Then, he once more returns to teaching pattern 151, and again copies each pattern (from 151 to 200) four times—but this time he copies them on a 9-dot map (even though yours— the one he copies from—continues to be drawn on 25-dot maps). When these have all been accomplished, the cycle is repeated except that he draws on a 5-dot map and, finally, on a 0-dot map.

The only exception to this routine occurs when a child initially places into the upper section of the teaching program—when his score on the TVAS is 11 or higher. For example, as the Placement Table shows, if the child's TVAS score is 11, he enters the instructional program with teaching pattern 160 and starts off copying your pattern on a 9-dot map. There is no need for him to engage in the simpler tasks, with the 17-dot map. Thus, after he has copied patterns 160 to 200 on a 9-dot map (each pattern oriented four different ways), he works his way through these same patterns again with a 5-dot map, and finally with a 0-dot map. If his TVAS score is 17, he starts off with pattern 185 on a 0-dot map and works through pattern 200. When that is accomplished, he is done with this program.

All this may sound very complicated, but once you get into it, the system will be apparent. It is designed to over-teach; to help the child establish a skill that he then can use almost automatically.* But it also is designed to avoid starting the child off at too easy a level and thereby lowering his enthusiasm for the experience.

Even now, before you have had a chance to really use the program, I think you will see that as the child progresses through the teaching program, he is learning to do better in the TVAS. In reality, of course, that is of no great consequence. But inasmuch as we know that improved performance in the TVAS means improved visual perceptual skills in general, and therefore improved classroom performance, it is a worthwhile goal.

Additional activities

Although the program just described forms the core of the visual perceptual skills instructional program, it can be expanded. This is advisable, both to add interest and enhance the child's general abilities. Any number of other manipulatives can be used. For example:

*To help him acquire this automatic level, encourage him to take fewer looks at the pattern as he copies it. Initially, of course, he will probably look at the pattern frequently. As he gets better at it, he should be able to take larger "bites." But do not rush into this at the expense of accuracy. That comes first.

PEGBOARDS

Pegboards are readily available from any local school-supply company and from many toy stores. Pegboards are devices that can be used in a variety of ways. Given a choice, purchase the kind that has 100 holes arranged in a 10 × 10 pattern. You will need two of these, along with 200 pegs—usually available in a variety of colors.

Start off by constructing patterns on your pegboard and having the child duplicate them on his pegboard. Recalling the general principles offered at the beginning of this section, you will, at the start, want to limit the complexity of the patterns you construct (use only a few pegs) and make available to the child whatever additional information he needs to meet the demands of the tasks. In this instance, that means you should start off by placing pegs in corners, where they are easiest to locate, and then in outside rows.

As the child catches on, make your patterns more complex and locate them more centrally—away from the edges. Later on, eliminate your pegboard and draw patterns on graph paper. Outline an area the equivalent of the pegboard by drawing a black border around a square of 100 (10 × 10) spaces and insert the sheet of graph paper into an acetate page protector. This way you can draw your pegboard patterns without having to use a lot of paper. Finally, when the child is reproducing fairly complex patterns on his pegboard, reverse the situation and have him draw what you construct.

When he starts to acquire some ability here, switch roles with him. He constructs the model—you match it and have him check your work. Slip in an occasional error or two. It will sharpen his eye and he will probably enjoy seeing that others can make errors too.

PARQUETRY BLOCKS

Parquetry blocks, also available at most toy counters, are another useful device. Purchase two sets. You construct patterns with your set; have the child duplicate them with his. Start with simple patterns and work toward more complex ones.

To add another dimension, and interest, teach the child to see more at a single look by exposing your parquetry block construction for only a limited time (five or ten seconds). Then cover it and have the child construct his from memory. Needless to say, keep these patterns very simple when you introduce this activity—at least until you see what he can do.*

OTHER MANIPULATIVES

Any number of other manipulatives—commercially prepared and homemade—can be used this way. For example, one-inch cubes arranged in patterns, or wooden beads that can be strung on a shoelace, are both appropriate here. Indeed, popsicle sticks and bottle caps are also suitable for constructing designs that the child can then copy. The important point to keep in mind is that you want to help the child learn how to view a pattern of things—whatever they may be—in an organized, analytical way. That is the essence of competent visual perceptual skills.

GAMES

In addition to the activities already described, there are a number of less formal activities that can be used effectively. I will describe some here. As you start to use them, and as you gain insight into their value, I am sure you will think of others.

- 1. Card games. These are helpful, especially those that involve making sets (pairs, for example), and remembering and following rules. Rummy, hearts, casino, and old

*This technique of limited exposure can be used with any activity. I suggest, however, that you do not use it until the child has acquired some basic competency. It is essential, first, that he learn *how* to analyze and organize the materials —then you can work for speed.

maid are all good. The many versions of solitaire are also useful.

- 2. Memory games with cards. Concentration is a good activity. Do you recall it? All you do is arrange a full deck (less than that, if you think it advisable), face down, in 13 rows—4 cards in each row. (This arrangement can be changed to suit your own taste.) The first player chooses two cards at random, looks at them, shows them to all players and, unless they are a matched pair, returns them, again face down, to their original positions. If they are a matched pair, he keeps them and chooses another pair. He keeps on choosing until he misses. The second player then chooses one card, turns it face up, and tries to choose a second one that matches it. Obviously, if the first card is a match to either of the two shown by the first player, it is helpful for him to remember where that card is. The game ends when all cards have been paired. The player with the most cards wins.

- 3. Memory games without cards. There are many of these and they are adaptable. This one can be played at the dining room table after dinner. Everyone should participate. All players study the table, generally laden with dishes, utensils, and condiments. Then, the first player closes his eyes while someone else removes one object from the table. The question to the first player, then, is, "What's missing?" As the game proceeds, the challenge lessens (and the table gets cleared!). *Note:* Start off with a limited assortment of objects. There is no need to make the game too difficult.

  "What's Missing?" can be played anywhere, with any assortment of objects: playing cards, household objects, candy, or whatever is handy. It can also be modified to "Which one was moved?" or "Which one was just added?" and so forth.

- 4. Robot. The goal here is to have the child tell you what to do in performing some act. To do this properly, he has to analyze that behavior into its parts and sequence them

125

accurately. For example, show him a single letter, a geometric design, a block construction, an arrangement of sticks, or whatever else fits the situation, and have him tell you how to reproduce it, step-by-step. You, in turn, are to follow his directions precisely, doing just what he tells you to do, one step at a time. Start with easy tasks. This activity can be very difficult, even for competent adults. (Try telling someone how to draw a spiral. Remember, no hands.) At the onset, allow the child to use his hands, in addition to oral language, to describe what you are to do, but help him learn the words to replace those hand movements. For ·example, he may not know such words as *perpendicular, right angle*, and so forth, even though he can express them with his hands. Here, as always, the rule is "organize for success." Start with what the child can do and progress from there.

- 5. Board games. Checkers, chess, Monopoly, are all good. So are tic-tac-toe, cribbage, and the various dice games and map games sold at toy counters.

- 6. Construction activities. Tinker toys, Erector sets, Lego, Lincoln Logs, and so on. Follow the general sequence described earlier. That is, if the child cannot follow the drawn patterns that come with the set, start off by having him superimpose pieces on top of other pieces that you have positioned. Then, have him build easy constructions alongside your constructions. Then have him build from drawn plans.

- 7. Sorting. Use any materials that are available in different sizes, shapes, and colors. The child's job is to sort these according to one attribute. (For example, color: "Put all the *red* shapes in one pile and the *blue* shapes in another.") Then, if the materials are appropriate, have him sort them according to two attributes. (For example, color and shape: "Put all the *red squares* in one pile and the *blue circles* in another pile.") Coins are good for this. They can be sorted according to their value and their date. (For example, "Put all the pennies together," then, "Put all the 1972 pennies in one pile." There are many other attributes you can focus on—weight, thickness, texture.

• 8. Time-telling. This is difficult for most children who are not yet well into the second grade, so go easy. Obtain an old, large alarm clock that has an easily read dial and use it to teach the child the following things:

a) One hand is long—it is called the minute hand; one hand is short—it is called the hour hand.

b) The short hand (hour hand) points to the hour.

c) The long hand (minute hand) tells the number of minutes after or before the hour.

d) Start off by teaching the child how to read the clock when it is at the hour (e.g., one o'clock, two o'clock).

e) Have him move the minute hand (using the proper knob on the back of the clock) and observe how it makes one complete rotation for each hourly shift of the hour hand.

f) Then teach him how to read the half-hour—"30 minutes after" and "30 minutes before." (Teach him to read minutes as *after* until the minute hand reaches the half-past mark, and then, for the remainder of the hour, as *before*.)

g) Keep your language consistent. Do not use "quarter after" in place of "15 minutes after." There is time for all of this later.

h) Give him lots of practice and be patient with his confusion.

• 9. Chalkboard activities. The chalkboard is a remarkably useful device. It is large, can be erased easily, and is fun to use. (You can make one by painting a 4' x 4' section of smooth plywood with chalkboard paint.) Encourage the child to use it to draw pictures, print numerals and letters, play tic-tac-toe, and other things.

One game children seem to enjoy is Squiggles. One of you draws a single line or shape on the chalkboard. The other player then draws a picture that includes the initial line or shape. (See Figure 44.) Change roles each time.

FIGURE 44

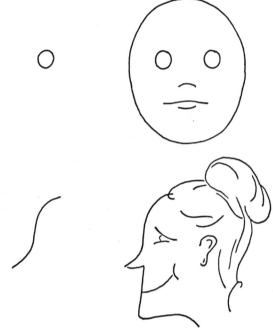

- 10. Teach him to use a calendar. Point out its organization—months and days of the week, and have him learn their names and their sequences. A good starting point is his birthday, or Christmas, or today. Each of these provides some focal point. Then, when he has established the basic facts, introduce the concepts of "day before," "day after," and so forth, by playing such games as "What day comes after Thursday; before Tuesday?" "What is today's date?"
- 11. How do you get there? Have him tell you how to get from one place to another. For example, from the kitchen to the living room, from home to school, to grandmother's house, and so forth. Teach him to read simple road maps, tracing the route between two points. Then, when he can, have him tell you how to get from *here* to *there* by consulting the map. As a variation, you describe a specific route but do not designate the destination; have him do that.

128

• 12. Analyze a story (or television show, or movie, or a real event). Get the child to tell you about one of his favorite stories or television shows and help him analyze and organize it by questioning him—*one question at a time.* For example, have him (a) identify the main and lesser characters; (b) identify their interrelationships; (c) describe the circumstances—place and time; (d) describe the events, emphasizing the pertinent points. Map out the story on a chalkboard, using simple symbols such as X's and O's for people, places, and events. Position them to reflect relationships. For example, if two people are closely connected, put their symbols closer together; if one person is larger than another, make his symbol larger.

This activity list could be extended, but I think you have the idea by now. The goal has been stated repeatedly—teach the child to analyze and organize spatial information (patterns) or, in these last suggestions, teach the child to analyze information that can then be organized spatially into patterns. Start with large units of information and very gross relationships. Work toward having him recognize refined units of information, and discrete and intricate interrelationships. (There will be more about this in the section devoted to teaching reading comprehension skills.)

One word of caution. Present all these activities as games —not as treatments. Let the child know that the formal program he is engaged in (the geoboard and map activities) is to be done on a scheduled basis; something he *must* do daily. These activities, in contrast, should be fun; they are not prescribed and formalized. These are the kinds of things you should do casually, while sitting around a fireplace, riding in a car, having dinner. If he begs off, allow him that privilege. He will play when he is ready, or when the activity is sufficiently interesting, or when he thinks he has a chance of succeeding. We all enjoy doing what we do well, so long as it is not too easy or too difficult. We all like to succeed. Give him plenty of opportunities to do so.

129

TEACHING AUDITORY PERCEPTUAL SKILLS

The central goal of an auditory perceptual skills program should be to teach the child how to analyze spoken language into its separate parts and recognize the sequence of those parts. As the goal is achieved, the child will become increasingly familiar with the individual sounds in words; sounds that are represented by letters in reading and spelling. The value of this will be evident not only in how capably the child discriminates sounds in spoken language but, more importantly, in how readily he learns to read and spell.

There are a number of programs available for teaching auditory perceptual skills. Some devote a great deal of attention to teaching the child to discriminate—to hear the difference—between various nonverbal sounds; for example, between the sound of an airplane motor and the sound of a vacuum sweeper. The rationale, apparently, is that poor listeners tend to be as much confused by nonverbal as by verbal sounds. The fallacy, however, is that though this may be true, there is no practical value in devoting time to nonverbal sounds. It may be effective and the child may become expert at noticing the difference between door bells and telephone bells, but there is no evidence to suggest that the effect of instruction will be apparent when the child faces the task of analyzing verbal sounds—spoken language. It will not help him learn to read.

There are other programs, a little closer to the mark, that are designed to teach children to discriminate between similar spoken sounds; for example, between *bear* and *dare*; *mat*, *met*, and *mit*; *laugh* and *lath*. These, again, do not go far enough in that the child can answer correctly without doing a thorough analysis of the words.

The program I am going to suggest focuses on teaching the child to take words apart into their individual sounds. But first I want to give you a general idea of its design. Then we will take a closer look at the various procedures.

The auditory skills program is based on the same set of principles put forth in the visual skills section. I will repeat them here, and illustrate how they pertain to teaching auditory perceptual skills.

- 1. Organize for success.
- 2. Provide the child with whatever additional information—hints—he needs to understand the task; then teach him how to do the task without this help.
- 3. Encourage the child to use all his senses to obtain additional information about what he is hearing—by examining it vocally as well as with his ears.

The first requires no explanation. It means exactly what it did in the last section. Simply, do not overplace or underplace the child; avoid giving him tasks that are too hard or too easy. The organization of the program I will describe deals effectively with that concern. What about the other two principles? How do they apply here?

One major difficulty that confronts the youngster who lacks capable auditory perceptual skills is that spoken sounds are so temporary. Once uttered, they are gone. They cannot be studied further unless they are remembered, written down, or restated by the speaker. It is extremely difficult to remember what you have not had time to organize and it is extremely irritating to a speaker to have to repeat himself very often; especially when the speaker is a teacher and the listener is a poorly performing child.

As a result, the child with substandard auditory perceptual skills faces a dilemma. On the one hand, he needs more time and exposure to what was said, in order to organize the information. On the other hand, he cannot remember the sounds easily, nor is it practical to assume they will be repeated a sufficient number of times to enable him to accomplish this feat. Therefore, any method that assists him in remembering what was said, so that he has additional time to organize it, will be helpful. In addition, anything that makes the separate parts of spoken language more apparent to him will be equally useful.

How can this be accomplished? Recall the second principle? What kind of additional information will make the task easier for the child? One way is to have him watch your mouth as you speak, and you, of course, should speak distinctly, enunciating all the sounds. For example, suppose the youngster is experiencing difficulty identifying the /m/ sound in the word *smack*. Would it not be helpful to have him watch your mouth as you say the word? Particularly if you emphasize the /m/ sound with your lips as you pronounce it—and have him repeat the word just after he has watched you do it? It certainly would. It is always easier to hear sounds if they can be seen at the same time.

Now to the third principle—teaching the child to examine sounds vocally; that is, to say them and simultaneously take note of what he hears and how his mouth feels. In a real sense, the speech production mechanism is the counterpart of the hands in that it enables you to "touch" vocal sounds the way the hands can manipulate visual information. Even as adults, how else can we analyze fairly long words into parts—syllables? Words that are too long to visualize. For example, how many syllables are there in the word *hippopotamus*? You will not be able to answer accurately if you do not say the word, either aloud or to yourself. Saying words aloud—even relatively short and simple words—helps the child identify its separate sounds, particularly if he speaks distinctly, pronouncing all of the sounds.

This last point is sensitive. The debate regarding whether or not to try to do something about a child's dialect continues to be heard around the country. One group argues that standard English and standard English pronunciation of words is desirable if only because it is the standard. The other group retorts that a dialect is the manifestation of the child's culture, and to try to eliminate it is tantamount to attacking that culture. I seek no quarrel with either group. But purely from a pragmatic basis, I must assert that a dialect can have a detrimental effect on a child's ability to identify all of the component parts—the individual sounds —of a spoken word. If he does not pronounce them, he will neither hear them nor feel them. How, then, can he identify them? Read them? Yes, he can read them—if he knows how to read. But that is not the kind of youngster we are worrying about here. The implications of a dialect, insofar as learning to read is concerned, are clear. This is especially so if the dialect is one wherein words are collapsed and word endings left off.

THE AUDITORY PERCEPTUAL SKILLS PROGRAM

Let us now look at specific instructional activities—what to do and when. Following the procedure we used earlier in the visual skills section, we will first look at how to place the child so that what he is asked to learn is neither too difficult nor too easy.

To determine where the youngster should begin his learning activities, take a look at how well he did on the Test of Auditory Analysis Skills (TAAS). What was his score?

The auditory skills program

Now look back at the chart on page 79. The chart shows that if the child is currently in kindergarten, he is expected to score a 3 on the TAAS—that is, pass the third item before getting two incorrects in a row. If he is in first grade, he is expected to score a 9, by the end of second he is expected to score an 11, and by the end of third grade he should be able to get through all the items and earn a score of 13.

You have now identified his instructional goal—the auditory perceptual skills level he should have achieved, given his current grade placement. The rule, as you know, is to start where he is. In other words, what was the most difficult task he was able to complete on the TAAS? That is where he is. Now he should learn how to solve the next item on the TAAS.

Getting started

A reexamination of the TAAS (see page 78) is now called for. As you will observe, the items are arranged in a specific sequence, going from easy to difficult. They fall into five categories. These are illustrated in the following chart.

FIGURE 45

LEVELS IN THE AUDITORY PROGRAM

LEVEL V
Identify and delete one consonant sound of a consonant blend.
Say **play**; now say it again, but don't say /**p**/

LEVEL IV
Identify and delete a final consonant sound in words where the consonant is preceded by a vowel.
Say **meat**; now say it again, but don't say /**t**/

LEVEL III
Identify and delete a beginning consonant sound in words where that sound is followed by a vowel.
Say **meat**; now say it again, but don't say /**m**/

LEVEL II
Identify and delete one syllable from a three-syllable word.
Say **cucumber**; now say it again, but don't say /**cu**/

LEVEL I
Identify and delete one syllable from a two-syllable compound word.
Say **cowboy**; now say it again, but don't say **boy**

The chart makes clear the five levels in the TAAS. You can see that placement is fairly simple. Items 1 and 2 fall into the lowest level (Level I) depicted on the chart. Item 3 belongs to the second category—Level II. Items 4-6 belong to Level III, 7-9 to Level IV, and 10-13 to the highest—Level V. Thus, the child's TAAS score tells us where he should get started. This is shown in the Auditory Program Placement Table.

AUDITORY PROGRAM PLACEMENT TABLE

TAAS SCORE	CHILD SHOULD WORK IN LEVEL
1	I
2	II
3	III
4	III
5	III
6	IV
7	IV
8	IV
9	V
10	V
11	V
12	V
13	no need to work in program

For example, suppose the child did very poorly in the TAAS; his score was 1. Consulting the Auditory Program Placement Table, you find that he should work in Level I, going on to more difficult levels only when he can demonstrate that he has learned the skills of that lowest level. What if the child's TAAS score was 5? Again consulting the Placement Table, it is evident that the child should work in

FIGURE 46 THE AUDITORY SKILLS PROGRAM

LEVEL	Clap hands to:	Draw and read dashes for:	Find the hidden:	Say the missing:	Say the word without the:	Substitute:
V			part of a consonant blend	part of a consonant blend	part of a consonant blend	part of a consonant blend
IV			final consonant sound	final consonant sound	final consonant sound	beginning and/or final consonant sounds
III			beginning consonant sound	beginning consonant sound	beginning consonant sound	
II	syllables in a three-syllable word	syllables in a three-syllable word	syllable in a three-syllable word	syllable in a three-syllable word	syllable in a three-syllable word	
I	syllables in a two-syllable compound word	syllables in a two-syllable compound word	syllable in a two-syllable compound word	syllable in a two-syllable compound word	syllable in a two-syllable compound word	

Level III, and remain there until he has learned the Level III skill. Then he will go on and work in Level IV.

All right, you now know how to place him in the program. What next? How do you teach him the auditory skills he needs to know?

The Auditory Skills Program is diagramed in Figure 46. In effect, this is a map of the skills he should learn in order to progress from where he is to where he should be. For instance, if he should be in Level V and, instead, is in Level II, the best way of getting him up to Level V is by teaching him all the skills shown on that chart between Levels II and V. That, of course, is the purpose of the Auditory Program. Once you have placed the child, the program is easy to use. Simply follow the procedures described on the following pages.

If the child is in Level I, teach him to:

- 1. Clap his hands in time to the syllables of a two-syllable compound word, saying them as he claps them. Say to the child, "Say *baseball*" (emphasizing the fact that there are two parts in that word). "Now say it again, and clap your hands once for each part of the word; clap and say the parts at the same time." (Use Level I words.*) When you see that he understands and can do this, move on. (His goal, here, is relatively simple—to show that he understands that words can be segmented into parts and that he can represent each part with a motor action—a clap.)

- 2. Draw a dash, from left to right, for each syllable in a two-syllable compound word, saying them as he draws the dashes. Say to the child, "Say *baseball*." (Emphasize the fact that there are two parts in that word.) "Now say it again, and draw a dash for each part while you say them." (Demonstrate to the child how the dashes are to be drawn; horizontally, from left to right; the first dash

*You may add to this list of Level I words if you wish, but do *not* use the words in the TAAS. Save those for testing to see whether he has learned what you set out to teach him.

being drawn as the first syllable is said—the second dash being drawn as the second syllable is said.)

Once he has grasped this, teach him to read the dashes in any order you designate. For example, if he drew two dashes for the word *baseball* and you then point to the first dash (the one to the left) and ask, "What does this one say?" his response should be "base." If you point to the right-hand dash, his response should be "ball."

When the child has learned to write (with dashes) and read the two-syllable words from the Level I list, it is time to move on to the next task.

- 3. Find hidden syllables. Ask him to "Say *baseball*"; then ask, "Did you say *ball*? Is the word *ball* hidden in the word *baseball*?" Or have him say *baseball*, then ask, "Is the word *doll* hidden in the word *baseball*?" The child's response in this activity is either yes or no. If he fails to grasp the concept, go back one step and have him

FIGURE 47

Say **more**	Is the word **more** hidden in the word	**morning?** **farmer?** **mortgage?** **morbid?**
Say **ball**	Is the word **ball** hidden in the word	**ballgame?** **baseball?** **cowboy?** **bolt?**
Say **bun**	Is the word **bun** hidden in the word	**bunny?** **thunder?** **bundle?** **bunk?**
Say **pay**	Is the word **pay** hidden in the word	**repay?** **paper?** **daytime?** **pain?**
Say **see**	Is the word **see** hidden in the word	**seesaw?** **seaman?** **saddle?** **seed?**
Say **miss**	Is the word **miss** hidden in the word	**mistake?** **mister?** **master?** **mistletoe?**

Say **car**	Is the word **car** hidden in the word	**cargo?** **card?** **scar?** **star?**
Say **all**	Is the word **all** hidden in the word	**always?** **recall?** **illness?** **ball?**
Say **ant**	Is the word **ant** hidden in the word	**anthill?** **antelope?** **andy?** **cant?**
Say **pick**	Is the word **pick** hidden in the word	**picnic?** **pickle?** **packet?** **picket?**
Say **ray**	Is the word **ray** hidden in the word	**Raymond?** **radio?** **rain?** **write?**
Say **won**	Is the word **won** hidden in the word	**wonder?** **once?** **window?** **wedding?**
Say **ban**	Is the word **ban** hidden in the word	**bandit?** **bank?** **Benny?** **banquet?**

draw dashes for the word before trying to decide whether a specific syllable is hidden in it. Figure 47 shows a list of word activities you can use for this step.

- 4. Say the part of the word that was missing. Say to the child, "Say *baseball*; now say *ball*. What did I leave out —what part is missing?" (The Level I list of words is suitable here. Vary the teaching pattern by omitting the first or second syllable in random fashion.)
- 5. Say the word without a specified syllable. Say to the child, "Say *baseball*." (Pause while he repeats *baseball*.) "Now say it again, but don't say *ball*—or, don't say *base*." (Use the Level I list of words.) If the child encounters confusion, back up a step or two.

When he shows that he understands what he is to do, test him with the first two items in the TAAS. If he passes these—and he should if he has gone through the above five steps—move on to Level II.

FIGURE 48

LEVEL I LIST

sunshine	seesaw	motion
baseball	oatmeal	virtue
someplace	window	morbid
steamship	recall	dispose
cowboy	paper	begin
mister	magic	defend
cupcake	after	bashful
into	dentist	cement
candy	monkey	muffler
person	sandwich	ocean
cartoon	shoeshine	murky
children	napkin	concert
sometime	daytime	vocal
bookcase	stingy	nasty
forget	upset	native
mountain	bargain	precise
doctor	surprise	measure
outside	himself	ordeal
daddy	mascot	selfish
doorbell	cardboard	vibrant
fancy	predict	indent
funny	airplane	famous
hunter	eyelash	protest
party	demon	except
business	hungry	obtain
garden	playmate	conceal
barber	ashtray	decay

If the child is in Level II, teach him to:

- 1. Clap his hands in time to the syllables of a three-syllable word, saying them as he claps them. Say to the child, "Say *cucumber*" (emphasizing the fact that there are three parts in the word). "Now say it again, and clap your hands once for each part of the word;" then, "Clap and say the parts at the same time." (Use Level II words.*) When you are able to see that he understands the concept of these words being constructed of parts, move on.
- 2. Draw a dash from left to right for each syllable in a three or more syllable word, saying them as he draws the dashes. Say to the child, "Say *cu cum ber*" (emphasizing the fact that there are three parts in that word). "Now say it again, and draw a dash for each part while you say them." (Show the child how the dashes are to be drawn; horizontally, from left to right; the first being drawn as the first syllable is said—the second being drawn as the second syllable is said—and so on.)

    Once he has grasped the idea, teach him to read the dashes in any order you designate. (Use Level II words.) For example, if he drew three dashes for the word *cucumber*, and you then point to the first dash (the one on the left) and ask, "What does this one say?" his response should be *cu*. If you point to the middle dash, his response should be *cum*, and so on.
- 3. Find the hidden syllable. Ask him to say "*cu cum ber*." Then ask, "Did I say /cue/? Is the sound /cue/ hidden in the word *cucumber*?" Or, "Is the sound /bum/ in *cucumber*?" The child's response will be either yes or no. If he fails to grasp the concept, go back one step and have him draw dashes for the word before trying to decide whether a specific syllable is hidden in it. Figure 49 shows a group of word activities you can use for this step:

---

*You may add to this list of Level II words if you wish, but do *not* use the words that are in the TAAS. Save those for testing to see whether he has learned what you set out to teach him.

FIGURE 49

Say **two** **toe** **row** **mar**	Is the word **two** **toe** **row** **mar**	hidden in the word **tomorrow?**
Say **car** **tar** **curb** **carp**	Is the word **car** **tar** **curb** **carp**	hidden in the word **carpenter?**
Say **man** **fish** **fast** **dish**	Is the word **man** **fish** **fast** **dish**	hidden in the word **fisherman?**
Say **knee** **noon** **moon** **honey**	Is the word **knee** **noon** **moon** **honey**	hidden in the word **honeymoon?**
Say **thunder** **stand** **under** **and**	Is the word **thunder** **stand** **under** **and**	hidden in the word **understand?**
Say **permit** **mint** **pep** **pop**	Is the word **permit** **mint** **pep** **pop**	hidden in the word **peppermint?**
Say **full** **once** **one** **fun**	Is the word **full** **once** **one** **fun**	hidden in the word **wonderful?**
Say **milk** **but** **bat** **tire**	Is the word **milk** **but** **bat** **tire**	hidden in the word **buttermilk?**
Say **ought** **melon** **water** **tear**	Is the word **ought** **melon** **water** **tear**	hidden in the word **watermelon?**
Say **pen** **on** **dent** **deeper**	Is the word **pen** **on** **dent** **deeper**	hidden in the word **Independent?**
Say **get** **full** **far** **for**	Is the word **get** **full** **far** **for**	hidden in the word **forgetful?**
Say **cut** **pill** **cat** **pillow**	Is the word **cut** **pill** **cat** **pillow**	hidden in the word **caterpillar?**

142

Say **fact**	Is the word **fact**	hidden in the word **manufacture?**
tear	**tear**	
man	**man**	
fit	**fit**	

- 4. Say the part of the word that is missing. Say to the child, "Say *cu cum ber*"; (Pause.) "Now say *cumber*." Then, "What did we leave out—what part is missing?" (The Level II list of words is suitable here. Vary the teaching pattern by omitting the first, or second, or third syllable in random fashion.)
- 5. Say the word without a specific syllable (first or last). Say to the child, "Say *cu cum ber*." (Pause while he repeats the word.) "Now say it again, but don't say /cue/ or don't say /ber/." (Avoid asking for omission of the middle syllable—work on the first or last only. Use the Level II word list.) If the child becomes confused, back up a step or two.

When he understands what he is to do, test him with the third item in the TAAS. If he passes this, as he should if he has worked through the above five steps, move on to Level III.

FIGURE 50

LEVEL II LIST

cantelope	refreshment	abdicate
basketball	emergency	diplomat
trampoline	peanut butter	workmanlike
important	destiny	clumsiness
defenseless	peninsula	excitement
memorize	introduce	evasive
mistaken	independent	emptiness
gorilla	classification	departure
carelessly	occupation	extravagant
yesterday	upside down	institute
cornerstone	newspaper	important

limosine	friendliness	substitute
September	silverware	impersonate
understand	decently	performance
remember	naturally	dedication
microphone	resonant	devotion
forgotten	ridiculous	undertake
gasoline	superlative	advantage
peppermint	pantaloon	represent
classical	favorite	vivacious
valentine	fanciful	atmosphere
buffalo	hardiness	indignant
babydoll	laboratory	enormous

If the child is in Level III, teach him to:

- 1. Find the hidden beginning sound of a word. Ask him to "Say *mat*." (Pause while he says it.) Then, "Does the word *mat* begin with a /m/ sound?" (Say the letter sound —*mmm*—not the letter name.) Encourage the child to think about how his mouth feels as he repeats the word.

   The following words are suitable for this activity:

FIGURE 51

Does the word begin with an /**m**/ sound? (as in mother)

mix	Monday	money	fame
mate	time	make	time
neat	misty	came	monastery
comb	ram	many	name
fame	seam	melt	milkshake

Does the word begin with an /**a**/ sound? (as in apron)

aid	apple	ace	animal
ape	awful	August	afraid
open	acorn	ant	ate

Does the word begin with an /e/ sound? (as in eel)

indian	evil	evict	team
eat	beef	ear	equal
even	every	sneeze	enemy

Does the word begin with an /i/ sound? (as in idea)

Indian	ice cream	find	grind
ant	item	icicle	ivy
ice	cry	plier	bike

Does the word begin with an /o/ sound? (as in open)

under	opera	omen	blow
over	know	bone	open
on	ocean	ox	boat

Does the word begin with an /u/ sound? (as in useful)

use	grew	union	unity
yeoman	usual	yule	ukelele
blue	umbrella	group	under

Does the word start with a /b/ sound? (as in big)

dig	boy	brown	breakfast
bag	drag	hag	slab
peg	basket	bicycle	crib

Does the word start with a /k/ sound? (as in cup)

cat	scare	kite	across
skin	castle	cartoon	smash
bake	color	lock	cash

Does the word start with a /d/ sound? (as in dog)

day	done	muddy	devil
sad	toad	door	blood
trip	drag	sled	danger

Does the word start with a /g/ sound? (as in go)

juggle	green	glow	ghost
dig	ragged	drag	glove
gold	gate	bag	grain

Does the word start with a /h/ sound? (as in hat)

home	hair	shove	show
omen	ahoy	him	history
hop	hang	they	hill

Does the word start with a /j/ sound? (as in joke)

Jane	rage	badge	Jim
jump	joy	chew	chase
goat	gyp	jar	cash

Does the word start with a /l/ sound? (as in lake)

lane	love	lend	lead
flood	pickle	glare	land
hill	log	flag	click

Does the word start with a /n/ sound? (as in neck)

snip	no	anthill	nevertheless
kneel	fan	in	instruct
onto	needless	nothing	needle

Does the word start with a /p/ sound? (as in pick)

spell	paint	stop	part
pray	drag	open	pill
plunge	blond	spill	clap

Does the word start with a /r/ sound? (as in ride)

real	bring	ride	far
dart	rag	drip	wrinkle
river	greave	rent	truck

Does the word start with a /**s**/ sound? (as in so)

sand	smack	misty	wrist
score	miss	spell	scold
zip	silly	whistle	stick

Does the word start with a /**v**/ sound? (as in very)

vote	victory	viking	win
wish	reef	love	vicious
vocal	vanish	fat	fish

Does the word start with a /**w**/ sound? (as in win)

swell	hole	wit	twine
twinkle	warm	vote	wedding
wag	wiggle	swim	wine

Does the word start with a /**y**/ sound? (as in yell)

yes	youth	hit	yard
win	twin	joke	beyond
hang	girl	yank	young

Does the word start with a /**z**/ sound? (as in zip)

zoo	zone	snip	tease
sow	zeal	zenith	zigzag
is	zoom	rose	toes

Does the word start with a /**ch**/ sound? (as in chew)

champ	ship	charge	jump
shoe	camp	general	chip
chunk	chuckle	show	school

Does the word start with a /**sh**/ sound? (as in ship)

shallow	see	chair	rash
soup	shave	jar	shun
chew	shine	shell	shrug

Does the word start with an /ĕ/ sound? (as in eskimo)

end	edit	ever	except
Esther	apple	into	up
eagle	empty	olive	elephant

Does the word start with an /ĭ/ sound? (as in igloo)

into	end	iodine	at
pet	illegal	if	ice
important	impact	up	tin

Does the word start with an /ŏ/ sound? (as in octopus)

opera	rod	under	pot
open	odd	old	object
apple	modern	on	officer

Does the word start with an /ŭ/ sound? (as in umbrella)

under	undermine	sun	urge
use	offer	hunter	bulge
unable	up	usual	ugly

Does the word start with an /ă/ sound? (as in apple)

ant	pen	add	ladder
cat	ask	attic	aide
ape	enter	ate	astronaut

Here is another activity related to this same skill:

Ask the child to print the beginning sound (to be more exact, the letter that *stands* for the beginning sound) of this word. Use the Level III word list.*

- 2. Say the sound that is missing. Ask the child to "Say *mat.*" "Now say *at.*" Then, "What sound is missing in *at* that you heard in *mat*?" (The answer, of course, is the /m/ sound.)

*You may add to the list of Level III words if you wish, but do *not* use words that are in the TAAS. Reserve those for testing, to see whether the child has learned what you set out to teach him.

Here are some suitable words. For more, see the Level III word list.

FIGURE 52

mat - at	tin - in	pin - in
mice - ice	four - or	fan - an
tan - an	ball - all	fall - all
pat - at	call - all	tall - all
date - ate	gone - on	nice - ice
mace - ace	Sam - am	tale - ail
ball - all	race - ace	sill - ill
my - eye	mask - ask	socks - ox
cart - art	pink - ink	sat - at
mice - ice	mad - add	tall - all
deal - eel	neat - eat	will - ill
mall - all	maim - aim	teach - each
faint - ain't	limp - imp	make - ache
sour - our	sad - add	wax - ax
gone - on	page - age	turn - earn
many - any	sold - old	supper - upper
hate - ate	came - aim	sink - ink
seat - eat	moan - own	mare - air
jar - are	fear - ear	mend - end
tan - an	tally - alley	tax - ax
lend - end	tile - I'll	bait - ate
till - ill	soil - oil	door - oar
nor - or	hand - and	gate - ate
sew - oh	jar - are	toe - oh
part - art	sigh - I	win - in
sought - ought	tape - ape	send - end
tease - ease	table - able	march - arch
made - ade	sash - ash	sand - and
tie - eye	fall - all	surge - urge

tear - air	told - old	mart - art
meeting - eating	tar - are	mold - old
tangle - angle	totter - otter	tone - own
mask - ask	sit - it	motto - Otto
mat - at	soften - often	slight - light
small - mall	tin - in	rise - eyes
merge - urge	tote - oat	mink - ink
moat - oat	meager - eager	marrow - arrow
mangle - angle	meal - eel	snip - nip
mate - ate	time - I'm	mow - owe

- 3. Say the word without the sound. Ask the child to "Say *mat*." (Pause) "Now say it again, but don't say the /m/ sound."

All the words on the Level III list are suitable for this activity. They are printed with parentheses around the beginning letters. For example, the first word on that list is (*n*)*or*. The child is told to "Say *nor*; now say it again, but don't say the /n/ sound."

When the child shows that he understands the process of deleting the beginning sound of a word, test him with items 4, 5, and 6 of the TAAS. If he passes, as he should if he has worked through the above three steps, start working on Level IV.

FIGURE 53

LEVEL III LIST

(n)or	(p)each	(w)oke	(p)itch	(m)ace
(b)urn	(b)ait	(p)ending	(n)ear	(m)ice
(h)eart	(h)arm	(r)ash	(f)ate	(s)our
(w)are	(d)oe	(w)onder	(b)eg	(l)ark

(p)ad	(j)oke	(d)are	(g)alley	(p)art
(r)oar	(g)ale	(h)ail	(b)all	(m)ake
(p)ink	(f)or	(r)each	(k)it	(f)all
(r)ant	(c)ash	(r)ally	(b)eat	(f)in
(c)all	(d)oubt	(w)ill	(h)aul	(m)at
(j)ar	(h)all	(h)ad	(l)ice	(f)an
(r)ail	(p)ouch	(p)air	(f)ern	(m)ill
(v)ery	(d)ate	(g)old	(h)am	(l)ake
(p)ace	(b)oil	(d)ad	(h)and	(w)all
(b)at	(c)art	(b)ad	(h)eat	(b)in
(l)ake	(l)ark	(l)ace	(l)ad	(r)an
(l)it	(p)up	(g)oat	(k)eel	(c)at
(f)ail	(d)art	(c)old	(n)ice	(p)ill
(f)ace	(f)ox	(c)ame	(l)eave	(c)all
(f)oul	(c)an't	(h)as	(l)ax	(s)in
(l)ash	(j)am	(d)ear	(h)older	(t)an
(g)ear	(l)ore	(d)ill	(w)age	(b)at
(l)earn	(b)and	(p)inch	(g)out	(s)ink
(v)an	(b)ake	(c)are	(w)itch	(m)all
(r)age	(r)amble	(b)ar	(v)owel	(s)eat
(t)one	(w)eave	(w)ink	(p)arch	(t)each
(m)are	(t)ax	(s)old	(p)age	(b)each

If the child is in Level IV, teach him to:

• 1. Find the hidden final sound of a word. Ask him to "Say *make*." (Pause while he says it.) Then, "Does the word *make* end with a /k/ sound?" (Say the letter sound, not the letter name.) Encourage the child to think about how his mouth feels as he repeats the word.

The following words are suitable for this activity:

FIGURE 54

Does the word end with a /**m**/ sound? (as in Sam)

bend	trim	mush	roam
limp	land	beam	bump
rhyme	steam	green	chum
stem	mean	dimple	mix
bump	came	come	time

Does the word end with a /**t**/ sound? (as in gate)

write	slot	hot	boat
hat	goat	mouth	toast
tame	fighter	had	sled

Does the word end with a /**k**/ sound? (as in make)

back	bag	sick	rack
rocker	lock	fig	crib
score	wrinkle	clap	rag

Does the word end with a /**b**/ sound? (as in bee)

big	bone	slab	bent
crab	dabble	bait	dent
dig	best	ribbon	web

Does the word end with a /**d**/ sound? (as in end)

dog	raid	rode	ladder
food	ditch	mouth	mustard
meet	sweet	loud	decide

Does the word end with a /**f**/ sound? (as in laugh)

love	with	live	growth
graph	stuff	cliff	sunfish
fame	fish	fancy	bluff

Does the word end with a /**g**/ sound? (as in pig)

bike	sling	lock	ghost
rag	haggle	fog	plug
grain	wag	page	stick

Does the word end with a /**j**/ sound? (as in edge)

lodge	bed	which	badge
generous	justice	magic	batch
wag	wage	wash	wish

Does the word end with a /**l**/ sound? (as in all)

long	hello	pail	silk
boil	star	pillow	steel
sill	a	listen	stolen

Does the word end with a /**n**/ sound? (as in in)

pin	grain	bend	team
stone	bandit	grim	gown
sandy	shine	nudge	something

Does the word end with a /**p**/ sound? (as in hop)

puzzle	ripple	tide	hopped
paper	trip	defend	heap
rope	raft	crib	feet

Does the word end with a /**r**/ sound? (as in or)

ball	sorry	park	race
fur	sir	tear	squirt
strip	read	furry	fire

Does the word end with a /**s**/ sound? (as in mess)

race	mist	base	toast
rash	sock	least	loose
rise	fasten	please	lose

Does the word end with a /sh/ sound? (as in push)

bush	mushy	squash	match
witch	latch	dash	wishing
rush	show	rubbish	lash

Does the word end with a /z/ sound? (as in eyes)

rise	froze	puzzle	choose
hose	loose	shoes	chosen
zoo	lose	splash	size

- 2. Say the sound that is missing. Ask the child to "Say *make*." (Pause.) "Now say *may*." Then, "What sound is missing in *may* that you heard in *make*?" (The answer, of course, is the /k/ sound. The following words are suitable here, as are the words in the Level IV* list.)

FIGURE 55

make - may	same - say	boat - bow
beat - be	mean - me	loaf - low
boil - boy	mate - may	storm - store
gate - gay	safe - say	time - tie
made - may	rode - row	type - tie
rope - row	soak - so	meat - me
soap - so	toad - toe	grape - gray
beam - be	ice - I	same - say
heat - he	pace - pay	time - tie
mate - may	race - ray	bite - by
home - hoe	dance - Dan	bait - bay
lame - lay	goat - go	team - tea
croak - crow	weight - way	late - lay

*You may add to this list of Level IV words, but do not use words that are in the TAAS. Reserve those for testing, to see whether the child has learned what you set out to teach him.

154

stake - stay	lime - lie	freak - free
boat - bow	like - lie	claim - clay
loom - Lou	mite - my	face - Fay
prime - pry	base - bay	feet - fee
rhyme - rye	awake - away	grace - gray
name - nay	firm - fur	pike - pie

- 3. Say the word without the sound. Ask the child to "Say *make.*" (Pause.) "Now say it again, but don't say the /k/ sound."

    (NOTE: You say the /k/ sound, not the letter name.)

    All the words in the Level IV list are suitable for this activity. They are printed with parentheses around the final sound. For example, the first word in that list is *wa(ke).* The child is asked to "Say *wake.*" (Pause.) "Now say it again, but don't say the /k/ sound." The answer is *way.* Proceed through all the words in this fashion.

FIGURE 56

LEVEL IV LIST

wa(ke)	tea(k)	see(n)	stai(n)
tri(te)	ra(ce)	mee(k)	law(n)
mea(l)	trai(n)	lea(gue)	pa(ge)
lo(be)	no(se)	grou(p)	si(de)
ja(de)	coi(l)	ho(pe)	hea(t)
di(re)	lo(pe)	see(k)	pa(ce)
kee(p)	plea(d)	ti(re)	wea(l)
wai(t)	boa(t)	gai(l)	coo(p)
no(te)	ty(ke)	mi(re)	li(fe)
bi(de)	hai(l)	joi(n)	ma(de)
fee(l)	pla(gue)	goa(t)	coi(n)

gra(ce)	sea(t)	ra(ke)	goe(s)
fu(se)	mo(de)	lea(p)	ra(ge)
ti(le)	frea(k)	ho(ne)	ho(se)
lea(se)	la(ce)	ma(te)	hi(de)
bi(ke)	sea(l)	bea(d)	tee(n)
sa(ne)	wa(ge)	ri(de)	ba(se)
boi(l)	du(ke)	grow(n)	sie(ge)
rai(n)	ha(ze)	coo(l)	gra(pe)
kee(n)	see(p)	mea(t)	loa(d)
new(t)	la(me)	ru(de)	soa(p)
rai(l)	mi(ne)	mi(le)	hai(l)
plea(t)	sa(ke)	pri(ze)	pi(le)
shi(ne)	mi(ght)	li(ke)	bea(m)
loa(m)	how(l)	ga(ze)	pla(te)
sta(ge)	loa(n)	hee(l)	lea(n)

Although the child will probably be able to pass the appropriate items on the TAAS when he completes the above, I suggest you also use the following activity before leaving this level.

- 4. Substitute beginning or final sounds. Ask the child to "Say *make*." (Pause.) "Now say it again, but instead of /m/ [say the 'm' sound, *not* the letter name], say /t/ [the 't' sound, *not* the letter name]," or "Say *make*; now say it again, but instead of /k/ say /t/."

The following word activities are appropriate for this step:

FIGURE 57

Say **sad**	Now say it again, but instead of /**s**/ say /**m**/	**mad**
Say **kale**	Now say it again, but instead of /**k**/ say /**s**/	**sale**
Say **tan**	Now say it again, but instead of /**t**/ say /**m**/	**man**
Say **sat**	Now say it again, but instead of /**s**/ say /**k**/	**cat**
Say **table**	Now say it again, but instead of /**t**/ say /**k**/	**cable**

Say **my**	Now say it again, but instead of /m/ say /s/	**sigh**
Say **make**	Now say it again, but instead of /m/ say /t/	**take**
Say **kill**	Now say it again, but instead of /k/ say /m/	**mill**
Say **mare**	Now say it again, but instead of /m/ say /k/	**care**
Say **milk**	Now say it again, but instead of /m/ say /s/	**silk**
Say **call**	Now say it again, but instead of /k/ say /t/	**tall**
Say **sit**	Now say it again, but instead of /s/ say /k/	**kit**
Say **task**	Now say it again, but instead of /t/ say /m/	**mast**
Say **cage**	Now say it again, but instead of /k/ say /s/	**sage**
Say **more**	Now say it again, but instead of /m/ say /t/	**tore**
Say **main**	Now say it again, but instead of /m/ say /k/	**cane**
Say **take**	Now say it again, but instead of /t/ say /s/	**sake**
Say **mend**	Now say it again, but instead of /m/ say /t/	**tend**
Say **tin**	Now say it again, but instead of /t/ say /k/	**kin**
Say **seal**	Now say it again, but instead of /s/ say /m/	**meal**
Say **cash**	Now say it again, but instead of /k/ say /s/	**sash**
Say **tangle**	Now say it again, but instead of /t/ say /m/	**mangle**
Say **sell**	Now say it again, but instead of /s/ say /t/	**tell**
Say **moat**	Now say it again, but instead of /m/ say /k/	**coat**
Say **tend**	Now say it again, but instead of /t/ say /s/	**send**
Say **fill**	Now say it again, but instead of /f/ say /h/	**hill**
Say **heart**	Now say it again, but instead of /h/ say /d/	**dart**
Say **lace**	Now say it again, but instead of /l/ say /p/	**pace**
Say **dart**	Now say it again, but instead of /d/ say /p/	**part**
Say **goat**	Now say it again, but instead of /g/ say /b/	**boat**
Say **fame**	Now say it again, but instead of /f/ say /g/	**game**
Say **hall**	Now say it again, but instead of /h/ say /w/	**wall**
Say **toss**	Now say it again, but instead of /s/ say /m/	**tom**
Say **boss**	Now say it again, but instead of /s/ say /t/	**bought**
Say **bait**	Now say it again, but instead of /t/ say /s/	**base**
Say **beam**	Now say it again, but instead of /m/ say /t/	**beat**
Say **lace**	Now say it again, but instead of /s/ say /t/	**late**
Say **lame**	Now say it again, but instead of /m/ say /s/	**lace**
Say **rack**	Now say it again, but instead of /k/ say /t/	**rat**
Say **rack**	Now say it again, but instead of /k/ say /m/	**ram**
Say **gate**	Now say it again, but instead of /t/ say /m/	**game**
Say **mate**	Now say it again, but instead of /t/ say /k/	**make**
Say **mite**	Now say it again, but instead of /t/ say /s/	**mice**
Say **bake**	Now say it again, but instead of /k/ say /s/	**base**

157

Say **seat**	Now say it again, but instead of /t/ say /k/	**seek**
Say **prime**	Now say it again, but instead of /m/ say /s/	**price**
Say **late**	Now say it again, but instead of /t/ say /m/	**lame**
Say **bite**	Now say it again, but instead of /t/ say /k/	**bike**
Say **fake**	Now say it again, but instead of /k/ say /s/	**face**
Say **base**	Now say it again, but instead of /s/ say /k/	**bake**
Say **leak**	Now say it again, but instead of /k/ say /s/	**lease**
Say **flame**	Now say it again, but instead of /m/ say /k/	**flake**
Say **face**	Now say it again, but instead of /s/ say /t/	**fate**
Say **well**	Now say it again, but instead of /l/ say /t/	**wet**
Say **steel**	Now say it again, but instead of /l/ say /p/	**steep**
Say **cash**	Now say it again, but instead of /sh/ say /n/	**can**
Say **cuff**	Now say it again, but instead of /f/ say /b/	**cub**
Say **drug**	Now say it again, but instead of /g/ say /m/	**drum**
Say **bead**	Now say it again, but instead of /d/ say /n/	**bean**
Say **safe**	Now say it again, but instead of /f/ say /j/	**sage**
Say **league**	Now say it again, but instead of /g/ say /n/	**lean**
Say **page**	Now say it again, but instead of /h/ say /l/	**pale**
Say **loaf**	Now say it again, but instead of /f/ say /d/	**load**
Say **stage**	Now say it again, but instead of /j/ say /t/	**state**
Say **grade**	Now say it again, but instead of /d/ say /n/	**grain**
Say **hope**	Now say it again, but instead of /p/ say /z/	**hose**
Say **gain**	Now say it again, but instead of /n/ say /z/	**gaze**
Say **hide**	Now say it again, but instead of /d/ say /r/	**hire**
Say **pan**	Now say it again, but instead of /n/ say /s/	**pass**
Say **win**	Now say it again, but instead of /n/ say /g/	**wig**
Say **plead**	Now say it again, but instead of /d/ say /z/	**please**
Say **fair**	Now say it again, but instead of /r/ say /l/	**fail**
Say **mall**	Now say it again, but instead of /l/ say /d/	**maid**

When the child has completed all these activities, he should be ready to be tested. Use the TAAS items 7, 8, and 9. If he passes, start working in Level V.

If the child is in Level V, teach him to:

• 1. Find the hidden sound that, in this level, may be anywhere in the word. Ask him to "Say *camel.*" (Pause while he says it.) Then, "Is there a /m/ sound [say the letter sound, *not* the letter name] in camel?" Encourage the child to repeat the word to himself and to think about how his mouth feels as he says it.

The following words are suitable for this activity:

FIGURE 58

Is there an /ă/ sound in this word? (as in pat)

wet	ladder	placid	shadow
racket	written	depend	dazzle
rake	sailboat	dancer	blade

Is there a /s/ sound in this word? (as in lacy)

beside	inside	wishes	placid
whistle	waste	luster	misty
brother	loses	mazes	muzzle

Is there a /t/ sound in this word? (as in attic)

brittle	handle	winter	paddle
waiter	weather	window	party
bother	model	alter	pathway

Is there a /b/ sound in this word? (as in cabin)

softball	super	sober	carpenter
soapy	laboratory	lipstick	mustard
gabby	grandpa	hamburger	applesauce

Is there a /d/ sound in this word? (as in odor)

midst	lately	muddy	comfortable
eighteen	stopwatch	pedigree	remainder
wonderful	codfish	weather	fracture

Is there an /ĕ/ sound in this word? (as in leg)

rest	feather	Wednesday	mint
wrist	window	defense	lend
meat	pin	domestic	handle

Is there a /f/ sound in this word? (as in defend)

baffle	wavy	defuse	prefer
weather	birthday	marvelous	wonderful
laughter	afterward	devise	pavement

Is there an /ĭ/ sound in this word? (as in mist)

listen	novel	mistletoe	master
western	whistle	lively	minister
lather	petal	wristwatch	messenger

Is there an /ŏ/ sound in this word? (as in log)

codfish	model	Boston	butterfly
shadow	bought	favor	poverty
showboat	protrude	strong	postpone

Is there an /ŭ/ sound in this word? (as in but)

nothing	mountain	insult	front
bought	blunt	subscribe	pendant
musty	instrument	design	horseman

2. Say the sound that is missing. Ask the child to "Say *slip*." (Pause.) "Now say *lip*." Then, "What sound is missing in *lip* that you heard in *slip*?" (The answer, of course, is the /s/ sound.) The following words are suitable here:

FIGURE 59

spider - cider	spoon - soon	snap - nap
slip - lip	stick - sick	stick - tick
stack - tack	slam - lamb	slam - Sam
spin - pin	swell - well	store - tore
stare - tear	flip - lip	black - back
best - bet	snip - nip	vest - vet

ghost - goat	mask - mack	best - bet
trap - rap	store - tore	wilt - will
best - bet	sunk - sun	bunt - but
slip - lip	stir - sir	scold - sold
trim - rim	scoop - soup	track - rack
stop - top	stake - sake	scale - sale
cork - core	swing - wing	bent - bet
snap - sap	bark - bar	beast - beat
rust - rut	bend - bed	boast - boat
skill - sill	clasp - clap	fern - fur
fork - for	cart - car	bank - back
try - rye	gland - glad	blow - low
felt - fell	hand - had	pest - pet
skein - sane	cast - cat	snip - sip
milk - mill	sent - set	hulk - hull
land - lad	start - star	lend - led
fluster - flutter	slag - sag	drown - down
drip - dip	spank - sank	string - sting
blow - bow	bright - bite	black - back
snap - sap	crow - row	just - jut
stack - sack	lint - lit	mark - mar
spin - sin	cram - ram	chart - char
store - sore	built - bill	west - wet
black - lack	fast - fat	roast - rote
fist - fit	triple - ripple	skip - sip
best - Bess	fend - fed	stick - sick
snap - sap	bent - Ben	sting - sing

- 3. Say the word without the sound. Ask the child to "Say *stick*." (Pause.) Now say it again, but don't say the /t/ sound. (Remember, you say the /t/ *sound*, not the letter name.)

All the words in the Level V list* are suitable for this activity. They are printed with parentheses around the sound that is to be deleted. For example, the first word in that list is *p(r)ay*. The child is to "Say *pray*; now say it again, but don't say the /r/ sound." Have him work through the entire list.

FIGURE 60

LEVEL V LIST

p(r)ay	(p)ray	(g)loss	(g)low
g(l)ow	(f)lap	(s)lap	s(l)ap
(s)lip	s(l)ip	(s)tick	s(t)ick
f(r)og	(f)lake	f(l)ake	buil(d)
ca(m)p	clam(p)	cla(m)p	cla(s)p
clas(p)	fi(s)t	bes(t)	be(s)t
e(n)d	fin(d)	fil(m)	fa(s)t
ha(s)te	p(l)y	s(t)y	be(n)d
be(l)t	b(l)onde	(b)rig	c(l)aim
bel(t)	b(l)ood	b(r)ig	(c)lash
be(n)t	(b)loom	(b)right	c(l)ash
ben(t)	b(l)oom	b(r)ight	cla(s)p
ben(ch)	(b)lot	(b)rim	(c)lass
(b)lack	(b)low	(b)ring	(c)lean
b(l)ack	b(l)ow	(b)room	c(l)ean
(b)lank	(b)race	b(r)oom	c(l)ing
b(l)ank	(b)rag	(b)rought	(c)lock
(b)lare	b(r)ag	b(r)ought	c(l)ock
b(l)are	(b)rain	(b)row	(c)olt
(b)leed	b(r)ain	b(r)ow	c(l)ot

*You may add to this list of Level V words, but do not use words that are in the TAAS. Reserve those for testing to see whether the child has learned what you set out to teach him.

b(l)eed	(b)rake	(b)rush	c(l)ub
(b)lend	(b)ranch	bui(l)d	c(l)utter
b(l)end	bran(ch)	buil(d)	(c)raft
ble(n)d	(b)rat	bui(l)t	(c)ramp
(b)less	b(r)at	buil(t)	c(r)amp
b(l)ess	(b)ray	ca(m)p	cra(m)p
(b)lest	b(r)ay	cam(p)	cram(p)
b(l)est	(b)read	can(t)	(c)rank
(b)light	b(r)ead	ca(n)t	cra(n)k
b(l)ight	(b)reed	(c)laim	(c)rash
b(l)ind	b(r)eed	c(l)aim	c(r)ash
b(l)oat	(b)rick	c(l)amp	(c)reep
(b)lock	(b)ride	(c)lamp	c(r)eep
(c)rest	d(r)ip	f(l)eet	(g)low
cres(t)	d(r)ive	(f)lier	g(l)ow
(c)rib	(d)rove	f(l)ier	(g)lue
c(r)ook	d(r)ove	(f)light	(g)race
(c)ruise	(d)rug	f(l)ight	(g)rade
(c)rush	d(r)ug	(f)lit	(g)raft
cu(l)t	(d)rum	f(l)it	(g)rail
(d)raft	d(r)um	f(l)oor	g(r)ail
d(r)aft	e(n)d	f(l)orist	(g)rain
(d)rag	fe(n)d	(f)low	g(r)ain
(d)rain	fen(d)	f(r)ame	(g)rasp
d(r)ain	fil(m)	f(r)og	g(r)asp
(d)raw	fin(d)	f(r)izzle	gras(p)
(d)rank	(f)lair	(f)lume	(g)rate
d(r)ank	f(l)air	f(r)ee	g(r)ate
d(r)awn	(f)lake	f(r)yer	(g)rave
(d)read	f(l)ake	ga(s)p	g(r)ave
d(r)ead	(f)lame	(g)lad	(g)reed

(d)ream	f(l)ame	(g)land	(g)rey
d(r)eam	(f)lash	(g)lade	g(r)ey
d(r)eary	f(l)at	(g)lare	(g)rill
(d)rill	(f)law	(g)lass	g(r)ill
d(r)ill	(f)lee	g(l)ass	(g)rip
(d)rink	f(l)ee	g(l)aze	(g)round
(d)rip	(f)leece	g(l)ide	(g)row
(g)rub	p(l)ain	ran(k)	s(l)ide
hal(t)	p(l)aint	ra(n)t	(t)rack
ha(n)d	(p)lank	ri(n)d	t(r)ack
ha(s)te	plan(t)	ski(m)p	(t)rap
he(l)d	(p)late	skim(p)	t(r)ap
he(l)m	p(l)ack	s(l)ed	(t)rim
he(m)p	(p)ly	(s)lid	t(r)im
hem(p)	p(l)y	s(l)id	(t)ry
hi(l)t	(p)rank	(s)lit	t(r)y
hum(p)	(p)ray	(s)lide	wi(l)t
li(l)t	p(r)ay	s(m)ell	wil(t)
(p)laid	(p)ry	s(p)un	s(l)it
p(l)aid	pu(m)p	(s)wing	(s)lim
(p)lain	ra(m)p	s(w)ing	(f)led

The child is now probably able to pass the last four items (10-13) of the TAAS. However, I suggest that you also use the following activity before ending the program.

- 4. Sound substitutions. Ask the child to "Say *pry*." (Pause.) "Now say it again, but instead of /p/ [say the /p/ sound, not the letter name], say /k/" (the /k/ sound, thus the word becomes *cry*) or "Say *cup*." (Pause.) "Now say it again, but instead of /ŭ/ [the short-u sound, as in cup], say ă [the short ă sound, as in at]." The word then becomes *cap*.

The following activities are appropriate for this step:

164

FIGURE 61

Say **bleed**	Now say it again, but instead of /l/ say /r/	breed
Say **blight**	Now say it again, but instead of /l/ say /r/	bright
Say **broom**	Now say it again, but instead of /r/ say /l/	bloom
Say **brake**	Now say it again, but instead of /ā/ say /ō/	broke
Say **clamp**	Now say it again, but instead of /m/ say /s/	clasp
Say **clock**	Now say it again, but instead of /ŏ/ say /ĭ/	click
Say **crash**	Now say it again, but instead of /r/ say /l/	crush
Say **crest**	Now say it again, but instead of /s/ say /p/	crept
Say **crash**	Now say it again, but instead of /r/ say /l/	clash
Say **draft**	Now say it again, but instead of /ă/ say /ĭ/	drift
Say **drink**	Now say it again, but instead of /ĭ/ say /ă/	drank
Say **drip**	Now say it again, but instead of /ĭ/ say /ŏ/	drop
Say **drive**	Now say it again, but instead of /ī/ say /ō/	drove
Say **flame**	Now say it again, but instead of /l/ say /r/	frame
Say **flash**	Now say it again, but instead of /ă/ say /ĕ/	flesh
Say **free**	Now say it again, but instead of /r/ say /l/	flee
Say **fryer**	Now say it again, but instead of /r/ say /l/	flyer
Say **gland**	Now say it again, but instead of /l/ say /r/	grand
Say **glass**	Now say it again, but instead of /l/ say /r/	grass
Say **glow**	Now say it again, but instead of /l/ say /r/	grow
Say **grain**	Now say it again, but instead of /ā/ say /ō/	groan
Say **grate**	Now say it again, but instead of /t/ say /n/	grain
Say **grip**	Now say it again, but instead of /ĭ/ say /ō/	grope
Say **lint**	Now say it again, but instead of /n/ say /s/	list
Say **plank**	Now say it again, but instead of /l/ say /r/	prank
Say **pray**	Now say it again, but instead of /r/ say /l/	play
Say **ramp**	Now say it again, but instead of /m/ say /s/	rasp
Say **sled**	Now say it again, but instead of /ĕ/ say /ĭ/	slid
Say **swing**	Now say it again, but instead of /w/ say /t/	sting
Say **track**	Now say it again, but instead of /ă/ say /ĭ/	trick
Say **trip**	Now say it again, but instead of /ĭ/ say /ă/	trap

When the child has completed all the above activities, he should be ready to be tested. Use the TAAS items 10, 11, 12, and 13. If he passes, he will be demonstrating that he has acquired auditory perceptual skills adequate to any primary-grade reading program. He will be able to analyze spoken words into their separate sounds and recognize the sequence of those sounds. Reading will be less of a guessing game to him. Matching sounds to letters will seem more reasonable than it once did.

Additional activities

The following activities are supplemental to the program of instruction just described. Use them casually, a few minutes at a time, in a car, at the dining table, whenever conditions are suitable. They all have one central goal; to teach the child to listen analytically to the sounds of spoken language.

- 1. Encourage him to talk and then *listen* to him. This is crucial. If he does not get much opportunity to speak, he will be deprived of the opportunity to manipulate the sounds in spoken language. If you do not listen to him, he will not speak very much. Explain the importance of this to his brothers and sisters. He is to have his turn to speak, and he should be listened to with the same attention given to everyone else.
- 2. Have him make up alliterative phrases. (An alliterative, as you know, is a string of words that begin with the same sound. "Peter Piper picked a peck of pickled peppers" is a good example.) Some may be silly, but see if they can be somewhat meaningful; at the start, they need not be long. "Alice's aunt" is a good beginning. Play a game to see how long a phrase he can come up with. You state the sound; he constructs the phrase.

   For example, you say, "Make up a phrase where all the words start with the /s/ sound." This is not difficult. For example, "Sam Smith sits sadly sewing Sarah's scarf." When he gets the idea, ask him to add words to a phrase you start, but do not tell him the sound. Let him figure it out. For example, you say, "My mother . . ." then have him say the next word.
- 3. "Who said the word that starts with '?' sound." This requires a few people; it is a good after-dinner, linger-at-

the-table game. One person is It (not always the child). It closes his eyes. Each of the others says a word. Then someone asks It, "Who said the word that starts with the '?' sound?"

For example, say there are five people at the table. Sam is It. Mary says *boat*, Jim says *cat*, Bill says *fish*, Ann says *plane*. Someone then asks Sam, "Who said the word that starts with the /f/ sound?" (Say the sound, not the letter name, to the child.) The child, of course, should answer, "Bill."

You can also play this with ending sounds. That is, "Who said the word that *ends* with the '?' sound?"

• 4. Mix up the syllables of a word and have the child figure out what word you have in mind. For example, "What word is this—*cuss-sir*?" The answer, of course, is *circus. Loaf-meat—meatloaf*; and so on. Use longer words also. For example, *zine-ga-ma—magazine*.

5. Rhyming words. State a familiar one-syllable word and see how many rhyming words the child can come up with. Do not insist that they all be meaningful words. It can be more fun if you allow the activity to be a little silly. For example, "What rhymes with 'tip'?" The answer—bip, cip, dip, fip, gip, and others.

• 6. Lipreading. Ask the child to figure out what you are saying just by watching your lips. You, of course, will have to emphasize your vocal motions so that they are apparent. Start easy—one word at a time. Also, trade places with him so that he gets a chance to overemphasize the speech production motions.

• 7. Slow motion speech. This one works well with a tape recorder that can be played at two different speeds. The goal is to speak slowly enough and in a deep enough voice so that when the tape is replayed at the faster speed, the taped message is still understandable. It takes practice and—most important—it requires the child to break the spoken message into parts and stretch those parts out so that they will be understandable when they are replayed at the faster speed.

167

- 8. Teach him to speak Pig-Latin. As you recall, this involves moving the beginning sounds of each word to the end of the word, and then adding *ay.* For example, *cat* becomes *atcay, boy* becomes *oybay,* and so forth. *Ildrenchay ovelay isthay.*
- 9. Imitate others' speech patterns. Everyone likes to mimic, but not everyone likes to be mimicked, so be careful not to insult someone who might be sensitive. The best approach is for you to assume some dialect (Spanish, British, Irish, French) and have the child converse with you—he, of course, using the same dialect. Do not worry about the authenticity of the dialect. The important thing is for the child to become sensitive to what he hears.
- 10. What word is this? First, say only one portion of a word (for example, a syllable or a single sound). With this small clue, the child is to guess the word you have in mind. If he is correct, fine; if he is wrong, add another clue (syllable or sound) and keep at it until he gets it. Then trade roles with him. For example, "What word is this?—/tine/ (rhymes with *mine*)." Then, "Not enough? Okay—here's another clue—/va/ [pause] /tine/." Then, "Still not enough? Okay /val/ [pause] /en/ [pause] /tine/ —Get it? Right! *Valentine.*" Start with simple, well-known words, such as his name, and increase the complexity as he catches on.
- 11. Coding sounds. This activity, similar to spelling, involves representing sounds with letters. Provide the child with four cards, each of which displays a single letter:

t a p s

Then make certain that he knows the sound of each letter (the *a* should be sounded /ă/ as in *cat*). Have him show you the card that says /t/. (He should show the *t* card.) Then ask him to add a card so that it says *at.* (Say the word, do not spell it for him. His job is to recognize what *sound* was added, and where it belongs in relation

168

to the *t* card.) Once this is accomplished, have him change it to *ta*; then to *sta*; then to *sat*; then to *ast*; then to *pat*; then to *taps*; and so on. Introduce additional sounds (cards) and more complex arrangements as he shows that he understands the concepts involved—that letters stand for sounds and that the left-to-right sequence of letters stands for the sequence of sounds.

- 12. How many spoken words can you think of that have a number hidden in them? For example *"wonder"* (one), *"Tuesday"* (two), *"before"* (four), *"date"* (eight).
- 13. How many spoken words can you think of that have a color hidden in them? For example, *"bread"* (red).

This activity list could be extended, but I think you have the idea by now. The goal is to teach children to analyze spoken language into component parts—first syllables and then individual sounds.

It is important that you treat these activities as games. Let the child know that the formal program, already described, is treatment; something he *must* do on a schedule. These activities, in contrast, are to be done when he feels like doing them. Engage in them casually. If he does not feel like playing, allow him that privilege. He will play when he thinks he can compete successfully.

TEACHING GENERAL-MOTOR SKILLS

The central goal of a general-motor skills instructional program should be to help the child recognize that his body is constructed of a number of movable parts that can be organized in a variety of ways. As the goal is achieved, the child will have better control over his movements—better not only in the preciseness of those movements but also in the ease with which he executes them. It is important to understand that the goal is not to teach a particular skill, such as hopping or skipping. Rather, the goal is to teach the child better coordination that he will then be able to display *by* hopping and skipping.

There are a variety of formal programs available for teaching general-motor skills. Some are very elaborate—too elaborate, in my opinion—calling for such sophisticated paraphernalia as trampolines and the like. There is no need to go to this extent.

Ideally, a variety of experiences should be provided in a variety of settings—ball fields, gymnasiums, swimming pools, and so on. YMCA and Boy Scout programs can be exceptionally effective in helping the child achieve better motor abilities and, at the same time, help him grow socially and emotionally, as well as cognitively.

Therefore, even though I will limit my suggestions to a few basic activities, be assured that there are many alternative approaches. I should emphasize that you are not concerned with sponsoring the development of exceptional athletic abilities. The general-motor skills that I identified as worthy of testing are, for the most part, those expected from an average six-year-old. Certainly, it is desirable for the child to acquire good motor skills—they will serve him well in a variety of situations—but, in the context of a discussion about perceptual skills as they relate to school learning, there is no justification for working toward motor skills that would make an Olympic participant proud.

The important question here, then, is when do you worry about the child's motor skills, and just what do you do about them? It might be useful to refer back to Figure 34 on page 90, which shows how general-motor skills link up with visual and auditory perceptual skills that, in turn, link up with reading, spelling, arithmetic, and writing. You may recall that I suggested that you should not worry too much about testing the child's general-motor skills until after you have tested his visual and auditory skills. If you found either of these to be inadequate, then you were to test those general-motor skills that are directly related. If, on the other hand, the child's visual and auditory skills were satisfactory, you were advised that you need not worry about his general-motor skills.

Now what? Suppose you found in your testing that the

child's visual or auditory perceptual skills were substandard, then you tested his general-motor skills and found these to be less than satisfactory. What should you do? You should help the child acquire the motor abilities he lacks, in accord with the test results. But, remember, it is not enough that he learns to hop, or balance, or what have you, by devoting full attention to the act. You want him to be able to do these things almost automatically, similar to the way an experienced driver controls an automobile.

That does not mean that the child should be able to show complete facility when he starts to acquire a skill. Obviously this will not be the case. For example, when he first starts to work on fine-motor finger skills, such as cutting with scissors, he may very well have to devote as much attention to handling the scissors as the new driver does to handling his car. This level of operation is a start, of course, but not enough—he should be able to perform easily, and the only way this can ordinarily be brought about is through lots of practice. So, in teaching general-motor skills, the three principles, already defined, apply once more:

- 1. Organize for success. For example, if the child's goal is to learn to use a scissors effectively, it is not wise to have him start by trying to cut out intricate shapes. Start with a simple straight line and increase the complexity of the task as he acquires skill.

- 2. Provide the child with whatever additional support he needs to complete the task; then teach him how to do it without this help. When we were discussing visual and auditory skills, this help generally came in the form of providing additional information. When dealing with motor skills, the help will ordinarily be in the form of physical support. For example, if the child cannot hop on one foot unless he holds onto something (a chair, your hand) then allow him to do so; encourage him, in fact. Then wean him from that support as he shows improvement.

- 3. Encourage the child to use all his senses to obtain additional information about what he is doing—by looking and listening as he acts. Put simply, this suggests that the child will improve his motor skills more rapidly if he takes the time to look at and listen to what he is doing. This is true in all of the areas discussed here, but it is especially true in fine-motor abilities; watching the hands and what they are doing, listening as alliteratives are spoken, will increase the effectiveness of the activities.

Suggested activities

There are literally thousands of general-motor activities. I will limit my suggestions to a representative sampling. Try to make the activities pleasurable. Give them a game format—a game that the child has a chance of winning, at least often enough to keep him interested.

The activities described here are organized according to the general categories of balance and movement skills, hand skills, oculomotor skills, vocomotor skills, and rhythmic skills. As such, the first three relate more closely to visual perceptual skills, the last two to auditory perceptual skills.

BALANCE AND MOVEMENT SKILLS

The activities in this category all present the same general goal to the child: movement that shows he understands his body is made up of a number of movable parts and that he knows how these parts work together.

- 1. Walk like a:
  a) duck—squat on both feet and walk forward, backward, and sideways.
  b) rabbit—hands and feet on floor, move both hands forward together, then both feet, and so on.
  c) kangaroo—take large hops, both feet together.
  d) crab—chest up away from floor, hands and feet on floor, walk forward and backward without collapsing.
  e) elephant—walk on all fours, slowly and ponderously.

- 2. Roll across the room. Lie down on the floor, then roll over sideways, attempting to maintain the desired direction.
- 3. Hop scotch. This well-known game involves hopping, jumping, and balancing.
- 4. Jump rope. Start simply. It will be easier for the child to learn to jump rope if two others hold the rope. Start off by marking an X on the ground to show the spot where the child is to stand. Then the two persons holding the rope should swing it back and forth slowly and rhythmically while the child jumps over it. Do not swing it completely around him at first. Just keep it very close to the ground and swing at a pace that is manageable for the child—one that he is able to deal with effectively. When he is able to do this, extend the task by extending the swing of the rope. Do not try to impose difficult conditions on him until *he* knows that he can handle them.
- 5. Ball games. There is no need to describe any of these here. There are many and they are well known. One hint, however—it might be wise to start off using an inflated balloon rather than trying to teach the youngster to catch and hit a fast-moving object. A balloon is better than a ball because it moves much more slowly, is larger, and generally easier to manage. A good place to start is to have the child try to keep the balloon afloat by tapping it with his hand, or head, or foot, while you keep track of the time. Perhaps the child will be interested in beating his record, especially if you reward that feat.

  Avoid organized and competitive sports until after he has acquired some basic skills. *Do not involve him in Little League,* or the like, until you are sure he has *some* chance of participating without embarrassment. He is experiencing enough failure in the classroom; do not seek it elsewhere as well.
- 6. Obstacle course. This may be any homemade activity —outdoors or in—that involves whatever objects are handy. Simply arrange a set of objects and instruct the child how he is to proceed through, over, under, or around them. For example, you might have him climb

over a table and under a chair or slide down a rope. Timing him, and keeping a chart of his progress, might be motivating.

- 7. Balance rail. Procure from a lumberyard a ten- or twelve-foot length of a wooden 2 x 4. Place it on the floor and have the child walk the length of it—forward, backward, sideways. His goal is to be able to walk it without stepping off. Once he can do this, complicate the task by having him walk the rail while he:

  a) places his hands on his hips, his head, his chest.

  b) walks heel to toe.

  c) holds a weight in one hand.

  d) balances a book on his head.

  e) looks somewhere other than at the walking rail, straight ahead or at you for example.

  Again, remember the basic principles for teaching these skills. If a twelve-foot walking rail is too long, use a shorter one. If he cannot get across the rail without some support—a hand to hold—give him that support, then slowly withdraw it.

- 8. As you can see, this list of activities could be longer. You can take it from here, I am sure. Just keep the basic goals in mind. You want him to be able to pass the tests described on pages 92-94. These are not difficult tasks and should be accomplished fairly quickly. If you and he want to work for more elaborate skills, go ahead. It will do him no harm; but I do not think it will do much good, either, in terms of directly helping him to become a better reader, speller, calculator, or writer.

FINGER SKILLS

The following suggested activities are again but a sampling of what could be a long list. They are designed for the same general purpose: to teach the child how to use his hands (fingers) in precise, controllable ways.

- 1. Move *this* finger. Designate one finger (touch it or name it) and have the child extend it, keeping all of the others out of the way. (Note: He may want to use his thumb to restrain the other fingers; this is acceptable.) Then have him extend the same finger on the other hand. Start slowly; work on speed after he has learned the basic movements.

- 2. Fold paper. Origami activities are excellent. You should be able to find a book on origami in your library or local bookstore.
- 3. Crochet, or knit, or weave. These are valuable activities, particularly since a pattern is usually followed, thereby providing some instruction in visual perceptual skills as well.
- 4. Identify objects with the hands. Place familiar objects in the child's hand(s) for him to identify without seeing them. Common household objects work well. So do coins of various denominations, cardboard or plastic geometric shapes, and buttons of various sizes.
- 5. Cutting, pasting, painting, or coloring. All are worthwhile activities that children tend to enjoy. Avoid activities that are too demanding. Do not give him tasks that depend upon facile fine-motor skills, that you know, in advance, he cannot handle. Find uncluttered coloring pages.* There is time enough to give him intricate tasks after he learns the basic skills.

6. Buttoning buttons, zipping zippers, tying bows, and lacing laces. This implies that the child should dress himself, feed himself, and butter his own bread. And it is meant to. This is very important, even if it means that he will have to get out of bed a half hour earlier in the morning, or clean up a spilled glass of milk occasionally.

- 7. A walk through any toy store will provide countless ideas—construction toys, games that require drawing, and so forth. But you need not invest in a lot of commercial games. There are any number of materials around the house that will serve quite well. Anything that requires the child to use his individual fingers precisely

*I recognize that many people believe that coloring books will have a detrimental effect on the child's creative abilities. I do not think so. Our most creative artists were well acquainted with their craft and media first. *Then* they were creative— able to express their thoughts and feelings through some medium.

rather than his whole fist will probably be useful—folding napkins and sorting buttons are good examples. And if, at the same time, he has to follow a pattern—thus employing his visual perceptual skills—all the better.

OCULOMOTOR SKILLS

These activities are not in any way intended to be a substitute for a vision specialist. As I suggested earlier, if your child's eyes do not appear to be normal, either in how well he sees or how well he controls them, seek advice from a professional. (Remember, it is advisable to have a visual evaluation done when you first suspect a learning problem —even if his eyes seem to be free of problems.) The activities suggested below are a sampling of the kinds of general activities that can serve to foster better control of eye movement.

- 1. Follow a smoothly moving target. Suspend a rubber ball from the ceiling on a string so that it is at about the level of the child's lower chest. Although size is not critical, something approximating baseball-size is fine. A variety of activities can be engaged in with this setup.
  a) Remove the strings from an old badminton racket (or fashion a similar loop from a coat hanger) and have the child keep the loop of the racket around—but not touching—the ball, as the ball swings in a variety of motions. Also have him take the racket away, then return it to its position around the ball, without touching the ball.
  b) Have the child use his hands instead of the racket. He is to cup them near, but not touching the ball as it swings.
  c) Bunt the ball with a broomstick handle. The ball should be at the child's chest height. The child holds the broomstick handle at his chest with both hands and makes contact with (bunts) the ball. He maintains this bunting pattern as long as he can. The activity can be made more complicated and involve more complex

eye movements by having the child lie down on the floor, face up, and do his bunting from there. (Obviously, the ball will have to be lowered.) As the child improves, encourage him to move his eyes, not his head, as he follows the ball.

- 2. Making the eyes hop. Contrary to popular belief, your eyes do not move smoothly across the page when you read. Rather, they hop across, stopping periodically to look at the words. You do not read when the eyes are in motion—only when they stop. So, one way to improve reading ability is to make the eyes hop more accurately; if they land where they are not supposed to, you stand the chance of skipping a word or a line or, at best, wasting time finding your place.

The following activity can be conducted in any room containing furniture or other objects. Tell the child that, as you name an object in that room, he is to look directly at that object and keep looking at it until you name another object. When you do, he is then to move his eyes directly to that second object, then a third as it is named, and so on. If he takes his eyes from the object before he is told to, it is a miss. (Keeping score adds interest.) Do not make unreasonable demands on him. That is, do not call out a new object every second or two. That is too fast. Likewise, do not delay overly long between calls. Keep the pace somewhat irregular, but reasonable. If he needs additional support, have him point at the object with his finger as he looks at it. This will help him control his eye movements.

VOCOMOTOR (SPEECH) SKILLS

These activities are not in any way intended to be a substitute for a speech therapist. They are a sampling of the general activities that might foster more precise speech production skills. If your child shows any signs of a speech problem, seek professional advice.

As you will note, all the activities are designed to teach the child better control of his lips, tongue, and jaws.

177

- 1. Whistle through puckered lips.
- 2. Inflate balloons.
- 3. Play tabletop soccer with a Ping-Pong ball and straws, propelling the ball with air blown through the straws.
- 4. Click tongue against roof of mouth; click teeth; produce odd noises with vocal cords.
- 5. Say alliteratives rapidly. For example, "She sells seashells by the seashore."

RHYTHMIC SKILLS

The rhythmic skills we are concerned about here are those that require the child to coordinate his two body sides in a synchronized way. This is not the same as tapping out rhythms with one hand, although there is nothing wrong with doing that also.

- 1. Bongo drums are useful in generating interest, but not necessary. The child is to:
  a) tap one time with his right hand, then one time with his left, then his right, and so on (about one tap per second).
  b) tap two times with his right hand, two times with his left, two times with his right, and so on (same tempo).
  c) tap once with his right hand, twice with his left, once with his right, and so on (same tempo).
  d) then do the reverse; twice with his right hand, once with his left, and so on (same tempo).

At first the child may have to count to himself as he engages in these various rhythms, saying "one-two, one-two," then "one, one-two, one, one-two." If he has to, fine, encourage him to do so. But his goal is to be able to tap these rhythms without losing the beat when he switches hands—while at the same time carrying on a conversation. This will take practice.

Once he has the rhythmic pattern established, start asking him simple questions, like his age or his birthday. The questions can get more complex in time. The goal here is for him to be able to tap any of the rhythms upon request while simultaneously carrying on a conversation.

HELPING THE CHILD WITH HIS SCHOOL SUBJECTS

Up to here, I have been discussing perceptual skills—readiness abilities that, in varying degrees, are called for by all elementary school reading, arithmetic, and spelling instructional programs. I have traced the development of these skills in children and described how they can be tested and taught.

However, most of you are probably concerned about a particular youngster; and chances are that he is well beyond the readiness stage. As such, you are interested in finding out what can be done for a second, third, sixth, or even tenth grader who has a history of school failure.

In other words, what about the fourth-grade child who is reading at a second-grade level, or whose arithmetic skills are far below what they should be? What do you do about him? Will he be "cured" if you test him properly, find out what perceptual skills he needs help with, and then work on those skills? Probably not. Unfortunately, it is not that simple—and the older the child the more complex the problem.

First of all, the perceptual skills program may not be as effective as we would hope. Some small percentage of children display persistent perceptual skills deficits, despite extensive attempts to teach them—not because the teaching was improper, but because whatever caused the problem in the first place continues to cause trouble.

In most cases, however, the effort is effective. The child acquires the perceptual skills he originally lacked. He is now better prepared to profit from instruction. But if he is past the age of six or seven, he is probably already far behind in one or more of his school subjects. Learning better perceptual skills will not close that gap. Nothing will, other than effective instruction and plenty of it. In other words, the child who is lagging behind in school needs more than a perceptual skills program. He needs to be taught what he does not know, in a way that takes into account the skills he has and the skills he lacks.

The goal of this next section is to suggest ways that children in such circumstances should be taught, taking into consideration the strengths and weaknesses of their existing skills.* To achieve that goal, we must first determine what reading, arithmetic, spelling, and writing require of the child—what he has to be able to *do* in order to make progress in those subjects. Then we can design ways to teach him how to do it. (Going back to the example of teaching the blind child to read, what he had to be able to *do* was relate spoken language to symbols. Braille was a way designed to teach him how to do it.)

General goals

Before we do that, however, we should spend some time considering certain general concepts that apply to all subject areas. As the previous section stressed, the way to improve a child's perceptual skills is to have him break patterns down into their parts and then teach him how to recognize the way those parts fit together. For example, teach him to recognize that meaningful spoken words are made up of nonmeaningful sounds connected in a specific sequence. If he learns this, he is less likely to be confused by the concept that those sounds can be represented—

---

*This does not mean that we are going to determine whether the child is a visual or an auditory learner, and then teach him through the better modality. That is a gross misconception, although one that continues to be popular. The concept got started because it seemed so logical. Blind children do not see. So teach them through an intact modality—their fingers. What is overlooked in that reasoning is what is involved in learning to read. Reading requires relating spoken language (sounds) to symbols. Since blind children cannot recognize visual symbols, tactile ones are used. It works because the process is not altered; only the nature of the symbols is changed. They are presented to the fingers instead of the eyes; the basic task is still one of translating symbols into language. But generalizing from this and arguing that when a child's auditory skills are inadequate, he should be taught through his eyes, is wrong. It ignores what reading is all about.

coded—with letters. Teach him to recognize that spatial patterns—geometric designs, arrangements of objects—are made up of nonmeaningful lines that fit together in precise ways. If he learns this, he is less likely to be confused by the concept that the quantity and relative differences of those lines (length or width, for example) can be represented with numerals. These are *analysis* processes.

Learning to read, spell, calculate, and write is different. They involve *assembling* processes. In each of these, the child has to learn to put together small units into larger units, so that he has time to interpret the abstract information represented by the letters and numerals. You cannot very well think about how to solve a practical arithmetic problem if you have to work through the basic arithmetic in the problem by counting on your fingers or in your head. Working through a reading or arithmetic task this way would rule out your chances of interpreting anything. It would consume too much time and mental energy. You would lose your train of thought. You would not be able to remember enough about the beginning of the reading paragraph or the arithmetic problem when you finally got to the end. The information would not be meaningful; it would have no unity; it would be a collection of segments.

The key words here are *larger units* and *remember*. Psychologists talk about two kinds of memory: long-term and short-term. Both are crucial to successful learning; both are needed to assemble small units of information into larger units.

Both are what their names suggest. When you remember your telephone number, or what you did last Christmas, you are using your long-term memory. It is information that you are not likely to forget—at least, not for a while. It is information you have memorized. If you ignore it long enough—if you get a new telephone number—it will be shoved aside for other, more pertinent information.

You use your short-term memory to store information for the moment—it is information that may or may not eventually be transferred to long-term memory, depending on what it is, how much you use it, and how unique it is. For example, when you look up someone's number in the telephone book, you remember it long enough to use it. Then you forget it, unless you use it frequently, memorize it intentionally, or (and this is most relevant to our concerns) associate it with something already memorized. (There are, of course, those isolated experiences, sufficiently unique, that seem to go directly into one's long-term memory; these are usually events that have strong emotional impact.)

There is a limit to the amount of information one can hold in short-term memory at any one time. Psychologists suggest that seven units is about it; a 7-digit number, for example. Given that fact, how can we possibly hope to help a child learn to interpret sentences that contain more than seven words; for that matter, how do we do it?

We do it, not by remembering *more* units of information but by remembering *larger* units—chunks—made up of familiar patterns of smaller units. Then, when we encounter a set of new information that contains these chunks, we recognize them—remember them—with relative ease; thereby reducing the amount of new information that has to be remembered in that situation; thereby enhancing what we remember of that situation.

I presume, for example, that you can remember quite a bit of what you have read so far in this book. (At least, I hope so.) How have you managed it? Surely, not by memorizing the words as you read them. You have done it by using at least two strategies:

- 1. You have not read every word—you chunked the words; you read fast enough to take your information in large, meaningful bites.
- 2. You attached the information contained in this book to knowledge you had already stored in your memory. Not all that I have said is new to you. What part do you remember least? That part that was most novel—probably the sections devoted to testing and teaching perceptu-

al skills. There you probably had to deal with the information in smaller bites, and thus can hardly be expected to recall very many of the details.

To achieve in school, the child has to learn to do these same things. If he approaches each learning situation with a clean slate, and attempts to remember each piece of information without attaching or relating it to something already remembered, he will fail. The only way to profit from today's lesson is to see how it relates (is different—is the same) to all previous lessons. Thus, each new lesson, if it is properly designed, is not a big step beyond the previous ones. In fact, in terms of what the child is to *do*, it should be remarkably similar; only the material he does it with should change—get more complex.

This is the general guideline that underlies all the activities you will use. By definition, the child with a learning difficulty does not have the ability to organize information effectively and see how separate segments fit together. He is slower to see a system—a pattern. (Do you see how this relates to perceptual skills? The better the skills, the better the ability to recognize patterns.) That will be your job: to make sure that the child sees the important patterns and devises ways to remember them. His teacher and his school will continue to decide what information he is to learn, using that systematic approach.

READING

First, we will identify some of the basic processes involved in learning to read—what learning to read requires of the child. Then we will compare what is known about good learners of reading, poor learners of reading, and the various school programs for teaching reading. After this we will be able to think logically about how best to help the child who is having trouble learning to read, taking into consideration the demands made on him by the reading program used in his school.

The three stages

Reading can be defined in many different ways. For our purposes, consider reading as the translation of visual symbols into language that the reader already understands. Using this definition, it is apparent that in order to read the child must be able to do certain things. These can be described as components of reading—stages. He must be able to:

STAGE I

Recognize the letters and the conventions that govern their use; that is, the left to right sequence; the use of capitals and periods.

STAGE II

Translate the letters into verbal language—"decode" them—either letter by letter into separate sounds that are then blended into words; or as whole words from the start, where initially little attention is paid to the separate sounds; or perhaps something in-between. (We will discuss these different approaches shortly.)

STAGE III

Understand the individual words, or at least enough of them so that he can take an educated guess at the rest, and assemble them into clusters that enable him to get meaning from the text.

These three stages may be conceived to occur in sequence, as shown in Figure 62.

Not only must the child be able to do these three things, he must be able to do them efficiently—fast enough and with sufficient ease so that the process does not break down before the third stage has been achieved. The faster he is able to do them, the better his reading will be. If he cannot do all of them efficiently, you can anticipate trouble.

For example, if he has not mastered Stage I—if he is not

FIGURE 62

READING

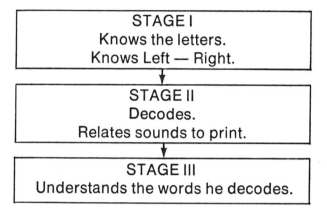

STAGE I Knows the letters. Knows Left — Right.
STAGE II Decodes. Relates sounds to print.
STAGE III Understands the words he decodes.

sufficiently familiar with the letters that constitute the words he is trying to read, and cannot recognize them with facility—it is bound to affect his ability to decode them (Stage II). If he tends to confuse the letters, he is apt to generate the wrong sounds (for example, *big* instead of *dig*). If he is slow at recognizing the letters, it will take him too long to get through a word; he will have trouble remembering the first part of the word when he finally gets to the last part, and the first part of a sentence when he finally gets to its end (Stage III). He will have a reading problem.

Suppose he does recognize the letters accurately and easily, and does understand that when he reads he is to start on the left and move toward the right? Well, he will at least be past the first stage, but he may still encounter difficulty with decoding. He not only has to recognize the letters, he also has to translate them into sounds. If he lacks the ability to do this both accurately and rapidly, you can still expect trouble. If he says the wrong sounds, he will produce the wrong word. If he produces the correct sounds too slowly, he again will have difficulty remembering the front part of the word when he finally gets to the last part. Thus, once more, it is not very likely that he will understand what he reads. He will have a reading problem.

Within each stage, he must learn to deal with larger units of information, progressing in one way or another (depending on the reading system), from individual letters and sounds, to printed and spoken words, to strings of words—phrases and sentences.

Here is an illustration of that point:

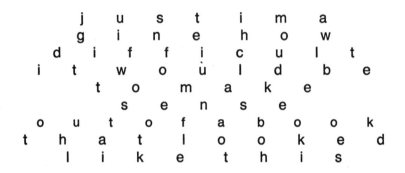

Sure you can do it, by going through it one letter at a time, then going back and chunking those into larger units —words. But, despite the fact that you can already read, it slows you down considerably. If you were not already a competent reader, it would be a trying task indeed, and would probably destroy any chance you had of comprehending the text unless you took the time to read it over and over again—to merge it into units that had meaning.

As another illustration, turn this book upside down and read the text in that position. You will be able to do it, but once more your reading will be slowed down. You will probably find it necessary to revert to a less efficient reading style where you decode word by word; where you deal with smaller chunks. See what that does to your reading speed and comprehension.

As a child acquires the abilities identified here as belonging to Stage I, he learns to deal effectively with small units —letters and sounds. As he progresses and masters Stage II, the units become larger—he chunks the units he dealt with at Stage I into printed/spoken words and, in fact, stops seeing and hearing the separate letters and sounds. As he acquires Stage III skills, the units become even larger and, with each step, his ability to understand what he reads increases. He has to devote less time to the mechanics of the lower stages. He has more time and energy available to spend on the higher level aspects of reading—that is, to thinking about what he is decoding. Do you recall the student driver illustration? It fits here.

Now, let us examine the difference between what children who learn to read easily do, and what children who encounter difficulty in learning to read do, and how different reading programs place different demands on the learner. This should help us determine the best way to help a child with a reading problem.

The very good learner, upon being shown a printed word and told what it says, analyzes the word's printed and spoken patterns into their respective component parts, recognizes certain pertinent features in both, and relates the two. For example, upon being shown the printed word *cat* and told what it says, the *very* good learner (and there really are only a relative few of these around) recognizes that the spoken word *cat* is made up of three sounds. He links the printed *c* to the /k/ sound, the printed *a* to the /ă/ sound, and the printed *t* to the /t/ sound. Coding—recognizing that the letters can stand for specific sounds—makes sense to him. Thus, decoding also seems reasonable. He virtually teaches himself.

This, of course, is not a very common situation. Most children, even good learners, are not that competent. Most need to have at least some of the letter-sound rules pointed out to them, either directly or by inference. For example, some can be taught that the printed letters *at* stand for the sound /at/, that the printed *c* stands for the /k/ sound, and the printed *m* for the /m/ sound. And from this information base, they will probably be able to read the words *mat* and *cat*. Or, it could occur the other way around. The child could be taught to read *cat* and *mat* and apply this knowledge to reading the words *can* and *man* immediately after being taught the sound of the letter *n*. Once taught some basic principles, he can apply them generally.

The poor learner is, by definition, not so aware. That, in fact, is the major reason he is called a poor learner. Upon being shown a printed word (*cat* for example) and told what it says, he does not notice pertinent visual and auditory details. He does not necessarily see that there are three letters in the word, that the letters occur in a specific sequence, and that the spoken word *cat* is constructed of three sounds that are in some way connected with the three printed letters. Since he does not perceive all this on his own, someone else has to make it apparent to him. And even after he is taught these concepts, he has trouble applying them generally to other words containing the same letters.

WHICH READING PROGRAM IS BEST?

There are a number of systems for teaching children to read. Many are similar, but some of them do differ greatly. On the one extreme, for example, there is the so-called "Look—Say" method—a system that continues to be popular although it has been modified substantially over the past ten years. I described this system, to some extent, in an earlier part of the book, but some additional remarks are called for here.

In that system, the children are taught to recognize whole words as whole words; in a sense, to read the words as though the letters constituted a picture. Individual letter sounds are ignored for the most part.*

The child has to memorize whole words from sight—indeed, they are known as sight words. For example, the child is taught to read the words *look* and *oh*, after which he can read a line in his first reading book: "Look, look, oh look!" Then he is taught the words *see* and *Spot* and *jump*. Now another sentence can be read. The stories are accompanied by a number of pictures—these, not only to make the text more interesting, but also to help the reader re-

---

*It is interesting that the rationale for this system appears to have been based on the fact that good learners were able to learn to read this way. The assumption was that the system would therefore make good learners out of everybody. Strange reasoning—but popular at one time.

member those words he has not yet been able to memorize. The pictures are cues or prompts.

At the other extreme are the phonics programs. Generally, with these the child is taught that individual letters represent individual sounds and that words comprise strings of these sounds, blended together. For example, the letters *s*, *i*, and *t* might be taught first, each one separately. The child is instructed that each letter makes a specific sound: the *s* as in the word *see*, the *i* as in the word *igloo*, and the *t* as in the word *to*. He practices reading these letters separately—saying their sounds—and is then taught to blend them—put them together. Having learned these three sounds and how to blend them, he should be able to read three words: *it*, *sit*, and *its*. Additional letters and their sounds are then taught—perhaps the *a*, as in *at*; the *m* and the *p*. Now the child is expected to be able to read more words: *sat*, *tap*, *mat*, *mit*, *tip*, *pat*, and so on.

As you can see, a phonics program depends a great deal less on the child's memory and his ability to analyze words into their component parts. He is, in fact, introduced to reading by being taught the component parts first; then he learns how to put them together into words. All he has to memorize are the letter-sound combinations, and at the onset he is not exposed to very many. With this information, he will be able to read a fair number of words; far more than if he had to memorize each word separately.

Both systems have their faults. In the first—the sight method—the burden placed upon the child's memory is overwhelming unless he figures out for himself (or someone teaches him) that letters stand for sounds. If he truly has to memorize all reading words as though they are pictures, looking at none of the separate letters for phonics cues, there will be a distinct limit on the number of words he can learn and retain during a school year. This is why so many children depend heavily upon the pictures in their reading books—it helps them guess at the words they do not remember and, as a result, teaches a lot of children to guess instead of to read; not a very good substitute.

Only the good learner—the child with competent visual and auditory perceptual skills—is served well by the sight method. Since, by definition, he can readily analyze printed words into their parts (letters) and spoken words into their parts (individual sounds), he is likely to discover at least some of the letter-sound relationships without their having to be taught. All other children—particularly those whose auditory perceptual skills are not superior—are not served well by the sight method. They need something different.

However, the sight method is not all bad. It does have certain good features. First, meaningfully related words can be taught from the beginning; simple stories that have some point can be used from the first lesson on, thereby stressing the concept of reading for meaning. Second, the child learns to read whole words, even whole sentences, from the beginning; he does not learn to decipher each word letter-by-letter before he reads it—a process that, if it persists, tends to wipe out any chance of getting meaning from print.

The pure phonics approach is not all good nor all bad either. On the plus side, as already mentioned, the program does not require superior auditory skills from the child, nor does he have to memorize very much to get started—usually only about eight consonants, two vowels, and a sound for each. His first reading words are constructed from these.

On the negative side, however, the child's beginning reading vocabulary tends to be limited to very short words. As such, he may not get enough experience in blending extended chains of individual sounds as rapidly as is needed to acquire fluent reading ability. It is quite a while, in many phonics programs, before the child is asked to read multisyllable words, or words where the letter sounds are not regular.

That last point is important. As you know, letter-sound relationships are not consistent in the English language. Consider the letter *a* and its sounds in the following words: *mat*, *mate*, *above*, *law*, and *meat*; four different sounds and, in the last word, no sound at all! Here is another mind-boggler: What understandable rules can explain how to sound out such words as *said, their, eight*, and the like? And there are plenty of these in our language. Thus, learning to read through a pure phonics approach has its problems. There are too many irregular words—words where the letter-sound relationships are exceptions to the rules.

It is clear, then, that neither system is perfect. Both have their good features and their faults. The child with substandard perceptual skills will encounter trouble with both, although you can be sure that he will have much less *initial* confusion with the phonics-based program than with the sight method.

All right, then, how about some other system? One that takes into account the differences children display in their perceptual skills; one that takes what is good from both the sight method and the phonics method, and avoids what is not good in them.

The perfect system has yet to be developed and probably never will be. Yes, better systems can be designed. Most of those in use today are better than what was available ten years ago, and even better ones are on the way. But it is unrealistic to foresee a *single* system that serves *all* children equally well.

There is still one other type of reading problem that should be mentioned. This is the one where the child can recognize all the letters, does understand the left to right organization of printed language, and can decode satisfactorily. His problem appears to be with Stage III skills. What he cannot do well is comprehend what he reads, even though he knows all the words. When he reads aloud, he sounds the way a good reader sounds; it is not the halting, error-filled reading of the child with a Stage II decoding problem. This one is a puzzler. Fortunately, there are not too many like this, but there are enough.

His problem is difficult to explain. It seems to be the result of an inability to organize and associate the information contained in the text. Relationships are not perceived. I will not attempt to speculate about cause, but I have observed enough of these children to know that closely related to their reading comprehension problem is an inadequate set of visual perceptual skills. It is as though their failure to see relationships between concrete objects is reflected in their reading—and I know of no reading system, now available, that meets their needs.

In summary, then, it seems obvious that the answer to children's reading problems will not be found in a system, although a good system can be a powerful help. The answer will be found in making certain that the children have the basic prerequisite skills *before* they enter into a program of reading instruction, and then once entered, in monitoring closely their progress—making sure they learn enough at each stage to meet the requirements of the next.

In other words, the answer is in preventing failure—but more about that in the final section. What we have to do now, since this book is primarily focused on children who are already experiencing school failure, is to face the problems they are displaying. What can be done for them? How can they be helped?

Helping the poor reader

This section contains a number of activities that will help the poor reader. They do not constitute a complete reading program that can replace his school program. Rather, they focus on specific skills that are vital to satisfactory reading.

It is essential, when you use these procedures, to coordinate your efforts with your child's teacher. If the activity calls for a list of words appropriate to his grade or abilities, they should be obtained from his teacher. If key words are used to help the child remember certain letter sounds, they should be the same words his teacher uses.

The activities are all based on the same instructional principles that I cited earlier in the discussion about teaching visual and auditory skills. I will restate them here, with examples of how they pertain to helping a child learn to read.

- 1. Organize for success. Teach the child what he is ready to learn. Do not expect him to be able to profit from a lesson based on fifth-grade material when he has the skills of a second grader. He can learn only if he can connect what you are teaching him to some already established base of information. If what you are teaching him depends upon prior knowledge that he does not have, the outcome will be failure and frustration, and he is already too familiar with those. Therefore, make certain that the child can perform Stage I operations fairly well before you go to Stage II. There is no sense in trying to teach him to decode when he does not know the letters he will encounter in that lesson. And, likewise, there is no sense in worrying about his reading comprehension (Stage III) until he is able to string at least some words together well enough to conceive of the string as a unit of information, not a segmented chain of individual units.*

Remember the diagram, shown at the beginning of this section, that displayed the three stages? Your goal, as you work with the child, is to merge those three stages. Stage I abilities should become so well established that they require virtually no attention from the child—he can perform them instantaneously. Then, in time, Stage II abilities should reach that same level of virtually automatic performance. Then, finally, Stage III as well. When this happens, the diagram would no longer show three boxes, each one representing a separate stage. Rather, it would show a single box that represented the merging of all three into a single, complex ability called reading— the translation of visual symbols into language the child already understands.

- 2. Provide the child with whatever information—*hints*— he needs to understand the task; then teach him how to do the task without this help. I will discuss some ways of doing this—color cues, for example—and recommend their use. It is better to have the child start to decode successfully—albeit with hints—and then work toward

---

*This does not mean that you should work at one stage until he is perfect before going on. Once the child knows *some* letters he can be taught to decode *some* words and to interpret whatever information they represent. Thus, he can and should be working on all three stages at the same time.

eliminating these hints, than to have him fail miserably. The one way offers nothing of value. With the other, the child has a chance; a good chance.

- 3. Encourage the child to make use of all his senses; not just his eyes. In other words, if it helps him to point with his finger or to move his lips while reading, allow him to do so. In fact, insist upon it.

Suggested activities

The following activities are organized according to the skills they teach and the stages to which they belong. Test him informally to see where he should start. For example, if the child is already familiar with all the letters, if he displays no reversal tendencies (confusing *b* and *d*; reading *was* for *saw*), if he understands the purpose of a capital letter and a period, there is no reason to use the activities listed under Stage I. Likewise, if he can already decode with facility, Stage II activities may be omitted. Finally, if he comprehends oral and visual information efficiently and if he remembers and understands what he sees and hears on television, at the dining room table, in school, and can demonstrate this by relating that information in an organized way—identifying main points and lesser ones, and how they fit together—then you probably do not have to spend much time on Stage III activities.*

Stage I suggestions: Helping the child who has difficulty recognizing the letters and the left to right sequence.

- 1. Stage I reading skills are based, to a great extent, on adequate visual perceptual skills. If you have not already

---

*Do not conclude that because the child's Stage III (comprehension) skills are competent, there is no need to work on Stage II (decoding) skills. That assumption is incorrect. The child may comprehend well as long as he does not have to do the decoding. That is why you should test him orally. If he is able to comprehend oral and pictorial information (television, movies, and so on), it is very likely that he will also comprehend written information once he learns how to decode it efficiently. On the other hand, if he is poor at comprehending oral and pictorial information, he will also be poor with written information, no matter how well he decodes it. Hence, it is quite possible that you will use just Stage II activities, or just Stage III activities or, indeed, both.

done so, test his visual skills with the TVAS and, if they are not up to the expected level, devote some of your time to teaching them. This can go on at the same time that you are helping the child with his reading.

- 2. Determine which letters the child already knows— both capitals and lower case. To be certain, have him print them from dictation. Teach him the ones he does not know; and teach him the letter names at the same time.*

Teach the capital letters first. They are less confusing and easier to print. Then teach the lowercase letters, in clusters, based on their construction—not their relative position in the alphabet.

Teachers have long known that it helps some children if you point out to them that the letter *c* is embedded (hidden) in certain other letters. These are

a d e g o q

There is a *c* hidden in each of these and, in addition, if

---

*There continues to be much debate among reading experts over the value of learning letter names. Some argue that this is a needless, perhaps even distracting step; that children do not need to learn letter names. Rather, they insist, children should be taught simply to connect the letter shapes with the sounds they make.

On the surface, this seems to be a valid argument. And it is, if the child displays the characteristics of a good learner that I described earlier. If, however, he does not belong to that group (and if he did, you probably would not be reading this), it will be easier for him to learn the sounds that the letters represent if he first learns the letter names.

Consider this analogous situation. Suppose you are introduced to three men: Jim, John, and Sam, and told that you are to remember the sounds of their voices and relate it to their faces—that you will shortly be asked to use this information to solve a problem. In a second situation, you are introduced to three other men: Tim, Tom, and Charles, and asked to do the same thing. Suppose that the only difference between these two situations is that you are given some time to study photographs of this latter trio before they are introduced, and told their names— learning which one is Tim, which is Tom, which is Charles. As a result, by the time they are introduced, you are completely familiar with each one's identity. You do nothing like that prior to meeting the first trio. With which group will you do a more accurate and rapid job of associating sound (of voice) with appearance (of man)? With the latter trio, obviously. There, you have only one new thing to learn about each of them. With the first trio, you have to sort out the three as well as relate face to sound. Teach the letter names as you teach the letter shapes—before you teach letter sounds.

the letter does contain a vertical line, it is positioned to the *right* of the *c*—it comes *after* the *c*—just as the *d* comes after the *c* in the alphabet. This point should be stressed to the child. Two more letters can be added to this group, even though they do not contain the *c*. These are the *j* and the *u*. The former because it can be thought of as the *g* with the *c* removed; the latter because its vertical line is to the *right* of the body of the letter—the only other one, aside from those already identified, where this is so.

Once these have been learned fairly well, additional letters should be taught. Learned, however, means more than being able to discriminate one from another, although that is a good place to start. Discrimination skills can usually be taught by playing card games, where each card contains a letter (you can either purchase such cards or make your own). Play matching games—concentration (see page 125)—or variations of rummy. If the child has difficulty matching the letters, cut out pairs of cardboard letters and have him start off by placing his letters on top of your letters, and then alongside (as described in the visual skills program).

The next step in teaching the letters, once he can *match* them, is to teach him to identify—*point to*—the appropriate letter when it is named. You can use your deck of cards here, too.

This, again, is insufficient evidence of mastery, as is the next step—having the child *name* the letters when they are shown to him. (Once more the deck is useful.)

As I said before, do not assume that the child knows the letters until he can print them accurately from dictation. Start him off at a chalkboard. Then work on lined paper. (For more about this, see the section on Writing.)*

---

*I should acknowledge that the good learner does not need all this attention. He can be dealt with in a less structured way, skipping steps without too much risk. By definition, he sees the important details, recognizes how they relate to other details, and has a good memory; it is likely that he will continue to learn even after lessons are over for the day. He does not have to be taught as much. The poor learner will not do the same. Someone has to teach him in a way that recognizes his problem.

Another cluster of lowercase letters that appear to belong together are those that stem from the lowercase *r*, and if they contain a vertical line, it is located to the *left* of the main body of the letter. These, of course, are:

b h m n p k f

Once again, these should be taught to the point where the child can print them from dictation, built on a base of first matching shapes, then pointing to them when someone else states their names, and thirdly, naming them when someone else shows them.

The third cluster includes all those that remain. These are:

i l s t v w x y z

As with the others, these also should be taught to the point where the child knows them well enough to print them from dictation.

One additional point should be made here. Teach each group of letters separately, and be especially careful to avoid teaching the group that is related to the *r* until the group that is related to the *c* is well established. In fact, you really should teach the *r* group last.

Or, said another way, do not teach the *d* by pointing out to the child how it differs from the *b*. Yes, the differences are very obvious when the two mirror-image letters are shown in juxtaposition. But your goal is not to have the child be able to see differences; your goal is to have him be able to print and read the letters accurately, without confusion. There is less likelihood of the child becoming confused by *b*'s and *d*'s if he learns one of them thoroughly before the other is introduced. This way, he has an established frame of reference; a standard to use for comparisons.

Consider this illustration. Suppose, in one situation, you already know Jim very well and are then introduced to someone who strongly resembles him, named Tim.

Now, moving to a second situation, suppose you are introduced to both Jim and Tim at the same party. Where are you apt to get their identities confused, in the first or second situation? The inference should be clear. Teach one—I like to teach the *d* first—and make sure the child has learned it well before you teach the other.

- 3. For children who already know the letters, but continue to confuse the *b* and the *d*, supply unambiguous hints where they appear to help.

Underline with blue pencil every *b* in the child's reader. Point out to the child that the pencil is *blue*—stress the /b/ sound. Do not mark the *d* in any way. A single hint is fine. As soon as there are two—one for the *b* and one for the *d*—the child is faced with the problem of keeping the hints straight.

Granted, it is probably unreasonable to suggest that someone take the trouble to underline every *b* in the child's reader—or is it? If this is an effective way of helping to eliminate a major source of confusion, and if a simpler way cannot be invented, then it is not so unreasonable. In fact, the job can be given to the child himself and, in that way, turned into a learning experience rather than a tedious chore for some adult.

Simply provide the child with a model—a clearly printed *b*—and a sharpened blue pencil, and instruct him to start on page one, line one, and track across each line, drawing a blue line under every *b* that he can find, saying *b* (the letter name) each time he does so. Monitor him, at least for a while, to make certain he understands the task, and do not assign too much work at any one sitting. It can even be turned into a game of sorts by imposing a time factor—seeing how many *b*'s he can find in a fixed amount of time; two minutes say. Keep track of his daily performance by plotting it on a graph. Reward him appropriately when he surpasses his previous record.

- 4. Draw a blue vertical line down the left-hand side of every page the child is to read, and every page on which he is to write. This provides a consistent and reliable ref-

erence point, in terms of direction. Explain its purpose—
that he is always to begin reading and writing at the side
of the page where the line is, and proceed across the page,
away from it. (And, stress the /b/ sound in *blue*—point
out that the blue line is on the same side of the page as
the straight line in the letter *b*.)

- 5. If the *b* and *d* confusion is firmly established (or any
  other letter, for that matter) provide the child with a
  large model of the letter you want him to learn and have
  him trace over it with his index finger (with the same
  hand that he uses for printing) as he says its name. Also,
  point out the distinctive features of the letter. Do not
  wait for him to discover them on his own. In other words,
  if he is working on the *d*, call his attention to the position
  of the line in relation to the circle. Sandpaper letters may
  be used, but they are rarely necessary. Remember, do not
  include both letters in the same lesson. Teach one only,
  and stay with it until it is memorized.

- 6. If the child is unable to discriminate between the lowercase letters without a great deal of extra help, but is
  familiar with the capital letters, use only capital letters
  until he learns the lowercase group. Again, this requires
  constructing lessons by hand—retyping or printing his
  reader in capital letters. But the effort will be worthwhile
  if it enables the child to start to learn. (This procedure is
  not needed very often. Most children will master the lowercase letters in a reasonable period of time.)

- 7. If the child tends to lose his place on the page, instruct
  him to use his index finger as a pointer. Insist that he
  always use the same hand—the one he prints with. Teach
  him to synchronize the movement of that finger with his
  eyes and his voice; in other words, the finger is to be
  pointing directly at the word he is looking at and reading,
  nowhere else. His finger is a source of support and will
  direct his eyes—show them where to look. If he needs further help, try listing the words vertically instead of horizontally. It is a lot harder to lose your place under those
  conditions and, although it will probably slow down his

reading, it will be worthwhile if only to demonstrate to him that he *can* control his eye movements.

For

example,

it

takes

more

time

to

read

this

list,

but it is easier to keep your place.

- 8. Teach the child that each new sentence starts with a capital letter and ends with a period. Do not assume he knows that until he demonstrates it for you. If you have any doubts, find a paragraph that he can read and have him read it aloud. Does he read in sentences? Does his voice show that he understands the concept of a sentence? If so, fine. If not, teach him—tell him—that sentences start with capitals, end with periods (or question marks or exclamation points), and have him identify some sentences in that paragraph, and elsewhere. [Have him draw brackets around a few so that you can be sure he has the idea.]

- 9. Organize cluttered pages in his workbooks by drawing a border around important portions of the page and masking out other sections. He will not learn from pages that are too disorganized.

- 10. This final one is a general suggestion. Take advantage of casual situations wherever they occur. For example, have him search for and count specific letters on license plates, or on billboards while riding in the car. Turn it into a game. Assign a letter to him and a different letter to yourself, and see who can discover 10 or more of "their" letter first. You can also do this with a newspaper page, a book, while shopping in a supermarket, or while watching TV commercials.

You can vary this activity by assigning two or three letters that must be found in sequence. For example, "Find a C, then a J, and then a D." Or, have him look for a newly learned and common word, such as *the*.

As you can see, there are lots of variations. My concern, here, is that you take advantage of those casual moments, when they do come along, and give him the opportunity to practice newly learned abilities. Make it fun, of course, but also make it meaningful.

Stage II suggestions: Helping the child who has difficulty decoding—relating the printed letters to spoken sounds.

- 1. Stage II reading skills are based to a great extent on adequate auditory perceptual skills and adequate Stage I skills. Therefore, if you have not already done so, test his auditory skills with the TAAS. If they are not up to an expected level, teach them. But at the same time, start to use the suggestions listed here.
- 2. Make absolutely certain that he knows that letters stand for sounds, that words contain strings of sounds, and that clusters of letters stand for spoken words. He will also have to know that the statement "letters stand for specific sounds" is not always true in the English language—that some letters stand for more than one sound, and sometimes a letter will stand for no sound at all—but hold off on that until after you are convinced he knows the basic concepts.

His teacher will be able to tell you whether he needs help here. Ask her, and while you are at it, if he does have a problem in this area, find out which letter-sound combinations he should work on.

You can test his skills yourself, informally, although this will not be as reliable as having his teacher tell you. Simply have him read the following lists of words, and take notice of his errors. If the child has established a basic understanding of letter-sound correspondence, he should be able to read all these words correctly:*

Caution: These lists do not represent *all* the letter-sound combinations. Therefore, even if he reads them all correctly, do not conclude that he has no problem in this area—check with his teacher.

pad	pig	pup
sit	rot	sad
red	dig	rid
bat	fan	hat
cup	get	man
rag	lap	rug
pot	sun	pen
tan	net	win

The following words are somewhat harder for some children because they contain a silent letter and a long vowel:

bite	cane	date
fine	hope	joke
code	late	mine
game	pale	note
rope	tame	safe
wake	vote	rule

And the following are even more difficult for most children because they contain blends—where two consonant sounds are merged into something resembling a single sound:

slap	twin	crab
gift	snag	stick
can't	clip	trip
fist	spot	spill
dress	skip	felt
stop	grin	smell
glad	tent	plan
swim	flag	drop

And, finally, the following—which contain consonant combinations called *digraphs* (where the two letters take on a single sound, such as the "ch" and "sh") and *diphthongs* (vowel blends that stand for a single sound) : *

mouth	boy	owl
shape	wish	this
chop	when	spring
thank	bath	catch
chicken	stretch	rushing
shout	coin	cow

That is enough to give you some sense of the child's decoding abilities. If he read all the preceding words fluently, you can assume that he has at least some of the necessary basic skills. If he stumbled, misread, or read them in a sounding-out way (letter-by-letter, sound-by-sound), assume that he does not have adequate skills. (Again, I remind you that the best way to find out what he should work on is to ask his teacher.)

Now, how can the child be helped, assuming he needs it? The obvious answer is by teaching him the letter-sound combinations he does not know. I agree with that, but with one modification. Teach him by adapting the auditory analysis procedures described earlier; teach him the letter sounds by having him analyze spoken and written words rather than by teaching the letter sounds in isolation.

• 3. Use the teaching activities from Levels III, IV, and V in the auditory program (see pages 144-165), where the child is taught to say the missing sound. Thus, when the child is asked to, "Say *dear*; now say *ear*. What sound did we

*Some may question the value of talking to parents about diphthongs and digraphs. In my judgment, the more parents know about these things, the more able they will be to point out to the child those aspects of the written language that are consistent—for which he can learn a rule—and those aspects that are irregular. As literate adults, reading seems to be a simple, obvious kind of act. It is *not*—especially for the child we are concerned with here.

leave out?" add the request, "Print the letter *or letters* that stand for that sound." This way you will be teaching the child both auditory and reading skills (and spelling skills too, for that matter) at the same time.*

- 4. The sound substitution teaching activities of Levels IV and V of the auditory program work well here also. You print the word that is introduced first; *mat,* for example. Then, when the child is asked to "Say it again, but instead of /m/ say /f/," have him print the new word as well as say it. A chalkboard is good for this activity, because he can easily erase the *m* and replace it with the *f.*

This same activity can be used for teaching vowels. As just described, you print the original word, then have the child print and say the new word. For example, you print the word *pat,* tell the child what it says, if he does not know it, and ask him to "Say *pat,*" then; "Say it again, but instead of /ă/ (as in *pat*), say /ĕ/ (as in *eskimo*)." Once he responds orally, have him print the new word by erasing the *a* and inserting an *e* in its place (if this is done on a chalkboard) or, if done on paper, have him print the new word *pet* below the original one *pat.*

You can use the word lists supplied with the auditory program, or you can use the child's own word list obtained from his teacher. The words in the program are unique in that they continue to be meaningful (when heard, that is, not necessarily when read) even after a sound is omitted or substituted. For example, *bake-ake* (pronounced *ache*), *meat-mea* (pronounced *me*), *slip-lip*; *desk-dek* (pronounced *deck*). Some of the child's words may not have that characteristic, but this is not that important with children beyond the age of six or seven. Use his words, even though the word without the sound is not meaningful. (For example, "Say *pretty*; now say *retty*; what sound did we leave out? Print the letter that stands for that sound.")

Caution: As always, do not try to cover too much at one time. Work on one or two sounds until they are well established. Then start on another, and so on, until he knows them all.

- 5. When you teach the child to blend the sounds of a word, have him pronounce the beginning consonant sound and the vowel sound that follows it as a unit. Then have him add the other sounds. Do not have him pronounce these first two separately and then try to join them.

  For example, in the word *bat*, teach him to start to read it by saying /ba/ and then adding the /t/ (/ba/ . . . /t/; ba . . t/; /bat/). Do not teach him to say /b/ . . . /a/ . . . /t/ separately, and then try to join them.

- 6. During all this (and if he does not know many letter-sound combinations to start with, it will take quite a few sessions to teach them), you should be giving the child some experience reading words that contain the sounds he is learning. Your child's teacher and the local librarian will be able to help you. If necessary, or if you feel like it, write your own stories. You may want stories with sentences such as "Ed met Ted," "The cat sat in the hat," and so on. (*The* is a word that cannot be sounded out too successfully. Teach it to him as a sight word; a word that is read like a picture.) Avoid stories that use a lot of sight words until he has established basic fluency with the regular words—words that can be sounded out in a straightforward fashion. (More about sight words in a moment.)

  It will probably be useful to teach him some word families when he gets to this point. For example, have him read these lists of words:

fist	ban	bit	bag	bet	bake	cot
list	can	fit	hag	get	cake	dot
mist	dan	hit	lag	let	fake	hot
	fan	lit	nag	met	lake	lot
	man	mit	rag	net	make	not
	pan	pit	sag	set	rake	pot
	ran	sit	tag	wet	sake	rot
	tan	wit	wag		take	tot
	van				wake	

As you can see, these lists are easy to construct. Give him practice on a variety of them.

- 7. Test him on his knowledge of sight words. (This list will vary according to his grade level. Ask his teacher for a list that is appropriate for him.) The following words are apt to appear on most lists. Ask him to read these:

by	I	goes	all
the	one	are	flew
said	does	though	large
was	two	bought	field
their	who	new	could
they	right	boy	would
were	laugh	shoe	which
say	eight	first	move
know	does	eight	because
light	warm	where	write

It is essential that the child be able to read sight words. To teach a sight word, first point out to the child those letters in the word that *do* represent their sounds. These, at least, will not have to be memorized. For example, if he knows the sound of the letter *s*, he knows the first sound of the words *said* and *saw*. All he has to do now is memorize the remainder of those words. If he knows the sound of the *d*, he also knows the last sound in the word *said*. Hence, there is not very much left to memorize (and, in fact, he can now start to explore various vowel sounds systematically until he finds one that fits).

Once you have pointed out the consistent letter-sound combinations in the word, tell him what the word says and have him copy the entire word as he, himself, spells it aloud. He is to do this often enough so that he can print the word correctly without copying it. Then go one step further. Have him print it with his eyes closed, thinking about what his hand is doing as he spells the word. (Teach only a few sight words at a time. When these are learned, go on to others.)

If pointing out the important parts of a sight word is not enough, help him further by underlining them, thereby lessening even more the demands placed on the child's memory. For example, show him the word: "light" looking like this, and have him sound out the underlined letters: the l, the i, and the t—pausing where there is a space between the underlines. This will be a significant help. In fact, in this instance it is all he needs to read the word since the *gh* is silent.

I had better respond to critics who will now rush to remind me that a child should not learn to depend on such supports because, after all, they are not ordinarily available and "he does have to learn sometime!" I agree. He should not get dependent on the underlines. But, on the other hand, I see no harm in giving some hints that will facilitate his progress, so that he will stay on the job and ultimately learn to read without that help. I am not advocating that you tell him the sounds, merely that you call his attention to the letters in the word that can be translated directly into sounds; that you teach him a technique that you and I use all the time when we are faced with reading an unfamiliar word.

Here are some additional examples of how the underlining procedure works:

beautiful	goes	saw
believe	weight	thought
breathe	language	their
wrist	warm	should
flight	was	learn

Obviously this does not solve the problem completely. Even with the underlines, the child still has to memorize some portion of each word. But there is one immediate and beneficial effect derived from the technique. It forces the child to look at more than the first letter of the word. (If you have had any experience with a poor reader—and I recognize that you probably have—you are familiar with their tendency to say the beginning sound of the word correctly, and guess at the rest.)

The underlining procedure makes the child direct his attention to middle and final sounds as well as beginning sounds. As a result, his chances for reading the word correctly improve significantly.

- 8. Test his ability to break printed words down into parts (syllables) so that they can be read one part at a time. (Or, better yet, ask his teacher if he can do this.) For example, if he is to be able to read the word *several*, he will have to attack it one portion at a time, then combine the parts. (Obviously, if the word is not in his speaking vocabulary, he is not very likely to be successful in sounding it out, so start with words that he knows orally.) Use the following list as a starter, but ask his teacher to help you identify suitable words. Show him the words one at a time, and say, "What does this word say?"

something	valentine
telescope	understand
animal	birthday
cabinet	telephone
grandmother	beautiful
beginning	anywhere
fisherman	hundred
airplane	woodcutter
below	forget
children	interrupt
classroom	without
summer	remember
basket	brother
sister	overhead

To teach him the words he does not know, first go back to the procedures described in Levels I and II of the auditory program and have the child *clap, draw dashes,* and *read dashes* for these multisyllable words. (You say them; he does the rest.) Once you are satisfied that he can do these fundamental tasks, show him a multisyllable word that he is to sound out, but underline its syllables before you present it to him. For example, show him the word *cab i net,* and have him sound it out, part by part, and then put it together.

It is important that the child continue to practice this skill until he reads words as units, not as a string of syllables. If his first effort at reading the word *cabinet* results in the sounding out of *cab . . . . i . . . . net,* that is fine for the first effort. But, keep him at it until a meaningful word is produced; a word he knows to be a word. Then eliminate the underlines. You do not want him to stay at the segmented level. Remember the earlier discussion about memory. Your goal is to teach him to be fluent, to be able to construct chunks of ever-increasing size.

- 9. Periodically have him print single words and short sentences from dictation. Start off with easy words. Then move up to sentences.

Sources of additional support

As already noted, the above procedures are intended to teach the child to decode printed language with facility, so that he will read fluently—the only kind of reading that will enable him to comprehend what he reads. These procedures focus on the child learning the consistent letter-sound combinations of our language and applying that knowledge to those irregular words where the rules do not apply; where a certain amount of memorization is necessary. It is important for him to realize that no word has to be fully memorized. Every sight word contains some letters that stand for their sounds.

It is very difficult for some children to keep all of the

letter-sound combinations—and letters with nonsounds—straight, especially at the start. This is where supports in the form of hints are helpful. But be careful; do not give too many hints at one time. Add them one at a time and stop when there are enough. Do not assume the more, the better.

The following supports are designed to help the child learn to decode. You do not have to use them all. Use what works until it is no longer needed.

- 1. Vocalizing—saying aloud what he is reading—will often be a great help. As you recall, this is the only way someone can "get his hands on" the sounds—feel them as well as hear them. The poor decoder almost invariably is a poor analyzer of spoken words. That is why vocalizing is helpful

  Be prepared, though, to listen to arguments from some experts who will tell you that vocalizing must be eliminated because it drastically limits reading speed. This last part is correct. If you say the words as you read them, or simply move your lips, or even if you say them to yourself without moving your lips, you will not read any faster than you can speak—and that is not very fast in terms of reading speeds. However, we are concerned here about the severely impaired reader who, if he does not move his lips, will have difficulty learning to read at any speed. Preventing him from moving his lips—from getting the support it will provide in analyzing words into sounds—will not speed up his reading. On the contrary, it will probably prevent him from learning. Tell him to move his lips—to read aloud, listen to what he is saying, and think about how his mouth feels as he is doing this. He can work on eliminating this support, and on reading faster, *once he learns to read.*

- 2. Use color to signal a certain vowel sound. For example, some children experience confusion keeping the short $\breve{e}$ (*eskimo*) and $\breve{\imath}$ (*igloo*) sounds straight. If so, go through his book with a red felt-tipped pen, coloring over every $\breve{e}$

READING

that should be given the short sound pronunciation. (Use
a pen that merely colors but does not obscure the letter.)
This will help him make the distinction. Point out that
the *red* color (and stress the short ĕ sound in *red* when
you say the word) means he is to say /ĕ/, as in *red*.

- 3. Teach him key words that will help keep the short
  vowel sounds straight. Use words that are easy to picture
  in the mind's eye. For example, teach the child to think
  of an:*

> *apple* for the (short) ă sound
> *eskimo* for the (short) ĕ sound
> *igloo* for the (short) ĭ sound
> *octopus* for the (short) ŏ sound
> *umbrella* for the (short) ŭ sound

Have him memorize these; quiz him regularly to keep
them fresh in his memory.

- 4. Draw a slash through silent letters that occur at the
  end of words (as in *came*). These slashes can be eliminated when they are no longer needed.
- 5. There are some commercially available reading programs that are specifically designed to provide additional
  visual information and thereby help the child learn to
  decode. I do not suggest you use any of these, unless they
  are also used in the child's school.

The Initial Teaching Alphabet (i.t.a.) is an example
of such a program. It uses an expanded alphabet where
there is a letter—a symbol—for virtually every sound.
For example, there is a symbol for the short ă and another for the long ā (*a* and *ae*). The i.t.a. is a good idea,
if the child has the visual perceptual skills needed to deal
with the demands made by the additional symbols. Some
of these extra symbols are potentially confusing and,
since the youngster will not see these additional symbols
anywhere else, he may have trouble learning them. The

*Find out what key words his teacher is using, and use the same ones.

211

i.t.a., in my opinion, should not be used with children who have less than satisfactory visual perceptual skills.

- 6. Do not stop working on Stage II activities until the child demonstrates adequate decoding skills. (Remember, however, that he should also be working on comprehension—Stage III skills—at this same time.) Have him read something daily, and have him strive for fluency, if only for a short sentence or two. As one activity during his daily reading, have him first read a sentence silently. Tell him that if he comes across a word he does not know, he is to figure it out or ask for help. Then, when he is sure that he can read *all* the words in that sentence (and only then), he is to read the sentence aloud, fluently, as a sentence. Then he may go on to the next sentence and follow the same procedure. His goal is to shorten the time between   sentences.   If   he persists   in   reading   in   a   laborious,   segment-. ed   way,   he   will   never   be able   to   get   meaning   from   text. How   well   do   you   think you   could   comprehend   a   paragraph   such as   this   if   you   read   it   once   and   then put   it   down?   And you can read!

Also, point out to him that paying attention to the meaning of a sentence will help him figure out some of the difficult words. If the text is meaningful, the words will all go together, and a child with decent language and comprehension skills can usually tell when a word is suitable and when it is not. Thus, he can often reject a word that he might start to misread because it just does not fit. For example, the word *saw* in "The boy *saw* a dog" makes sense. If he confuses *saw* for *was*, the resulting sentence does not make sense and, if the child is alert to meaning as he reads, he will realize the error and reexamine the sentence. Certainly, even as adults, we misread an occasional word, then reread the sentence because it did not make sense.

Stage III suggestions: Helping the child who has difficulty comprehending what he reads.

- 1. Stage III skills are closely related to decoding abilities (Stage II) and higher level visual perceptual skills. If the child's visual perceptual skills are below what is expected for his grade level (see page 69), you should spend some time working on them. At the same time, of course, you should be using the procedures discussed below (and Stage II activities as well, if those skills are not up to an adequate level).

- 2. Provide interesting reading material for him. Find out what he would like to read about and then ask his teacher or your local librarian what is available on that topic and appropriate for the child's ability. If he is interested in comic books, use those. The goal here is to get him to read well—worry about the quality of the content after he has learned to read.

- 3. Discuss stories with the child and use questions to direct his attention to the fact that stories contain both important and not-so-important details that relate to other information—information contained within the same story as well as drawn from the child's background of experiences. Do not introduce too many details until you are sure he can deal with the main ones. If the child's responses to questions indicate that he missed the important details, point them out to him and explain how they interrelate.

- 4. Teach the child to read in chunks larger than single words by having him engage in the following activity. Provide a paragraph that he can read, a pencil, and a sheet of lined paper. Say to him, "Let's see how much of this you can copy in two minutes. I'll say 'Go' when it's time, and 'Stop' at the end of two minutes. Ready? Go."

Stop him at the end of two minutes and count (a) the number of words copied, and (b) the number of spelling errors and omissions. Now graph both scores as shown in figures 63 and 64.

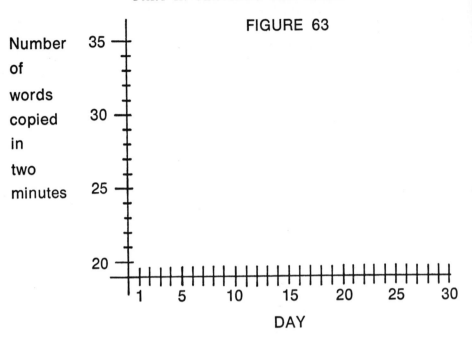

FIGURE 63

Number of words copied in two minutes

DAY

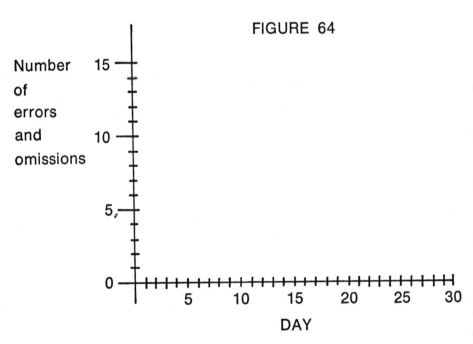

FIGURE 64

Number of errors and omissions

DAY

Do this daily, keeping track of his performance on the graphs. If his speed improves, the line on the first graph will move upward. If his error and omission rate improves, the line on the second graph will move downward. Point out to the child that he can copy more if he will take larger bites (more words at one time), and he will keep each bite in his memory better if he repeats it to himself as he writes it on the page. (Just as you will repeat a phone number to yourself as you go from telephone book to telephone.)

The goal here is to help the child improve his short-term memory and his reading speed. Repeating information to himself helps the former. Taking bigger bites helps the latter.

- 5. Show him how the information in a story can be classified—and usually in more than one way.

The poor comprehender lacks organization. He tends to lump information together. For example, suppose the child has just read a story about a boy named Jim who has a pet, a dog named Spot; a girl named Ann who has a pet, a cat named Tiger. The story relates how Spot chased Tiger; Ann became frightened; Jim laughed; Ann became angry with Jim; Spot stopped chasing Tiger; Ann and Jim became friends.

The very poor comprehender will remember assorted details in some random, nonassociated array. At best, he may be able to identify the children, the animals, and perhaps some events. But he will not be able to report how these separate details fit together. The diagram in Figure 65 attempts to illustrate how he might classify the information in his memory.

The better comprehender is more likely to organize the important details of the story into a linear sequence that is similar to the way the story was written—what occurred first, second, and so on. This is depicted in Figure 66.

The best comprehender will have a variety of ways to organize the story. He may very well do it as illustrated above, but he will also be able to reorganize the details and think of them as in Figure 67.

FIGURE 65

FIGURE 66

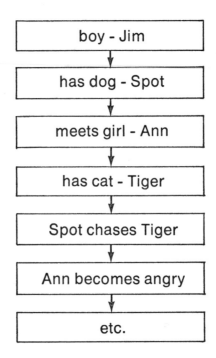

FIGURE 67

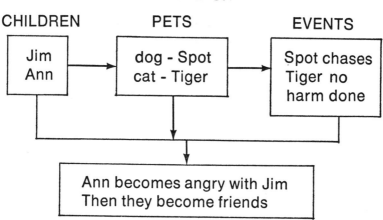

In other words, a good comprehender is able to organize and reorganize information so that various aspects of the story can be related in a number of different ways. His ability to associate information effectively enables him to see abstract ideas.

Teach your child to sort out and organize information; then teach him to reorganize it. A good place to start is with the family. Show him a family tree, as in Figure 68.

FIGURE 68

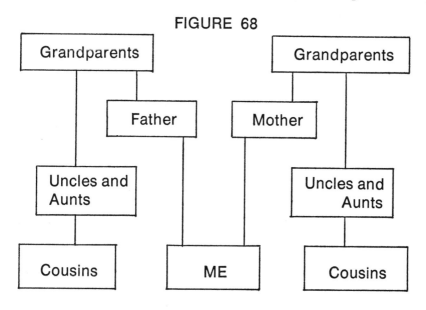

Then, show him another organization, as in Figure 69 and discuss with him how this same information can be arranged in different ways.

FIGURE 69

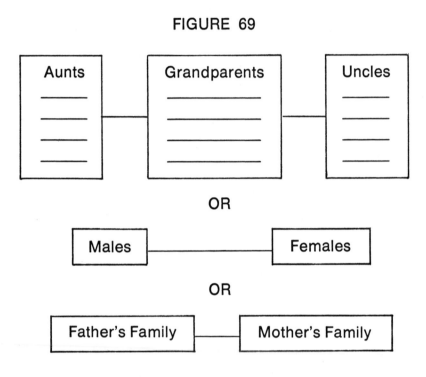

Do the same with other topics in which he has an interest; animals, perhaps. Animals can be classified in a variety of ways: size (large-small); habitat (air-land-water); color (light-dark, or specific colors); relationship with humans (domestic-wild); and so on. Engage him in the task. Have him think of ways to classify information. That is the basic skill you are trying to teach.

Your primary goal in these activities is to teach the child that information can be organized, after it has been sorted, and that there is more than one way to classify the same set of information; that a classification scheme can range from simple to complex and that it also can be multidimensional. Animals can be sorted according to both their size and their habitat, for example. They can be large and live in water, or large and live on land, or small and live in water, and so on.

When he is ready, try to chart these on a two-dimensional map, using either pictures of the animals, or their names, in the cells of the map. Figure 70 illustrates this:

FIGURE 70

		SIZE	
		Large	Small
HABITAT	Air	eagle	hummingbird
	Sea	whale	goldfish
	Land	elephant	mouse

Have him practice doing this. It will be a worthwhile concept for him to learn. There are lots of things around that can be used in this kind of activity. For example, you can classify household objects according to location in the house, color, size, usage, or clothing according to size, color, weight, specificity to one sex, and so on.

When he has the idea, start using it with television stories, movies, and the material he has to read for school. Have him classify the main ideas, the people, and the events in ways that show he understands how it all fits together. Continue to lay out this information in charts until he is able to do it in his head without the charts.

- 6. Foster his language development. Teach him new words and encourage him to use them. The larger his vocabulary, the better off he will be. Read to him, tell him stories, and have him tell you stories. Get him to write stories, and be suitably impressed when he does; do not criticize anything, including his spelling and handwriting.

ARITHMETIC

First we will identify some of the basic processes—what learning elementary arithmetic requires of the child. Then we will contrast what we know about good learners of arithmetic, poor learners of arithmetic, and the way that arithmetic is taught.

Elementary school arithmetic programs invariably involve learning to use a relatively limited set of symbols to perform various operations: addition, subtraction, multiplication, and division. To progress in such a program, the child must be able to:

- 1. Count aloud in correct sequence. Ordinarily, this is quite limited at first—such as counting from 1 to 10—and gets more extensive as the child acquires additional skills.
- 2. Recognize and print numerals.
- 3. Count things, at first to a maximum of 10 things, then to 100, and so on.
- 4. Relate printed numerals to specific quantities. For example, to understand that the numeral 3 represents a quantity of 3 things. No more, no less.
- 5. Recognize that the equal sign(=) stands for: "is the same as."
- 6. Recognize that single things or groups of things can be combined and that the operation can be represented with numerals and other symbols: a plus sign (+) and an equal sign (=). Thus, *1* thing combined with *1* thing forms a group or collection of *2* things; see Figure 71.

220

• 7. Recognize that collections of things can be taken apart
—that things can be removed from the original group—
and that the operation can be represented with numerals
and other symbols: a minus sign (–) and an equal sign
(=). Thus, given a group of 2 things from which 1 thing
is removed, the remainder is 1 thing; see Figure 72.

FIGURE 71

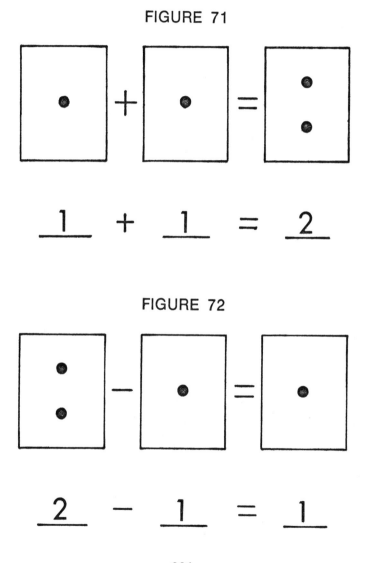

1 + 1 = 2

FIGURE 72

2 – 1 = 1

- 8. Recognize that symbols can be used to represent the operation of combining equal groups (where each group comprises the same quantity of things): a multiplication sign ($\times$) and an equal sign ($=$). For example,.when one wants to show the total quantity of things contained in 3 groups, where each group contains 2 things; see Figure 73.

FIGURE 73

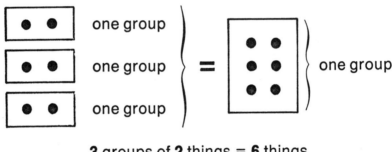

3 groups of **2** things = **6** things
3 × 2 = 6

FIGURE 74

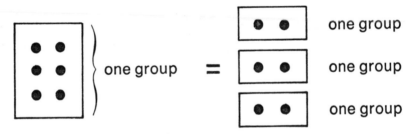

A group of **6** things divided into groups
containing **2** things each = **3** groups
6 ÷ 2 = 3

- 9. Recognize that symbols can be used to represent the operation of reorganizing a collection of things into a quantity of smaller, equal groups: a division sign ($\div$) and an equal sign ($=$). For example, when one wants to show the number of subgroups created when a group of *6* things is broken down into smaller subgroups, each containing *2* things; see Figure 74.

All these operations have to do with counting and coding quantities with symbols. Multiplication, in a sense, is a system for adding rapidly; division is a system for sorting things out rapidly. The function of numerals in these operations is very straightforward. They provide a way for coding finite quantities of things.

But the child must know more than this if he is to make adequate progress in an elementary school arithmetic program. He must know that numerals can represent something other than specific quantities; that they can also represent precise relationships. For example,

- 1. The numeral *1* can represent the *first* something in a sequence of somethings; *2*, the *second*; and so on.
- 2. The numeral *1* has a fixed relationship to the numeral *2*, and vice versa. Four things are 2 times (2 ×) as many as 2 things and 2 things are one-half (½) as many as 4 things; 10 things are 2 times (2 ×) 5 things and vice versa; and so on. The need to understand that numerals can serve two functions—that they can represent both absolute and relative values—causes great confusion for certain children.*

---

*This is where the close connection between visual perceptual skills and arithmetic becomes evident. Remember the operational definition of visual perceptual skills . . . the ability to analyze spatial patterns into their separate parts and to recognize the interrelationships of those parts?

To achieve the first nine steps listed above, the child only needs to have reached the level in visual perceptual skills development where he can analyze a spatial pattern into its parts. If he can do that, he will be able to count accurately and, given sufficient time, to add, subtract, multiply, and divide. He needs time to perform these calculations because he has to count all the things in all the groups.

If he has not reached the level of visual perceptual skills development where he can also recognize the interrelationships of the parts, counting will be the *only* way he will be able to add, subtract, multiply, and divide—unless he memorizes all of the so-called "number facts." And the task of memorizing them will be extremely difficult, because he will not see how they interrelate. They will be an assortment of separate, unrelated facts.

The child who does not see relationships is forced to deal with every arithmetic problem as a new problem. Even though he may just have solved "6+9=?" he probably will have to start all over again solving "7+9=?" and again for "9+7=?" And, if you watch him, you will see him counting from 1 each time. That is, counting aloud, or on his fingers, or to himself—but counting, nonetheless: "1-2-3-4-5-6"; then "1-2-3-4-5-6-7-8-9"; then, combining these, and counting "1-2-3-4-5-6-7-8-9-10-11-12-13-14-15." What an expenditure of time and energy! What an open invitation to error, given the number of things he has to count and the number of times he has to count them!

Now put yourself in the situation this child faces with the problem "7×8+?" and visualize his method of solution. He will either draw 7 rows of things (pencil marks), each row containing 8 things, and then count them all, or he will count from 1 to 8 on his fingers (or in his head), then from 9 to 16, then from 17 to 24, and so on. In either case, the results are generally disastrous. The chance of making a counting error is very high and the time required to do the operation is too great. He will fall behind his classmates.

To the child with competent visual perceptual skills, arithmetic makes sense. Numerals provide a logical system for coding a variety of things—quantity, relative position in a series (first, second, third . . .), and relative difference in some measurable characteristic (such as 2 times as many inches, 3 times as many pounds). To the child with inadequate visual perceptual skills, arithmetic does not make sense. It is a *nonsystem* that forces him to memorize an enormous variety of unrelated number facts. His solution? Memorize as much as possible and guess at the rest. And, to make matters worse, even his guesses are not based on reason.

The three stages

What skills does the child need? Although the sequence of arithmetic abilities are not so neat as they are in reading, we can map them, as shown in Figure 75.

In a way, Stage I here resembles Stage I in reading; it focuses on familiarizing the child with the coding elements and conventions—the numerals, the signs, and how they should be used. Stage II is also comparable in that it involves coding and decoding the symbols in a series of straightforward operations. Stage III is akin to comprehension. In reading, comprehension means understanding what has been decoded. The same general definition applies in arithmetic.

FIGURE 75

ARITHMETIC

STAGE I
Counts "things" accurately and records the quantity with numerals.

STAGE II
Recognizes that groups of "things" can be combined into a large group or broken up into smaller groups, all of which can be represented with symbols. (=) (+) (-) (÷)

STAGE III
Recognizes that numerals can code relationships as well as absolute quantities.

WHICH MATH PROGRAM IS BEST?

I have avoided the argument that is currently gathering momentum among educators about modern math—good or bad? In my judgment, the discussion is not worthwhile. Just as with reading programs, it is foolish to attempt to identify *the best* arithmetic approach. The child with competent visual perceptual skills will learn arithmetic with *any* system, although he will probably progress more rapidly with the so-called modern math approach since he is able to discover so much on his own. The child with substandard visual perceptual skills may be able to do fairly well in modern math *at first*. You see, at first all he has to do is learn how to count and use numerals to represent those quantities. But if it is difficult for him to see relationships, he will fail to see the way numbers organize into patterns. As a result, he will start to slip behind his more competent classmates as he enters second, or perhaps third grade and has to solve problems involving larger numbers. Modern math is not bad for him. It offers him one benefit in that it gives him a system for doing arithmetic problems. The trouble arises in that the system—counting things—is too slow for classroom standards, unless he sees relationships, thereby learning to chunk information into larger units.

Helping the poor arithmetic learner

This section contains a number of activities that will help the child who is having difficulty with arithmetic. If you use these procedures, you should coordinate your efforts with the child's teacher.

The activities are organized according to the three sets of basic abilities outlined in Figure 75. Namely, Stage I, the child's ability (a) to count by rote; (b) to recognize and print symbols (numerals, equal sign, plus sign, and others); and (c) to count things and record the quantity with numerals; in Stage II, the child's ability to add, subtract, multiply, and divide, through organizing and reorganizing groups of things and then counting them; in Stage III, the child's ability to recognize relationships and code those relationships with numerals.

The three instructional principles that applied in other areas are also to be kept in mind here.

- 1. Organize for success. As always, teach the child what he is ready to learn. Do not expect him to see a relationship between 27 and 54 if he really does not see one between 10 and 20. If he is unsure about the symbols, and confuses the 6 and the 9, do not try to teach him complex arithmetic skills. This does not mean that he must. be perfect in Stage I abilities before you move onto the next, but it does mean that he should have the fundamentals fairly well established.

- 2. Provide the child with whatever information—hints— he needs to understand the task; then teach him how to do the task without this help. Here we will consider various procedures that will enable the child to solve problems with real materials; procedures that make relationships apparent rather than merely implied.

- 3. Encourage the child to make use of all his senses, not just his eyes. As in every other instance where this principle has been stated, it refers to the fact that tangible information—information that can be handled—is more reliable than nontangible information. Exploit this fact to its fullest. Having a child touch 4 blocks as he counts 4, and touch 2 blocks as he counts 2, will enhance his understanding of the relationship between 2 and 4.

Suggested activities

The following activities are organized according to the skills they teach; the stages to which they belong. Test him informally to decide where he should start. For example, if the child is already familiar with the numerals and other common arithmetic symbols, if he can accurately count a collection of up to 100 things and record that amount with numerals, there will be little need for Stage I activities.

It is more difficult to separate the activities of Stages II and III. Stage III procedures are designed to teach the child to do the same calculations he learned at Stage II, but in a different, more efficient, way. I recommend, therefore, that you do not omit the Stage II activities, even if the child can already add, subtract, and so forth, unless he is also competent with Stage III tasks. And if he is, there is nothing more for him in this section of the book.

Stage I suggestions: Helping the child who cannot accurately count or record quantities with numerals.

- 1. Visual perceptual skills are closely linked with learning arithmetic. If you have not already done so, test the child's skills with the TVAS. If they are below the expected level, spend some time teaching them to him while, at the same time, you are using the procedures listed in this section.

- 2. Make certain that the child is completely familiar with the numerals, 0 to 9. Completely familiar, in this instance, means that he can:

   a) match numeral shapes.
   b) point to the proper numeral upon request.
   c) name the numerals correctly when they are shown to him in some random order.
   d) print the numerals from dictation.

   If he cannot do this last, find out what he can do in that sequence of abilities and teach him from that point on. In other words, if he cannot print them accurately, but can name them when they are shown to him, then set about teaching him to print them. If, on the other hand, he can do no better than match up printed numerals, then do not start teaching him to print them. Rather, teach him first to identify them—then move on.

   How do you teach him? Drill and practice. Fortunately, there are only ten symbols to start with, so the task is fairly well defined. Here are some suggestions, arranged according to the sequence I just described.

   (1) To teach matching skills. Play card games, concentration, board games that use a spinner, and other games involving printed numerals.

   (2) To teach the names of the numerals. This usually comes about quite readily by playing the games, but if extra help is needed, provide it. Although drill and practice will work, a game format makes it more interesting for the child. If you own one of the small electronic hand calculators that have recently be-

come so popular, use it. Simply call out a single number and have the child find it on the calculator. To add interest and some extra value to the activity, call out two, three, or even four numbers in succession and see if he can also keep the sequence straight while finding the proper buttons. If you do not have a calculator, use a typewriter and, if there is not one available, simply use homemade cards (playing-card size) on which numerals have been printed.

(3) To teach him to print the numerals. There is only one good way—give him a pencil, a crayon, or a piece of chalk and set him to work. To facilitate the process, have him first trace over numerals that you print. Then have him copy numerals alongside ones that you print. Finally, have him print them while his eyes are closed, thinking about what his hand is doing.

- 3. Make certain that he can count up to 100.

    a) Take walks and count steps. See how far 100 steps will take you. (Compare the outcome of taking long steps to taking short steps—in this way, you will be teaching relationships at the same time.)

    b) Have him count out 100 pennies or poker chips, or what-have-you.

    c) Have him bounce a ball 100 times or more, if he can, and keep score. Have him establish a record and then try to beat it. Once he has pretty well learned how to count to 100, start questioning him about "What number comes just after—?" or "What number comes just before—?"

- 4. Teach him to write the numerals from 0 to 100. Show him that when he gets past the 9, two digits are used, and that the first one written is a 1 from 10 to 19, then the first one becomes a 2 from 20 to 29, and so on. This is best done by aligning them vertically on graph paper, rather than horizontally. It is easier to see the system that way. For example:

1
2
3
4
5
6
7
8
9
10
11
12
13
14
15
16
17
18
19
20
21

is better than this:

1, 2, 3, 4, 5, 6, 7, 8, 9, 10, 11, etc.

Point out to him that once he is past the teens, the first number in the sequence is the one said first. For example, *twenty*-three, *sixty*-seven, and so on.

- 5. Teach him to record quantities—to count objects and write down the amount—ranging from 0 to 100.

   a) This can be added to the "take a walk and count the steps" activity described above. Have him develop

230

a set of directions—a map—for moving from one point in the house or the backyard to another. For example, ask him to measure the perimeter of your yard in footsteps, record it, and compare that to the neighbor's yard. (Measuring things and comparing them is excellent training for a variety of arithmetic skills.)

b) Have him, "Write down the number that comes just before or just after—."

c) Obtain 100 poker chips and a marking crayon. Number each of the chips from 1 to 100. Mix them up, then have the child arrange them in numerical sequence, stacked in piles of 10 chips each, with the lowest number in each pile on the top. He should end up, then, with 10 piles, where the chips on top of each pile look like that shown in Figure 76. Time him, and keep track of his improvement.

FIGURE 76

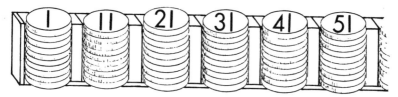

(NOTE: Draw a bar *under* each potentially ambiguous number, so that there is no difficulty distinguishing the 6 from the 9, the 61 from the 19, 81 from 18, and so on.)

Stage II suggestions: Helping the child who cannot accurately add, subtract, multiply, and divide.

All the activities in this section will use a homemade calculator. To construct it, you will need the poker chips just described—each one bearing a number from 1 to 100. In addition, you will need a map containing 100 squares, arranged in ten rows of ten squares each. This can be made with a piece of poster board, available from any art supply house, or for that matter, any piece of cardboard.

Draw the map so that each square is just large enough to contain one poker chip. The map should look like that shown in Figure 77.

FIGURE 77

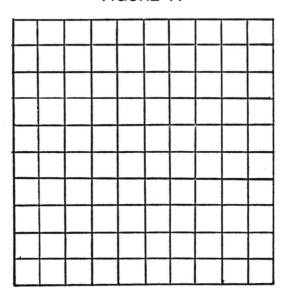

That is all the equipment you will need to get started.

- 1. To teach the child to add, say 4+5, show him a written statement of the problem and have him:

  a) remove the first 4 chips from the first pile of chips (those numbered 1, 2, 3, 4) and arrange them in sequence on the top line of the map, as in Figure 78.

FIGURE 78

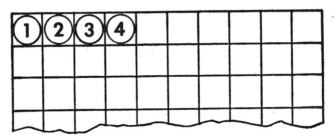

b) remove the next 5 chips from that same pile (those numbered 5, 6, 7, 8, 9), and arrange them in sequence on the second line of the map, beneath the first 4, as in Figure 79.

FIGURE 79

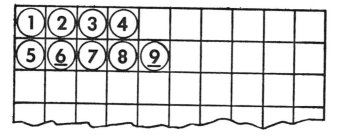

c) read and record the answer from the highest numbered chip—the last one in the sequence.

Start with the following problems, and then invent others. At first, they should be limited to adding single digit numerals, where the sum is 10 or less. Notice, by the way, that the problems are presented two ways. You should give the child experience in dealing with both formats:

1+6=	8+2=	7+3=
2+5=	4+3=	6+3=
2+6=	9+1=	4+4=
3+6=	8+1=	5+3=
3+5=	6+4=	3+5=
4+6=	6+3=	2+5=

$$\begin{array}{ccccccc} 5 & 3 & 4 & 5 & 5 & 6 & 7 \\ +5 & +7 & +6 & +5 & +4 & +3 & +2 \end{array}$$

As the child solves these problems, point out to him the pertinent relationships illustrated in the solution (in other words, some Stage III concerns).

233

To do this, leave the chips arranged the way they are at the completion of the problem in Figure 79, and have the child:

a) compare the size of the two groups, that is, tell you which is larger and by how many. For example, that 5 is *1 more* than 4.

b) then reorganize the chips so that all cells in the top line are filled first, then the second line, and so on. Hence, the map would now look like that shown in Figure 80.

FIGURE 80

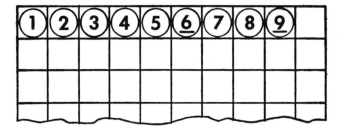

c) tell you how many less than 10 chips there are now in that top line (that is, 1).

There are two purposes for all of this. First, to illustrate to the child that when he adds, the answer not only refers to the total number of objects, but also to the fact that he is adding a certain number of things to an original number of things—that the last one counted (the ninth) represents the answer; that adding is, in fact, fast counting. The second purpose is to illustrate the relationships contained within the problem; relationships that, when recognized and remembered, will help him solve subsequent similar problems more rapidly. For example, that 5 is greater than 4 by a specific visible and tangible amount, and that 10 is greater than 9 by a specific visible and tangible amount.

Eventually you will want him to visualize the chips on the map—to pretend the chips are there—but this can wait until he has firmly established the basic skills using the chips and map.

We should try another illustration—one where the sum is more than 10 but less than 20. For example, given the problem 9+4=?, the child:

a) arranges his chips on the map as in Figure 81.

FIGURE 81

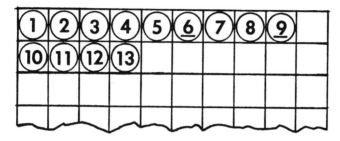

b) then as shown in Figure 82.

FIGURE 82

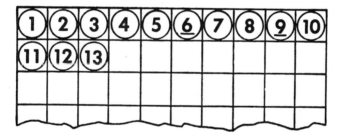

The answer remains the same in both configurations, obviously. But the regrouping is important—particularly as the child starts to recognize that 9+4 is the same as 10+3. And this should be pointed out, just in case he does not recognize it. Construct some problems for him at this level of difficulty and have him work them, always calling his attention to relationships.

Illustrating one more level of difficulty would be worthwhile, this time with a problem involving larger numbers.

For example, 16+18=?* Where the sum is more than 20, the child should:

a) count out and arrange the chips 'so that the map looks like that shown in Figure 83.

FIGURE 83

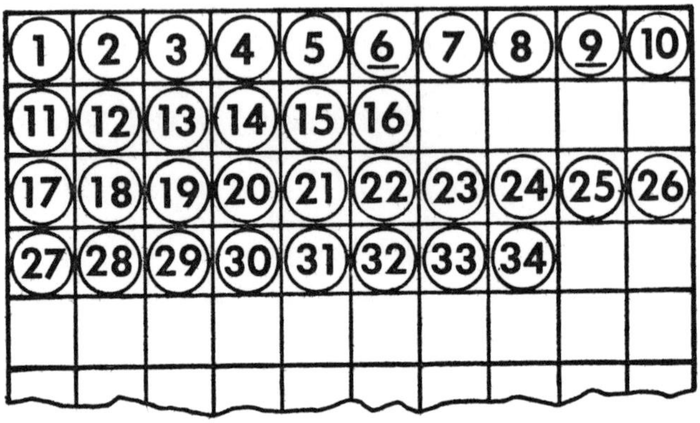

b) then be alerted to the fact that 16+18 is the same as 10+6+10+8; that in either instance, the answer remains 34.

c) then rearrange the chips so that the map looks like that shown in Figure 84.

FIGURE 84

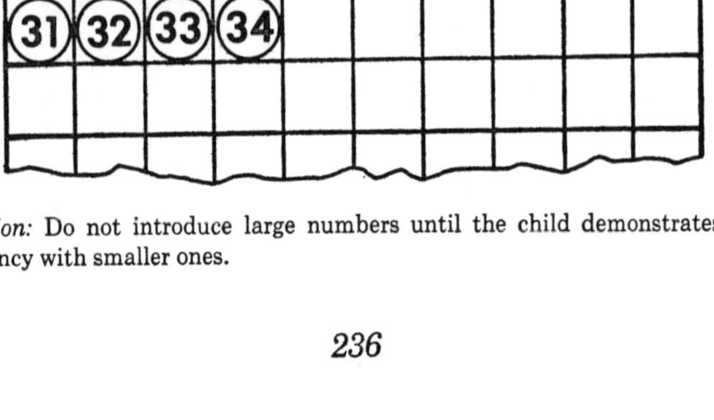

Caution: Do not introduce large numbers until the child demonstrates some proficiency with smaller ones.

The important point here is that the answer continues to be 34 even though the organization of the chips is now 10+10+10+4; that 34 chips may be organized in a variety of ways without changing the fact that the sum of them remains 34.

• 2. To teach the child to subtract, say 6 - 2, show him a written statement of the problem and have him:

    a) arrange chips 1, 2, 3, 4, 5, and 6 on the first line of the map.

    b) then remove the last two chips (chips 5 and 6) from their original position, and locate them in the first two cells of the third line—thus indicating that these are being removed or subtracted from the original set. The map will then look like that shown in Figure 85.

FIGURE 85

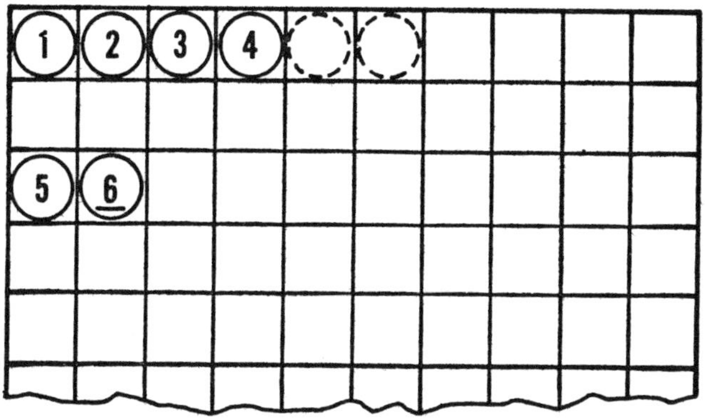

c) record the answer—that is, the number of chips remaining on the first line. Point out to him that subtraction is really the direct opposite of addition since the map is now almost set up to add: 4+2. All he has to do is move the lower line of chips up one line. You should also point out here how 4 chips differ from 2 chips (that 4 is 2 more than 2) and how 2, 4, and 6 interrelate (that it is really counting by 2's).

Give him a group of problems to solve that are representative of this level; that is, where no more than 10

237

chips are involved. Again, remember to show them in both formats:

$$
\begin{array}{r}
8 \\
\underline{-4}
\end{array}
\qquad \text{and} \qquad 8-4=
$$

Now move to more complex problems, where as many as 20 chips are involved, and go through the same procedures. For example, in the problem $19-10=?$, he should first arrange the 19 chips with 10 on the top line and 9 on the second. Then 10 chips should be subtracted from the set of 19 by positioning the last 10 chips (chips 10 through 19) on the third line. The remaining 9 chips on the top line indicate the answer to the problem.

But, as before, it is wise to point out (or better yet, have the child tell you) the difference between the 9 on the top line and the 10 on the third line—that there is *one more* in 10 than in 9. You might also try presenting the concept that when he subtracts, he is not really getting rid of a group of chips; he is simply taking them away from the original set. This might be too abstract for some children, but it is worth a try at this point. (That is why you leave the subtracted chips on the map.) Give him plenty of practice with written problems at this level —and with harder problems also—enough to be convinced that he can solve the problems by using the chips and the map. Later on you will eliminate the chips and have him do it in his head.

- 3. To teach the child to multiply. Make certain he can do addition problems before you get too involved here. Once he can solve the easiest level of addition problems, using the chips and the map but getting no additional assistance from you, introduce the easiest level of multiplication, where the answer is 10 or less.

For example, present the problem $3 \times 2 = ?$. (Even though you have followed the sequence described here, you should make sure that he knows the multiplication sign and differentiates it from the plus sign. To solve the problem, he should be told that 3×2 means 3 groups, each containing 2 things. With this information, he should place the first group of 2 chips on the top line, the next 2 chips on the second line, and the third group of 2 chips on the third line. The map should look like that shown in Figure 86.

FIGURE 86

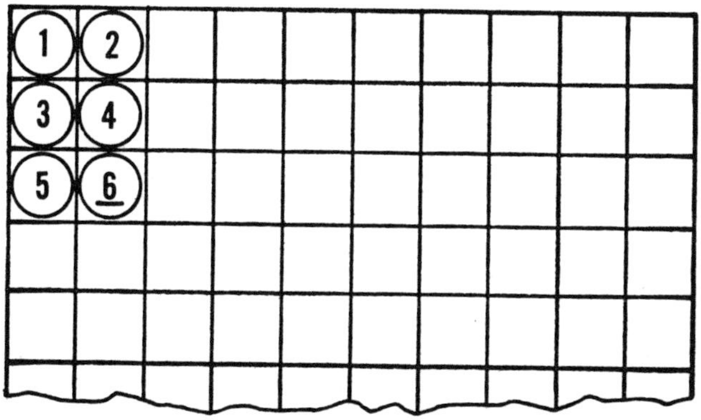

He can read the answer directly from the last chip, but while he is at it, you should point out that he can also find the answer to 1×2 and 2×2 by reading down that right-hand column of chips.

Give him a number of similar problems to solve with the chips and map. When he shows that he can do these without any help from you, introduce the concept that 3×2 is the same as 2×3, by rotating the map 1/4 turn counterclockwise. Of course, the chips will now be in an improper arrangement, but without rearranging them you can still point out how 3 groups (lines), each with 2 chips, is really the same as 2 groups (lines), each with 3 chips. Do not dwell on this concept, but point it out. You will do more of this later.

Now move to more difficult problems—they are not really more difficult, they simply involve more chips. Any multiplication problem up to 5×5 should be reasonable here (that is, where the answer is 25 or less). Follow the procedure described above and give the child plenty of practice solving written problems—and, after solving each one, point out the partial multiplication table apparent in the right-hand column of chips, then have him rotate the board and write the new problem. Hence, $4 \times 5 = 20$ will become $5 \times 4 = 20$.

Once you see evidence of understanding, introduce problems with higher numbers—up to 10×10—and give him practice with these. Remember, he is not memorizing the multiplication tables yet. He is merely solving problems and, at the same time, illustrating a concept that will help him considerably when he starts to memorize them.

This is probably a good place to talk about the number line—the nemesis of many children. The number line is another kind of calculator, similar in a way to the chips and map. However, it tends to be more abstract, as you will soon see. In my judgment it is representative of what is not good about modern math.

The number line is a good device, if you understand it. Good math learners use the number line capably because they are good math learners, and not the other way around. It confuses those who are less capable.

At any rate, your child will probably have to use a number line in school, so it may be wise for you to teach him how.

The number line looks like that shown in Figure 87.

FIGURE 87

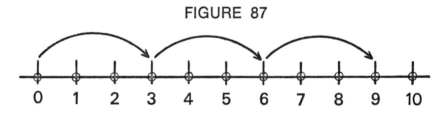

To calculate the answer to 3×3 on a number line, the child is to take 3 jumps of 3 spaces each. The confusion arises from the fact that he is jumping spaces while the marks on the number line are not the spaces, but rather the points that separate the spaces. Can you remember when you first learned to calculate the number of hours that elapsed between two points on a clock—say 9 A.M. and 12 A.M.? It may be easy for you now but at first you probably counted "9-10-11-12" and came up with the answer "4 hours." Many children encounter the same problem with the number line.

The chips and map can help. First, teach him to *jump* over chips. For example, 3×3 would look like that shown in Figure 88.

FIGURE 88

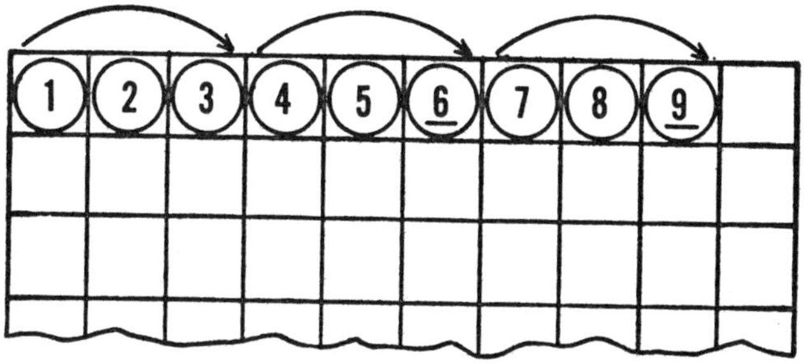

Then take away the chips and have him jump over the empty cells. Then substitute the number line for the cells, and tell him to pretend the chips are in those spaces between the marks on the number line. It takes practice, but it does work.

• 4. To teach the child to divide. Start at a simple level, after you are sure that he can multiply at this level. For example, if he can solve multiplication problems up to $3 \times 3 = ?$ introduce similar division problems.

Be careful how you word a division problem. For example, the problem $6 \div 3 = ?$ is to be stated as follows: "You start off with a group of 6 chips. You want to break this up—divide this—into smaller bunches, each containing 3 chips. *How many groups of 3 chips each will that make?*"

(Do *not* state the problem as, "Divide this group by 3." I agree that the two wordings are essentially the same, but it is much harder for the child to deal with this second wording.)

He is to start off by taking the first 6 chips from his pile and constructing groups of chips—3 in each; that is, placing 3 chips on the first line and 3 more on the second. He will then have used all his chips and the map will look like that shown in Figure 89.

FIGURE 89

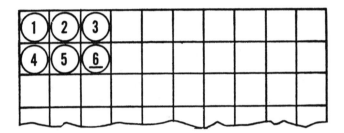

By counting the number of groups, he calculates the answer. But, also point out to him that $6 \div 3 = 2$ is very similar to $2 \times 3 = 6$, and also to $3 + 3 = 6$. Do not make too much of it yet, but by all means point it out. Also, rotate the map 90° (1/4 turn) and show him how $6 \div 3 = 2$ can also be described as $6 \div 2 = 3$, if he takes a different viewpoint.

After you have given him sufficient practice at this level, move up to more difficult problems—that is, where the upper limit is $25 \div 5 = ?$ The question is the same: "You start off with 25 chips. You want to divide this into smaller groups, each containing 5 chips. How many groups will that make?"

When he is ready, move up to the next level, where he is asked to solve problems as complex as $100 \div 10 = ?$ (These are not really more complex. The procedure is the same. It simply involves larger numbers.) Give plenty of practice at this level, always using the chips and the map.

Stage III suggestions: Helping the child who does not see relationships between quantities.

It is time to give up the calculator—the chips and map—and to pretend it is there. In other words, it is now important for the child to start to assemble the processes into chunks and perform them more rapidly. Manipulatives are useful, but the good arithmetic learner manipulates ideas, not poker chips. There really is only one way to accomplish this. That is, to practice pretending the chips and map are there to the point where he does not have to go through that step because the answer emerges almost automatically.

Prepare flash cards—index cards—each of which contains a single addition, subtraction, multiplication, or division problem. Use them regularly, by showing them to the child one at a time, and having him respond as rapidly as possible—but *do stress accuracy.* Guessing is not to be encouraged or, for that matter, even tolerated.

Tell him, at first, to pretend the chips and map are there, and to imagine that he sees them, the numbers on them, and the way they are grouped. If he does, and if he has had enough experience at Stage II, he will be able to see the answers in his mind's eye.

Practice this until he demonstrates competency. It might stimulate his interest if you use a stopwatch to measure the amount of time it takes to solve the flashcard problems. If so, use one, and record the times daily. He will enjoy trying to surpass his own record as the days go by.

Now is the time to teach him the multiplication and division tables; and teach them you should. To teach him a table (the 6 table, for example) instruct him to imagine how the map would look if he were working out the problem 10×6. If he can imagine the map, then all he has to do is read, in his mind's eye, the chips in the right-hand column. To teach him, have him actually construct the problem with chips on the map; then have him close his eyes and pretend he sees it. Give him as much practice as he needs. It is essential for him to become completely familiar with the tables.*

As an additional assist, give him sheets of paper organized the way the map is—10 lines, 10 blank cells in each line—and have him write a table in each, positioning the numbers in the correct cell. The 7 table would look like that shown in Figure 90.

FIGURE 90

1	2	3	4	5	6	7			
8	9	10	11	12	13	14			
15	16	17	18	19	20	21			
22	23	24	25	26	27	28			
29	30	31	32	33	34	35			
36	37	38	39	40	41	42			
43	44	45	46	47	48	49			

*Children tend to learn certain number facts more rapidly than they do others. For instance, most children will know that 6x6=36 long before they remember that 7x6=42. Take advantage of this by showing the child that he does not have to go all the way back to 1 when asked for a multiplication fact he does not remember. For example, if he does not know the answer to 7x8=? but does know that 7x7=49, then he should step back only to 7x7=49 and calculate the answer from that starting point. He should not return all the way back to the beginning. In other words, the child should be taught to exploit these easier-remembered facts; to use them as reliable landmarks. This will not only help him solve his daily arithmetic problems; these landmarks will serve as reference points around which the harder-to-remember number facts can cluster.

Additional suggestions

The following are auxiliary activities, not substitutes. They may be used at the same time you are using the map and chips. There is no good substitute for effective drill and practice, especially if the child is to acquire Stage III concepts as he practices.

- 1. The following activities call for a set of cubes; for example, the one-inch cubes commonly found in primary grade classes—although size is irrelevant, so long as all the cubes are the same size.

    a) Point to a single cube and say to the child, "This stands for 1." Then show him 2 cubes and ask, "How many does this stand for?" The answer, of course, is 2.

    b) Again show the child 1 cube but now say, "This now stands for 2." (If he is confused, give it more concrete meaning by saying, "Pretend this weighs 2 pounds.") Then show him 2 cubes and ask, "How many does this stand for now?" (Or, "How much does this weigh?") The answer should now be 4, since there are twice as many cubes.

    c) Continue in this way, assigning different values to one cube and then asking how many some multiple of that cube would stand for. (For example, if one cube stands for 3, then 3 cubes stand for 9.)

    d) Now alter conditions a bit and start off with more than 1 cube. For example, show him 3 cubes and say, "These stand for 3" (or "Altogether, these weigh 3 pounds"). Then show 2 cubes (or 1 cube) and ask what they (or it) stand for. Now show him the same 2 cubes and tell him that, together, they stand for 1 (or weigh 1 pound). Then ask, "What does 1 cube represent?" (1/2, of course).

    The goal you are after with these activities is for the child to recognize the interrelationships between numbers; that if something or some collection of things is 1, then twice that amount is 2, three times that amount is 3; one-half that amount is 1/2, and so on. These are not difficult abilities to acquire, but they do take some time and effort—particularly for children with poor visual analysis skills. Work on it—it will pay off.

- 2. Carry out this activity with a variety of materials. For example, use time as an illustration. Sixty seconds constitute 1 minute. Hence, 60=1. Following this concept, 120 would equal 2, and so on. Also use the concept of one (1) coin—the nickel—representing 5 coins or pennies, yet that same nickel representing only 1/2 the dime. Our environment is full of quantifiable items; our culture is a measuring and quantifying culture. Exploit that in your teaching.

- 3. Have him search for patterns in numbers; for example, that the 9 table is interesting in that the first number goes up 1 each time while the second number goes down 1 each time: 09—18—27—36, etc.

- 4. Have him solve puzzles involving number patterns. For example:

> 1, 2, 3 . . . what number comes next? (4, of course).
> 2, 4, 6 . . . what number comes next? (8).
> 1, 2, 4, 8 . . . what number comes next? (16).
> 1, 11, 21, 31 . . . what number comes next? (41).
> 5, 4, 10, 9 . . . what number comes next? (15).
> 2, 5, 4, 7, 6, 9 . . . what number comes next? (8).

As you can see, there is no limit to the number of puzzles you can develop. Your goal here is to teach him to use all available information when solving a problem, and to find organized patterns.

- 5. Any activity that is based on seeing patterns will be useful. These include:

a) construction toys and all the other materials already mentioned in the visual perceptual skills section of this book (pages 122-129).

b) playing a musical instrument—particularly a percussion instrument in a rhythm band. (This involves counting time, keeping his place, recognizing where he fits in.)

c) keeping score at athletic events.

SPELLING

There are many poor spellers. And not all of them have a learning disorder. Indeed, some of my most competent colleagues are poor spellers. Well then, is it worth worrying about—especially when the child we are discussing has so many other problems in school? Yes, it is worth worrying about—especially *because* he has so many other problems in school.

If the child's only problem was his spelling—if he was competent in reading and arithmetic—his teachers (and you) would probably shrug, smile, and acknowledge that no one is perfect. But if the youngster is a poor reader and a poor arithmetic problem solver in addition to being a poor speller, no one will smile. They may shrug, but its meaning will be different—"What's the use!"—and no one will even try to do anything about it.

Should they try? Yes. Good spelling instruction will probably help the child with his reading, and that makes it worthwhile.

What is it that makes a good speller? What does the good speller do that the poor speller does not do? It appears to be connected to some extent with reading skills, but certainly not completely. Not all good readers are good spellers; but, on the other hand, poor readers are never good spellers. So, good reading ability is part of the difference, but there is more to it than that.

The three stages

If we analyze the processes that underlie spelling, it appears that the good speller—the child who learns how to spell a vast assortment* of words—is able to:

---

*The word *assortment* implies that there are too many words to be memorized by rote—the way we memorize telephone numbers; as though the sounds of the spoken word had no direct relationship with the letters. We can memorize a certain number of spelling words this way, but that number is very limited. Good spellers do more than memorize.

247

STAGE I

Read the words—decode the letters into a spoken word. (He need not understand it, but, obviously, that is not undesirable.) If he cannot decode the word, then he has an additional mental task to contend with—one that is probably insurmountable if he is to learn more than a very few words.

STAGE II

Analyze the spoken word into its parts—sounds—and match those with the letters in the word. If there is a perfect match—if there is a sound for each letter in the word and the sounds are specific to those letters, and those letters alone—and if the child already knows those letter-sound combinations (Stage I skill), then the task is accomplished. The child will be able to spell the word. He will not have to memorize a thing. Words such as *mat, fit, run,* and *hot* belong in this category. If the match is not perfect —if there are inconsistencies or irregularities, such as there not being a sound for each letter, or if the letter used to code a sound is one that is not customarily associated with that sound—then a potential problem arises. The child will have to memorize the spelling of at least a part of the word. He will not spell it correctly if he simply sounds it out and then writes the letters that go with those sounds. There are plenty of words in this category; for example, *their, bought, blew, rough,* and *slice.*

STAGE III

Devise effective strategies for remembering those inconsistencies and irregularities.

These three stages are mapped in Figure 91.

Suppose we try to imagine how this sequence of abilities works. How does a child who learns to spell very easily deal with a new word? Take the word *consistent*—many adults have trouble with that one, often spelling it *consistant.* The very good speller reads the word (Stage I), pronouncing it clearly. Then he analyzes the word into its sounds, matching those individual sounds with individual letters.

FIGURE 91

SPELLING

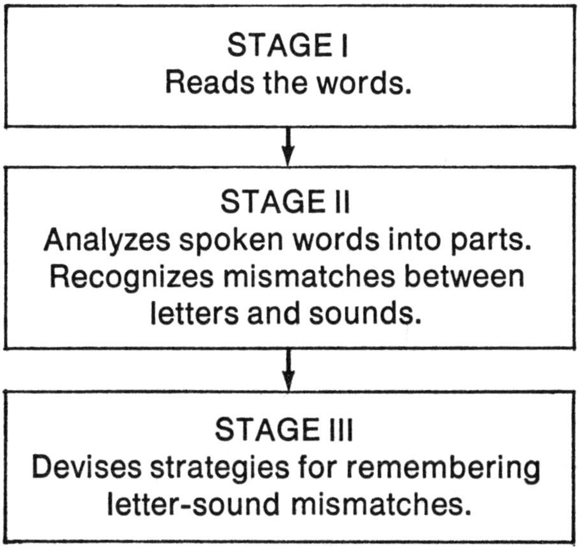

```
┌─────────────────────────────────────┐
│              STAGE I                 │
│          Reads the words.            │
└─────────────────────────────────────┘
                   │
                   ▼
┌─────────────────────────────────────┐
│              STAGE II                │
│   Analyzes spoken words into parts.  │
│    Recognizes mismatches between     │
│          letters and sounds.         │
└─────────────────────────────────────┘
                   │
                   ▼
┌─────────────────────────────────────┐
│             STAGE III                │
│   Devises strategies for remembering │
│       letter-sound mismatches.       │
└─────────────────────────────────────┘
```

Consistent turns out to be a fairly easy word for this part of the task; there is a sound for each letter. If he is careful to pronounce the word correctly, he notices that only the *o* and *a* stand for ambiguous sounds, sounds that could be coded by certain other letters. Both of these, in the word *consistent*, are schwa sounds.* The child (remember, he is a very good learner of spelling), having recognized these two potential trouble spots as the only parts of the word that he will not be able to sound out and then spell with complete confidence, devises a strategy to help him remember that the first schwa sound is coded by an *o*, and the second by an *e* (Stage III).

What is his strategy? It can vary, but with this word he

*The schwa is a very common sound in our language; it can be represented by virtually every printed vowel in the alphabet. For example: th*e*; *a*bove; nati*o*n.

probably pronounces the word to himself incorrectly, giving the *o* a short *ŏ* sound, and the *e* a short *ĕ* sound. That helps him remember. (We will examine various other strategies later in this section.)

We should try another word; one that has some different kinds of trouble spots. Take the word *receipt*—a sixth-grade spelling word in most schools. The very good speller reads the word (Stage I), breaks it down into its separate sounds, and recognizes that two of the letters in that word do not get sounded—the *i* and the *p* (Stage II). Having noticed these inconsistencies, he devises a strategy to help him remember to include these letters when he writes the word. He does not worry about the rest of the word. He can spell that part just by writing the sounds down in correct sequence.

There is one more step in learning to spell a word—this one, again, something that the very good speller does with virtually no outside assistance. He reads and he spells the word frequently, using whatever strategies he originally devised to help him spell it accurately. In time, he no longer has to think about the strategy. The word becomes a unit rather than a string of separate letters. He memorizes it. What originally required his special attention no longer does. He has chunked the letters into a word or a subcomponent of a word—a spelling unit*—and spells the word almost automatically.

In fact, the only time he stops to think about the separate letters is when someone asks him for assistance in spelling that word. Then he has to stop and think for a moment. Indeed, he may even have to write it down.**

What about the average speller; the child who does not

---

*The four letters *tion* is an example of a spelling unit. Once the child learns that these letters constitute a chunk that consistently represents the same sound, he no longer has to deal separately with the four letters.

**This is not dissimilar to many other skills we acquire. Take this question: "Is the vertical line positioned to the right or the left in the lowercase *d*?" Most of us would have to stop for a moment and mentally reconstruct the letter, or look at one already in view, even though we are very familiar with the letter. We are so familiar, in fact, that it has become something we do without thinking.

have too much trouble, but is not as good as the one we just described? Suppose he has to learn to spell *receipt*. Chances are he will be able to read it (Stage I). He is, after all, a fair student. He will also probably be able to break it down into its separate sounds, and he may even notice that the *i* and the *p* do not have sounds in the spoken word (Stage II). However, what happens if he does not notice it? If his spelling program is a good one, it will be designed to make those inconsistencies apparent to him. In other words, *receipt* will not be taught as an isolated word but, rather, as part of a group, all of which will share the same characteristics—the *ei* sequence. His teacher will call his attention to the similarity of the words in that group, thereby emphasizing it (for example, *receive, deceive*). And, in addition, she will devise a way to help him remember—perhaps "*i* before *e* except after *c*." She will also devise one for the silent *p*; perhaps she will have him pronounce the word with the *p* sound included, just to emphasize the fact that it is there— *recei-p-t*. Then, to top it off, she will have him practice spelling the word—writing it a number of times to help him remember it.

Now, what about the child with a severe spelling problem? What does he do when faced with the task of learning how to spell *receipt*?

First of all, he probably cannot read the word; his teacher has to read it to him. Thus, he is in trouble from the start— Stage I. Since he is a poor reader, it is predictable that he will be a poor sound analyzer; he will probably have difficulty breaking down the word into its individual sounds. He will also have real difficulty matching individual sounds to individual letters, even when the match is a regular one. The fact that this word is being taught as part of a group of words, all of which share the same characteristic, will not help him be aware of those characteristics. He will have trouble with all the words in the group, so no one of them helps him with the others (Stage II). There is too much to be aware of, let alone to memorize.

Finally, when his teacher shows him some strategies for keeping the irregularities straight in his mind, they are promptly forgotten. He is coping with a major and basic problem; he does not know how to match the regular sounds very well. Thus, talking to him about irregularities is useless; it is superfluous information—he has no way of understanding it, let alone using it. (It is a little like talking to a beginning swimmer about how to cup his hands in a particular way to get a little extra speed. He is devoting all his attention to staying afloat; there is little energy available for thinking about small subcomponents of the act.)

At any rate, suppose he has been through the lesson, and it is now time to practice writing the newly learned word. He practices, and may even manage to write it accurately a few times. But he is depending completely upon rote memorization of the *entire* word, not just certain strategic parts of it. It is just too much to remember. By tomorrow, the word will be gone and the youngster will fail again.

Helping the poor speller

This section contains a number of suggested activities that will help the poor speller. They do not constitute a complete spelling program that can replace his school program. Rather, they focus on skills that are vital to satisfactory spelling in general; skills that will help the child become a better speller.

As always, coordinate your efforts with your child's teacher. Ask her for spelling words that are appropriate for him. And show her what you are doing, so that she can add suggestions.

Once more the activities are based on the same instructional principles that have been cited repeatedly in this book.

- 1. Organize for success. Avoid overplacing the child. If he has not yet acquired Stage I skills—if he cannot read the words on his spelling list—spend time teaching him to do that. It is silly—no, cruel—to expect him to memorize his spelling words in their entirety. He will learn to spell only when he has acquired the skills that will enable him to limit memorization to certain small parts of every spelling word.

- 2. Provide the child with whatever information—hints—he needs to understand the task; then teach him how to do the task without this help. The good speller has no trouble identifying which portions of a spelling word require his special attention and which parts do not. The poor speller tries to memorize the entire word and, as a result, remembers very little and guesses a lot. We will discuss various ways to highlight those parts of the word that are most important.

- 3. Teach the child to make use of all his senses, not just his eyes. This pertains to the memory assist that writing and saying a spelling word provides.

Suggested activities

The following activities are organized according to the skills they teach; the stages to which they belong. As such, if the child is able to read the words he is trying to learn to spell, there is no reason to use the activities classified as Stage I. If he is able to analyze spoken words into their separate sounds and code those sounds with letters, and if he is able to recognize when mismatches arise—when coding the sounds of a word with letters does not result in a correctly spelled word—then Stage I and II activities may be omitted. If he is able to see those mismatches and devise, on his own, strategies for remembering them, then all the activities may be omitted. There is nothing in this section that will help him. Indeed, he does not need help, from this book or anywhere else, at least insofar as spelling is concerned.

Stage I suggestions: Helping the child who cannot decode his spelling words.

- 1. Stage I spelling skills are defined elsewhere in this book: in the sections devoted to helping the child acquire better reading skills (pp. 192-230), visual perceptual skills (pp. 113-129), and auditory perceptual skills (pp.

130-169). Check back to those. Test the child to determine what he needs, and do what you can. I recognize that it is easier to make that recommendation than to carry it out, but there is no use in trying to teach the child is spell words that he is unable to read on his own.

What you might do, and this is not a waste of time, is teach him to spell easier words—words that he can read, but that he cannot spell with consistent accuracy. The potential effects of this are twofold. One, it will help his spelling skills to some extent (although it will not do much about improving his spelling grade if he is in the sixth grade and you are working on third-grade words). Second, it will help his reading skills to the degree that becoming better acquainted with the letter-sound combinations is important to his reading.

Stage II suggestions: Helping the child analyze spoken words into sounds, code those sounds with letters, and recognize mismatches.

- 1. The importance of competent auditory analysis skills is obvious. Therefore, if you have not already done so, test the child with the TAAS (see p. 78) and, if he displays less than adequate skills, go to work with the auditory program. You may at the same time continue to work with the other suggestions listed here.
- 2. Coding individual sounds with letters was discussed thoroughly in the reading section. Use the suggestions listed in the Stage II portion of that section (pp. 201-212).
- 3. It is essential that the child learn to recognize mismatches between how a word appears when it is spelled phonetically (when the sounds are coded by the letters that customarily represent those sounds) and its regular spelling. The best way to teach this is to give certain exercises:

    a) Dictate a word from his spelling list and have him write it down the way he thinks it should be spelled. Have him say the word aloud, distinctly, and instruct him to put every sound down on paper. (If the child already knows how to spell the word correctly, do not insist that he spell it phonetically. You do not want him to practice incorrect spellings if they are not necessary.)

b) Now show him the correct spelling and have him compare his spelling with that. Do they agree? If not, do they differ only in those portions of the word where the letter-sound combination is irregular? (If there are other errors—if the child coded some regular sounds inaccurately—then he needs work on that part of the task. (See suggestion 2 above). Have him underline every letter in the correctly spelled word *except* those letters that caused him trouble—(1) letters for which there were no sounds (for example, the *e* in <u>came</u>, the *t* in <u>listen</u>, the first *d* and second *e* in <u>Wednesday</u>, the *a* and the final *e* in <u>leave</u>, the *b* in <u>doubt</u>), (2) letters that are not ordinarily used to code the sounds they are coding in this particular word (for example, the *gh* in <u>rough</u>, the *c* in <u>ocean</u>, the *o* and the *e* in <u>one</u>). Do you see the similarity between this and the Reading Stage II suggestions regarding sight words (pp. 206-207)?

Stage III suggestions: Helping the child devise strategies for remembering spellings that contain letter-sound mismatches.

- 1. This stage follows the activity just described. Here you want to teach the child how to remember the mismatches he found in the previous activity. There, he discovered problem areas and marked them by underlining all of the word except for those problem areas. Now you want to teach him to remember these potential trouble spots, because unless he memorizes them he will continue to make errors—errors that are not the result of poor auditory analysis and coding skills but, rather, due to the idiosyncrasies of the English language. Try any of the following techniques and, if necessary, use more than one of them.

a) Find a word he knows how to spell correctly that has the same characteristic as the word you are working on. For example, if he misspelled *motion* (moshun) and yet knows how to spell *station*, then use that latter word as a model to teach him that the syllable *tion* always (except in the word *shun*) is spelled *t-i-o-n*. (His teacher should be able to tell you where to obtain a book that lists all the spelling patterns that the elementary schoolchild is expected to learn.)

b) Have him pronounce *all* the letters in the word, even though they are not all sounded out when the word is read in customary fashion. For example, the word *knife*. If he reads it and says it aloud as /k/nife/ (pronouncing the *k* sound) when he learns to spell it, he is more apt to spell it correctly. He no longer has to memorize the *k* visually, so long as he pronounces it to himself when he writes it. As another example, consider the word *teach*. Have him read it as /t/e/ă/ch/—*tea-atch*. Sure, it is sort of silly, but that in itself will probably help him remember it, and therefore spell it correctly.

c) If the problem area he has identified can be explained by a rule, teach him the rule. The one I mentioned before, *i* before *e* except after *c*, is a good one, but even it is not foolproof (for example, *protein*). There are others, such as doubling a consonant when adding *ed* to the end of a word (as in occur-occurred; hop-hopped). Again, I suggest that you consult with his teacher for guidance on this. The rules you teach him should be consistent with the ones taught in school.

d) Rote memorization—not of the entire word, but rather of that portion of the word that cannot be sounded out accurately. For example, there is no reasonable explanation for the spelling of the word *once*, but that does not mean that the entire word has to be memorized. The *n* and the *c* fit—match the sounds of the word. Only the first and the last letters are difficult to explain through the principles of letter-sound rela-

256

tionships. They will have to be memorized—although, in keeping with suggestion b) above, if the child can spell *one*, then it would be wise to show him the similarity between <u>one</u> and <u>once</u>.

At any rate, to memorize a word spelling, follow this procedure:

(1) Show the child the word he is to learn to spell and have him read it. (If he cannot read it, he is placed way beyond where he should be. Stop this activity and move back to Stage I.) Have him say it aloud, first in the correct way, then pronouncing every letter.

(2) Now have him copy it, saying the letters aloud as he does. Repeat five times. When he can do this accurately go to the next step.

(3) Have him write it without copying; that is, from memory—spelling it aloud as he does. Repeat this five times. When this can be done accurately go to the next step.

(4) Have him write it five times, with his eyes closed —spelling it aloud as he does and thinking about what his hand is doing.

(5) Finally, have him write a sentence using the word appropriately. If he can make up the sentence, all the better.

- 2. Games. Scrabble, Spell-It, and Anagrams—all sold in book, variety, and department stores—are excellent activities. They do not teach spelling, but do make learning how to spell a little more fun.
- 3. Make small words out of larger words. For example, show the child the word *alligator* and ask him to construct as many words as he can, using the letters in that word:

all	gill	tail	rat	lit
goat	lot	grill	tall	till

WRITING

Almost every first-grade child is taught to print (manuscript), rather than to write (cursive). In some schools, cursive writing is introduced in the second grade; in others, in the third grade.

This was not always so. Years ago, only cursive was taught, and good penmanship was an important goal. Around thirty years ago, the emphasis started to shift to manuscript writing. "After all," the argument went, "the child has to learn to read manuscript—his books are printed, not written in longhand, and besides, manuscript can readily be converted to cursive writing by connecting the letters."

The reasoning seemed sensible, the switch occurred and, with it, additional sources of confusion for the children we are concerned with here.

First of all, teachers devoted less time to penmanship, to teaching and having the child practice how to write or print neatly. Secondly, directional confusions were experienced. It is not very difficult to remember the difference between a *b* and a *d*, but you certainly cannot say the same for their manuscript counterparts—the b and the d. Third, and not to be ignored, cursive writing is more efficient—less time consuming. You do not have to start and stop continuously. It is not a series of separate acts; it has a continuity and a rhythm that appear to make it a better system for some children.

Does that mean you should teach cursive writing to your first grader, and ignore manuscript? If you can do so without complicating his school life, yes, by all means. However, if doing so will only serve to get him into even deeper difficulty in his classroom, then, of course, the answer is No. Teach him better manuscript skills.

Is cursive writing harder to learn? And will he still be able to read his books? After all, they are printed. No, cursive writing is not more difficult to learn. It is a manual skill, as is manuscript, and if he is taught and if he practices, he will learn it. As for being able to read printed books, that too is not much of an additional burden for the child who learns cursive writing instead of manuscript. To read, he only has to recognize the letters. He does not have to know how to print them. And actually printing them is appreciably more difficult than recognizing them. (If you do not remember the distinction, go back to the section on visual perceptual skills.)

Enough, now, of the argument between manuscript and cursive. Find out from his teacher whether you have a choice. If you do, fine; teach him cursive, *if* he is also learning it in school. Do not, under any circumstances, try to teach him one system at home if he is being taught the other at school.

I will list some teaching suggestions in a moment, but first I want to lay out the stages you should attend to, and what they mean in practical terms.

The three stages

There are stages of proficiency in learning to write. First the child *draws* patterns—he is not printing letters until he thinks of them as symbols. Then, as he learns the individual letter names and their patterns—as he chunks individual elements into a larger unit—he *writes* or *prints* letters, but he has to think about them, and how to make his hand perform the necessary movements. As he practices, he acquires facility. Just as the new driver becomes the experienced driver and is able to stop thinking about what separate actions he is to perform, so too does the new writer become the experienced writer and stop thinking about how to control his hand. Surely you do not devote any significant amount of thought to executing the letters when you write. Rather, you think about what you want to say—to the thoughts you want to express. The mechanical aspects of the task have become automatic. What if they had not? Try to write backward and assess the effects. How does it affect your speed, your facility, your ability to think as you write? The effects will be apparent at once.

The stages may be diagrammed as shown in Figure 92.

FIGURE 92

WRITING

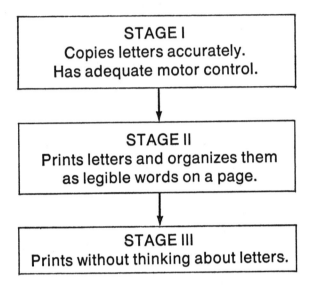

As always, it is an error to expect facility at a particular stage if the child has not established some degree of competency at the lower stages. As the child acquires the Stage I skills—as he learns to copy the letters accurately—Stage II abilities will require less conscious thought. As he acquires Stage II skills—as he becomes able to organize the letters he prints and the space in which he is printing them, so that what he produces is recognized as legible language—he will be better able to think about the meaning of what he is writing rather than its physical appearance (Stage III).

The stages will merge and the only time he will regress to a lower level of performance is when some disrupting factor is introduced into the activity—writing backward, for example, or, more realistically, writing neatly when that is not the normal pattern. When this occurs, performance deteriorates. The child's writing will become less neat and he will have to think more about the physical act of writing.

260

He will have less time available to think about what he is writing.

My point? Spend enough time practicing the lower level skills, so that they start to approximate automatic performance. If you ignore these basic stages, the outcome of your efforts—and the child's—will not be as satisfying.

I should also say something here about handedness. The child should always use the same hand, and it should be the hand he writes best with.* If you are uncertain about which one that is, test him. You do not need a formal test. Have him write or print with one hand, then the other, and compare the two. Almost invariably, one will be better than the other. That is the hand he should write with. If he tends to forget, and continues to switch hands from time to time, put a wrist band of some kind (a leather strap, a ribbon) on the side he is supposed to use and be firm in your directions to him. He is to use *that* hand for writing, and *only that hand.***

Helping the poor writer

This section contains a number of activities that will help the poor writer. They do not constitute a complete writing program that can replace his school program. They merely focus on certain skills that will help the child become a better writer.

As always, coordinate your efforts with his teacher. There

---

*This refers to school-aged children, children past their sixth birthday. Preschool children often alternate hands for various activities and, so far as is known, this is not bad—it is normal. However, by the time the child enters first grade, and is expected to learn to read, calculate, spell, and write, he should have developed a dominant hand. Otherwise he will experience much confusion with remembering the directional conventions of the language. That is, reading and writing from left to right; distinguishing a *b* from a *d*, and so forth.

**I have intentionally avoided discussing a so-called dominant eye and its relationship to a dominant hand. I stated very early in this book that the question I wanted to address was "How can I help the child do better in school?" not "What is the cause of his problem?" Even if I believed that a consistent hand-eye dominance was an important consideration—and at this date there is no substantive evidence to think so—it would still be irrelevant to this book.

is more than one writing program used in this country. For example, some schools teach this †, others teach this one †. Although it does not appear to be a crucial consideration in the long run, it is best if you teach the child to make the letter look the way it does in school. Ask his teacher to print or write the alphabet in the style she favors and use that as your guide.

Suggested activities

The following activities are arranged according to the skills they teach and the stages to which they belong. In theory, if the child has adequate motor control, you might think you should be able to skip Stage I activities and move on to Stage II. Do not. Start with Stage I activities and work through each stage in order.

Stage I suggestions: Helping the child acquire better motor control in writing.

A chalkboard is a necessity here. Paper and pencil will inhibit the motor facility you want the child to acquire.

- 1. Rhythmic writing. The goal of this activity is to have the child be able to draw repetitive patterns across the chalkboard in a fluent, rhythmic fashion. The fact that some of the patterns are letters is not relevant. But, at the same time, it is not accidental. Where letters make up the pattern, point them out to the child but do not stress the fact. Pay attention to smooth production of the patterns. Figure 93 shows the patterns you should use (although there is nothing wrong with modifying and adding to these).

  Draw the first pattern high on the chalkboard, repeating it across the entire board. Then ask the child to draw one like it lower on the chalkboard (at about his chin level). Show him how to hold the chalk, resting across the four fingers and secured by the thumb. Urge him to move his whole arm freely. You want neatness, but not at the expense of fluid movement. First work on ease of move-

FIGURE 93

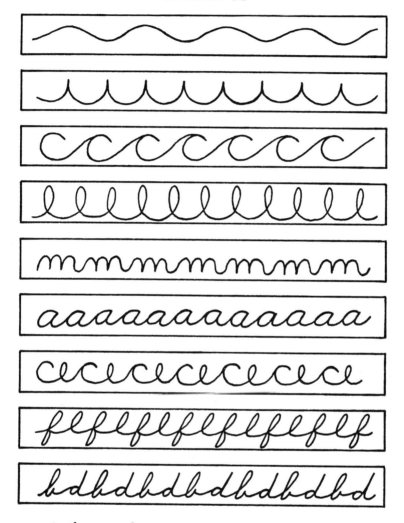

ment, then on the neatness. Some children move more freely to music. Try it if you wish, but it is not critical.

Have him erase his drawing and try again. Caution him to think about what his hand is doing, but again not at the expense of the rhythmic movement.

After about five or ten tries, his pattern should start to approximate yours. When it does, have him repeat the exercise with his eyes closed. Then move on to the second pattern. There is no need to remain on one pattern until it is perfect, although you should go back and review patterns from time to time. Be sure to comment on his improvement, if it is observable.

- 2. After he starts to show some facility at the chalkboard, introduce some pencil and paper activities.

a) Show him how to hold the pencil—with his thumb and index finger. And do not allow him to pinch the pencil at its point. His index finger should not extend beyond the painted portion of the pencil.

b) Show him how to position the paper—slanted so that it aligns with the writing hand. That is, this way for a right hander.

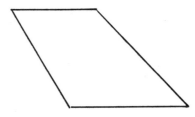

the opposite for a lefty:

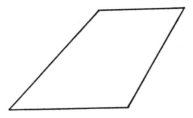

c) Show him how to hold the paper in position by placing his nonwriting hand at the top edge of the paper. If he cannot do this adequately, secure the paper to the desk in its correct position with masking tape.

d) Make certain that he is seated comfortably and properly. The desk top should be below chest level. He should be able to place his feet flat on the floor. A slant-top desk is desirable, but it is not essential.

e) Supply him with primary grade paper—the kind that has a middle line in addition to a top and bottom line.

f) Have him draw letter elements: circles; single vertical lines that extend from bottom line to top line as in *d* or *b*, and from the middle line to below the bottom line as in *p*; and diagonal lines as in the *w*, *m*, and *n*.

Stage II suggestions: Helping the child acquire more acceptable penmanship skills.

This goes beyond a concern for motor control. True, if the child lacks fine motor control, he is not apt to be a good printer. That is why Stage I activities focus on motor skills. But he will need more than fine motor control. He will also have to be sufficiently familiar with forming the letters and arranging them appropriately on a page so that it requires very little conscious thinking from him.

There is only one way to achieve this level. Practice. But practice without direction is foolish, at best. As always, a good teacher shows her skill by making certain that the student pays attention to what is important for him to see and hear. It is not enough to send the child to a chalkboard, show him a letter, and request that he copy it over and over again until he reaches some satisfactory level. That technique might very well work—especially if the child is both motivated and able to identify the important features. But we know too well that the child we are discussing usually lacks both of these attributes.

These activities, by the way, can be combined with teaching the child the letters themselves, as described in the Stage I portion of the section devoted to helping the child become a better reader (see p. 194-201):

- 1. Have the child stand at the chalkboard with his eyes closed or—if you want to and if he enjoys it—blindfold him. Place a piece of chalk in his writing hand, and guide his hand to produce a single letter. Make the letters large

—about six to ten inches high—and move his hand at a rate that approximates the speed at which you yourself print or write. The child's task is to answer the question, "What letter did we make?"

If necessary, describe what your hands (yours and his) are doing as the letter is being printed. In other words, if you are printing an *a*, say as you print, "We are starting at the top and drawing a circle—like this. Then we are adding a short straight line to the right side of the circle —like this." Your goal is to point out whatever it is he should pay attention to when he prints an *a*.

- 2. Include all of the letters—lowercase and capitals—in your activities. Work on one at a time, in random order, and review periodically. When the child is able to recognize the letters easily, start working with two in succession. In other words, you guide his hand in printing *at*, then ask, "What letters did we print?"

This procedure can also be used in conjunction with helping the child improve his spelling. Guide his hand in printing his spelling words. He then reads the word to you while still blindfolded.

You may extend this to include any number of sequenced letters (or, for that matter, numerals). Do not make the task unreasonably difficult. Remember, your foremost goal is to help the child reach the stage where he can execute the letters without having to think very much about what his hand is doing.

- 3. When the child is able to print or write both legibly and relatively rapidly at the chalkboard, then switch to paper and pencil. But do not try to direct his hand under these conditions. Modify the procedure so that he, alone, prints or writes while his eyes are closed. He is to strive for accuracy, neatness, and facility.

When he starts to approximate these goals, move on to Stage III.

Stage III suggestions: Helping the child print or write without conscious thought about what his hand is doing.

For some children, this final stage is difficult to achieve, but it is important if he is to progress satisfactorily in school. How can it be achieved? Once more—practice.

ˢ 1. Have him print or write while talking about something else. Start off simply. Show him a single letter—the *a*, for example—and have him print *a*'s on the chalkboard as he sings a very familiar song. Then, engage him in a simple conversation as he prints a row of a particular letter. Do not make the conversation abstract. Keep it on simple topics—but topics that do require some thinking—such as his favorite baseball team, a pet, a TV show.

As he demonstrates the ability to do both of these activities at the same time, increase the complexity of the copying task. Have him print or write a series of letters, repeatedly, as he converses. Three or four letters in repeated sequence is sufficiently complex (for example, *beta*).

• 2. Copy printed text from an appropriate book; a book that he can read and understand. His goal here is to copy the text both accurately and in a reasonable amount of time. This activity is identical to one described in the section devoted to helping the child improve his reading skills.

• 3. Save and date samples of his paper work. He will improve as you work with him, and comparing before and after samples often can be inspiring.

SUMMARY

In the last four sections, a fair amount of space has been devoted to examining how good learners differ from poor learners in various subject areas. I have focused on skills rather than on information; that is, on what it is the good learners can do that the poor learners cannot do. I have not paid nearly as much attention to how the two groups differ in terms of the factual information one group has acquired that the other has not. This is an important point; one worth explaining.

Obviously the good reader knows more words than the poor reader. It might seem reasonable, therefore, to assume that if you want to help the poor reader, you should set about teaching him all the words that the good reader knows. This same argument could be made about arithmetic and spelling.

Unfortunately, that approach does not work. Indeed, if the poor learner would only learn the information that the good learner has acquired—a large reading vocabulary, all the arithmetic facts—his troubles would be over. But he cannot, and that is why he has slipped so far behind in the first place. He does not have the skills needed to acquire and retain factual information very well because he has no system for reducing the amount of memorizing he has to do. Each new fact is a *totally new fact*, rather than a slight variation of something already learned and memorized.

The suggested activities are designed to help you accomplish two goals. One, to teach the child how to recognize what is common among certain facts—to recognize patterns—and, two, to teach the child how to remember what is uncommon—distinctive—among those same facts. If you achieve those two goals, you will help him enormously.

You will have to work with him daily. Arrange a schedule —five or six days each week; 30 to 40 minutes each day. That is total time, including time spent teaching perceptual skills. Do not get lured into scheduling more time in order to make faster headway. That will do more harm than good. The enterprise will become an overwhelming burden to you both, and will topple of its own weight.

Know that slow, steady progress is the only kind you can achieve—and be happy when you achieve it. Overnight miracle cures just do not occur. He needs more repetitive practice than most children; he needs to take smaller "bites"— steps—than most children; he needs to have important features pointed out—perhaps repeatedly; he needs to become more directly involved with the information—to see and touch; to hear and say—in order to remember and assimilate it. And, of course, he needs to *want to* learn—to be motivated. This last is crucial, basic to everything you have him do.

All children want to achieve—they are neither lazy nor perverse. They, like the rest of us, thrive on approval—from their parents, their peers, their teachers. But it must be honest approval. If they are at all sensitive to the world around them—and be assured that they are—they know when they have earned that approval, and it will motivate them to continue doing whatever earned it for them in the first place.

However, if they do not meet standards—at home, in their social group, in the classroom—they will not earn approval and will then react in one of two ways. They will perhaps try harder, and sometimes this works. Or, more realistically, they will give up and "tune out." They will adopt the attitude of "who cares?" even though they do care. What do we do in similar situations? Think about your own behavior when you are criticized by someone else —particularly someone whose opinion you value. You, too, will often say "who cares?" even though you do care. We all tend to protect ourselves—our feeling of personal worth, sometimes at a high cost. The old saying "Cut off your nose to spite your face" is not out of place here.

To motivate your child, give him successful learning experiences. That is what the organization of the suggested activities attempts to provide. Do it on a regular basis—one that allows him to recognize that though every day in his life will not be a hugely successful one, plenty of them will be. Think of motivation as the child's willingness to risk his reputation. He has to trust you before he will do this—and he has to trust himself. Create conditions so that this can happen.

Your task is not easy. Be prepared to devote a goodly number of hours to it. Be prepared to have discouraging days; days when you will be sure that the whole endeavor is for nothing. But be prepared also for those moments when you see real learning take place! When the child, for the first time in a particular circumstance, really understands what he is supposed to do. When he recognizes that school learning is based on a logical system and not on guessing. And there will be those occasions.

One last topic—the answers to the often-asked question "What if I do nothing . . . will he grow out of it?" That is a good question, but there is no single answer. First, what is *it*? If *it* is simply evidence of delayed maturation and, thus, a set of skills that will shortly be replaced by a more mature set of skills, then the answer is "Yes, he will grow out of it." If, on the other hand, *it* is due to some central problem, perhaps genetically acquired, perhaps the result of a very high fever during his first few years of life, then the answer is "I do not know," nor, so far as I am aware, does anyone else.

But suppose we forget that question for a moment and ask the next one: "Should we forget about special help and just retain him in his present grade in hopes that an additional year in the same grade will solve his problem?" The answer to the first part of the question is, *"Do something now."* Wait-and-see may in fact work, but if it does not, the problem will only be worse. And, ordinarily, the wait-and-see strategy does not work. As to the second part, certainly retain the child in his present grade if promoting him is going to mean increased demands with no other provisions to help him. There is no reason to think that promoting a failing third grader to the fourth grade will have any beneficial effects. But, neither is there any reason to expect him to overcome his problem by spending another year in the third grade.

Neither retention nor promotion is apt to solve his problem. The solution lies in doing something for the child— teaching him better perceptual skills where he lacks them; teaching him better reading, arithmetic, spelling, and writing skills where he lacks those. Basing hopes on a retention in grade is foolhardy. It evades the problem rather than faces it, and unless the problem is faced and dealt with, it will persist. Worse yet, it will grow.

PART III
PREVENTION

UP TO THIS POINT, we have focused our attention on the child who is already failing in school. I have described tests that he can be given, and discussed how to use the information derived from those tests to develop a plan of action—action designed to teach him the skills he needs to perform satisfactorily in school.

All this is useful, but it is far better to prevent the problem from ever occurring in the first place. That may be easier said than done, but there is little doubt that many learning problems can be prevented—and many others kept at a less severe level—if early action is taken. Said another way, there would be far fewer children with learning disabilities if, when they entered first grade, they were able to:

- 1. Analyze relatively complex spatial patterns into their component parts and recognize the way those parts fit together. Specifically, pass at least the first seven items of the TVAS.
- 2. Analyze relatively complex speech patterns into their component parts and recognize the sequence of those parts. Specifically, pass at least the first three items of the TAAS.
- 3. Print all the capital and lowercase letters from dictation.
- 4. Count as many as 10 objects accurately, and record that amount by printing the appropriate numerals.

The child who is able to display these four basic skills when he enters first grade is an extremely unlikely candidate for the label "learning disability." This does not imply that children who are unable to display these skills when they enter first grade will encounter learning problems. Many of them will do well in school, of course, just as most children did not contract polio even before there was a preventive vaccine. But, if prevention is your goal, then why leave his school progress to chance? *Teach your child the four basic skills listed above before he starts first grade.*

How should you go about this? There are two routes. If you have no reason to think that your preschooler is a high-risk child—a child who shows signs of being a learning problem—you may approach the task of teaching him the four basic skills in a casual, unplanned way. This is the way most children are taught much of what they learn before they start their formal schooling. If, on the other hand, you have reason to believe that your child is "high-risk," then your efforts should be more organized and intentional. In either instance, however, you should make the effort to teach him those basic skills.

Characteristics of a high-risk child

Although the high-risk child will display certain behavioral signs, there is no well-defined pattern. Some will display all the following characteristics, others will display only one or two. He may tend to be hyperactive—that is, unable to sit quietly for even short periods of time; distractible; generally awkward in both gross- and fine-motor actions—in walking and running as well as cutting, pasting, drawing, and manipulating an eating utensil. He may display poor speech and language development—that is, an inability to express himself verbally as well as most children his age, and his speech production skills may be less precise than is expected.

Many mothers have expressed it this way: "From the time he was an infant I knew something was wrong, but I

274

could never put my finger on it and no one else agreed with me. He seemed different from my other children, yet I knew he wasn't retarded or anything like that." In most cases, the "something" that was wrong was a set of behavioral characteristics that are more typical of a younger child. This is not easy for a parent to evaluate effectively. In a way, there is nothing really wrong with the child. He just seems to be immature; and even this is not completely consistent. Some days he seems fine; other days, not so fine.

To add to the dilemma, he often appears to be quite bright; to know all he should know. On those occasions, it is easy to say, "Oh well, he'll grow out of it." And indeed he might. But the important concern is whether his development timetable will match the school's—whether he will grow out of it before he enters the world of symbolic representation, the first grade. If he does, then fine. If he does not, there will be trouble; trouble that will mount as the child encounters daily failures and frustrations in the classroom.

What to do about the high-risk child

What should you do if your child shows signs of being high-risk? Insofar as you can, follow the testing plan that is described in the first portion of this book, and reviewed below.

TESTS

Medical

Ask your family physician, or pediatrician, if some health factor could explain the high-risk signs you have noticed, and ask also if the youngster is achieving his developmental milestones on schedule. It is fairly easy to get a reply to the first part of this question. He will be healthy or not, and if he is not, your physician will know what to do. Getting an assessment of his general development is not that easy in some places. Persist. If you cannot get it from your physi-

275

cian, call your County Medical Society or Public Health Agency and find out if there is a clinic operating in your area that can answer your question.

General development

Specifically, you will want to know whether the child's large muscle skills and small muscle skills are emerging as expected. In addition, you will want some opinion about his speech and language development, his social and emotional development, and his intellectual development. All of these can be evaluated and all are important. If they are all emerging as expected, be grateful. If they are not, go into action. Ask for help from whoever did the assessment and, in addition, start to use the activities I will list here.

Vision

Have his eyes examined. Do not settle for a visual screening by someone who is not an optometrist or ophthalmologist. Preschool children are very unreliable reporters, and screenings depend on the reliability of the patient. As I stressed earlier, you should find an eye doctor who will do more than assess the health of the child's eyes and the clarity of his eyesight. Both factors are important, of course, but they do not go far enough. Find someone who will assess visual function—how well the child uses his eyes, coordinates them, shifts and sustains focus. Both optometrists and ophthalmologists can do that, *if they will take the time and trouble.* Impress upon the one you choose that you want him to take the time and trouble, and do not settle for less. If no visual problem is found, be grateful. If a problem is identified, follow the doctor's advice.

Hearing

Then have his hearing tested. And, if there is reason, have someone evaluate his speech. Again, follow the professional's advice.

276

Perceptual skills

Now, how about his perceptual skills? Who should assess these? The visual (TVAS) and auditory (TAAS) tests, described earlier, are not really designed to be used with prekindergarten children and, although I could suggest some other tests for this age group, I hesitate to do so. As already mentioned, very young children are notoriously unreliable test takers—particularly if the tests are administered by nonprofessionals. So, if your child's visual or auditory perceptual skills are to be tested, and if he is younger than five, have a professional do it. Some optometrists and some psychologists test visual perceptual skills. Some speech and hearing people test auditory skills. See if you can find them in your community. If you can, good. If you cannot, then there is still something you can and should do. *Simply assume that the child's perceptual skills are not adequate when you design your plan of action.*

In other words, take nothing for granted—especially these crucial skills. If it turns out that you underestimated them, that his skills are adequate, then you caused no harm. It will soon become apparent what skills he has mastered. That is certainly more desirable than neglecting a deficit that ultimately will cause him to fail in school. In short, it is preferable to be overcautious than to ignore a significant problem. And do not delay. Act early.

Starting school

It is highly likely, in this era, that by the time a child is five years old, he will be enrolled in some kind of school. Many children start school at the age of three. You should choose your child's nursery school carefully, whether he is a high-risk or not. However, if he does show high-risk signs, you should be extra careful in your choice. Some nursery schools do not do well with distractible, inattentive children. They may be excellent schools, but not for him. He will taste failure there; he will lose much and gain nothing. Other nursery schools are just what the doctor ordered.

Their staff will know how to handle the high-risk child, directing his limited attention in productive ways, teaching him skills when they can, and helping him to feel an acceptable member of his group.

Another reason for the rush. Most children enter kindergarten at the age of five, and some—those whose birthdays fall in October, November, December, and in some places even January—at the age of four. The high-risk child should not enter a kindergarten that is part of a school system, unless everyone (you, his teacher, the school principal) agrees *in advance* that he will not start first grade one year later unless he is really ready—no matter how smart or tall or eager he may be; and that he will not be treated as a failure in kindergarten. The high-risk child can profit mightily from proper preprimary experiences. School is a good place for him to be. But it should be a school where he will be able to learn—to acquire skills—and not a school where, once in, he is excluded and classified as a failure.

That is the reason for the rush. If you are to prevent problems, you will have to choose his school wisely; sending him there earlier if they offer what he needs—delaying his entry if they do not.

Judging a preschool

How do you assess a school? That is a difficult question to answer. You visit it, you observe the class that your child would attend, you ask yourself, "Would *my* child do well here? Would this teacher be able to accept his periodic tendency to stop paying attention and start wandering about? Would they punish him, or merely refocus his attention?" And answer these questions *honestly*. Do not delude yourself into thinking that, once the child enters this classroom, he will change—become a young scholar—and everyone will live happily ever after. It might indeed happen, but do not count on it. If you get the strong impression that the class you are observing is tightly controlled and strictly disciplined, watch out. If you get the impression that, in con-

278

trast, the class is a chaotic mass of little bodies bouncing around, once again watch out. What you want for your child is a class where order and rules prevail—but order and rules that are flexible, adaptive to the differences among the children; where children may interact freely, but not disruptively; and where they are praised for positive actions rather than punished for negative ones.

USING THE VISUAL, AUDITORY, AND GENERAL-MOTOR PROGRAMS

If the child's visual and auditory perceptual skills are not satisfactory or if you are merely assuming that they are *not*, start using the visual, auditory, and general-motor programs described in the earlier sections. Do not concern yourself with placement tests. Just start the child with the easiest activities in each of the programs and work up to the more difficult ones as he shows progress. In other words, start him in the visual program with teaching pattern number 1 and a 5-pin geoboard (see p. 113); in the auditory program with clapping in time to spoken words (see p. 137); and in the general-motor program with activities designed to teach him how to balance, hop, skip, and use his hands, eyes, and speech production mechanisms more precisely (see page 172).

In addition, teach him how to count aloud from 1 to 10 and how to count from 1 to 10 objects and record that quantity with numerals. Teach him the letters of the alphabet. (See the reading and arithmetic suggested activities, pp. 194-197). Set up a five-day-a-week schedule and stick to it.

But do more than that. Take advantage of the fact that he is not yet in school where he is expected to learn to read, write, calculate, and spell. You can devote all your energy to teaching him basic skills rather than helping him with his homework. The pages that follow contain a variety of additional activities, appropriate for preschoolers, and organized according to whether they are pertinent to visual, auditory, or general-motor skills. They all have one characteristic in common—they are intended to make the child conscious of relevant details and the interrelationships of those details. In the section headed Visual Perceptual Skills, the details are embedded in various visual patterns. In the Auditory Perceptual Skills section, the details are acoustical. And, in the General-motor Skills portion, the details pertain to certain precise motor actions.

In most instances, the categories are not clear-cut; many visual perceptual skills procedures also involve motor actions. So, too, do many of the auditory skills procedures. That is not important and, in fact, if you think of a way to broaden a specific procedure—a visual task, for example, to also include an auditory component—all the better. You are not, after all, managing a research study. You are teaching your child a variety of skills to aid him in sorting out and organizing information—information that, in one way or another, he will be expected to learn how to represent with codes, letters, and numerals, when he enters school. The more sensitive he is to these details (within reason, of course), the more readily he will grasp the concepts of the codes. The more readily he does this, the more capable he will be at extracting information from the codes. Hence, the better a learner he will be.

It might be worth mentioning that, although these activities are designed for preschool children, they may also be used with older children, if they appear to offer some reasonable challenge. The order in which they are listed does not imply levels of difficulty. They vary and, in fact, any activity may be made simpler by reducing the amount of details involved, or more difficult by adding more details and demands.

How good is good enough?

One more point. How long should you use these activities —how much instruction should the child have? *He should receive regular instruction at least until he is able to display the four sets of basic skills listed at the beginning of this section.* When he can, you may stop teaching him if you and he wish. However, it will not harm him to go beyond that point, to acquire perceptual skills that are a little better than average so long as it is kept within reason.

So, unless teaching him creates an undesirable situation for either of you, continue to teach him beyond the very basic level. Obviously, once he reaches this point you may want to approach the task less formally and eliminate the schedule. That is all right. In fact, you will notice that your child will more and more *teach himself* as he engages in activities where he employs the basic skills you taught him; as he starts to use construction toys on his own, as he starts to use words with more facility, as he starts to see and hear details that he did not see or hear before.

ACTIVITIES TO TEACH VISUAL PERCEPTUAL SKILLS TO PRESCHOOL CHILDREN

• 1. Sorting tasks. There is a vast array of materials that may be used for this activity. Whatever you use, have the child organize the materials according to a characteristic that you identify. Have him do the following:

a) Sort buttons according to size. In every household there usually is a box full of buttons. Have the child sort these into containers—a specific size in a specific container.

b) Sort buttons according to color.

c) Sort buttons according to color *and* size. If you have enough buttons, this adds an extra dimension. Thus, one container will hold all the black buttons of a certain size, for example, and another container all the white buttons of the same size. This is a good place to teach the concept that things can be the same one way, yet different another way. Proceed with care. This can be a confusing concept. Do not stress it. Simply point it out periodically. He will catch on in time.

d) Sort playing cards according to suit, or according to numerical designation, or both.

e) Sort screws, nails, nuts, bolts, washers, and other hardware items according to size.

f) Sort paint chips (cards showing various colors; these are usually obtainable from a paint store) according to color. Homemade chips can be made with crayons.

g) Sort food cans according to size or according to the pictures on the labels.

h) Sort samples of fabric according to texture; for example, all smooth fabrics in one pile, all rough fabrics in another.

i) Sort shapes. You will probably have to prepare this yourself, but it is quite easy. Cut paper into a variety of shapes—circles, squares, and triangles—and have the child sort these according to shape, size, color. Add more shapes when he appears to be ready for more complex tasks. (You may also have him cut out the shapes himself.)

j) Sort silverware according to size, or function, or both.

k) Sort books according to size or color of cover.

l) Sort strands of yarn according to color, or length, or both.

m) Sort photographs of people according to their sex, their family relationships, or their ages.

n) Sort cards showing capital letters. You may have to make these yourself, but it is easy to do. All you need is a pencil and some paper. Cut the paper (or have the child do it) into playing-card size and print a capital letter on each. Start off with only two or three different letters and add to the assortment as he shows competency. For example, "Put all the A's in one pile, all the B's in another."

o) Sort bottles according to weight. Purchase a number of medicine bottles from your local drug store and wrap adhesive tape around them so that the contents cannot be seen, or use empty tin cans or soft drink bottles. Then pour sand (or salt, or sugar, or dried beans) into each container, so that even though they are equal in size, some are of one weight and others are either lighter or heavier.

This list could be extended, but I think you must have the idea by now. Any task is useful if it involves sorting objects that are similar in one way and vary in another—and if the child can figure it out.

- 2. Matching tasks. In all these activities, you construct a pattern and the child constructs one just like it, positioning his alongside yours. If he encounters difficulty matching your pattern, have him place his *on top* of yours rather than alongside. To add further interest, and to foster better visual memory, play "Flash" with him. To do this, hide your pattern from the child's view with a sheet of cardboard. Tell him to get ready, then flash your pattern for a brief period (count to 10, or 5, or 1, or whatever works), then cover it again. The child is to match your pattern from memory. Start with simple patterns. Increase their complexity as he displays the ability to deal with them.

a) Match playing cards. Line up 1, 2, or more playing cards and have the child match your pattern. (These need not be "lined up"; they can be arranged as a triangle, or what-have-you, so long as the child can manage the task.)

b) Match silverware. Line up a spoon, a fork, and knife, and have the child match your pattern.

c) Match a button pattern.

d) Match a color pattern, using crayons or other colored articles.

e) Match a hardware pattern made up of screws, bolts, nuts, washers, and so on.

f) Match letters. Construct your pattern with cards on which letters have been printed. Give similar cards to the child and have him match the pattern.

g) Match shapes. Parquetry blocks are particularly useful here. You can purchase these in most toy and variety stores. They include three basic shapes (square, triangle, diamond). Arrange them in patterns and have the child match the patterns. Caution: Do not use complex patterns until the child shows that he can match simple ones.

h) Match glassware. Drinking glasses of different shapes and sizes.

i) Match pipe-cleaner patterns.

j) Match toothpick patterns.

As you undoubtedly see by now, virtually any material can be used for this activity. Simply construct a pattern and have the child copy it. You can vary this by switching roles; have the child construct the pattern and you match it. He, of course, must then check your work for accuracy. Make an occasional error. He will enjoy finding them, and looking for them will sharpen his skills.

• 3. Organizing tasks. In these activities, the child is given materials and asked to organize them according to some attribute. Show him how; give him a model to follow. Then, in time, withdraw your model and encourage him to figure it out for himself. For example, have him:

a) Organize buttons according to size. Give the child a number of buttons, one of each size. He is to arrange them in a row, from smallest to largest. If necessary, start out with only three buttons and add to the task as he grasps the concept.

b) Organize playing cards according to their numerical designation. That is, arrange them in a line from the ace to the ten.

c) Organize bolts, screws, washers, or other hardware items according to size—from smallest to largest.

d) Organize shoes according to size. For example, Dad's, Mom's, big sister's, baby's.

e) Organize shapes according to size—squares, circles, triangles, and others.

f) Organize colors according to hue, for example, from light blue to dark blue.

g) Organize pictures according to time sequence. Show the child three pictures that are sequentially related; for example, drawings from a comic strip that shows (1) the sunrise and a rooster crowing; (2) a child awakening; (3) a child playing. Then have him arrange them in a logical sequence. (Other examples: pictures of articles of clothing to be arranged in the order in which he puts them on when getting dressed, or the order in which he removes them when getting undressed; pictures of food items—appetizers, main course items, desserts—and have him arrange them according to the sequence in which they are customarily eaten.)

h) Organize wood blocks according to thickness, ranging from thin to thick, like a staircase.

i) Measure objects, rooms, or people, and organize them according to size. He can measure with a ruler, a length of rope, a footstep.

Again it is apparent that the number of activities involving the organizing of information is virtually unlimited. The general skill you are trying to foster here is the ability to order information.

- 4. Classification tasks. This is an extension of what has already been described above. In these activities, the child is shown a picture and asked to classify it. For example, have him:

a) Classify food. Show him pictures cut out of magazines and have him classify them according to whether they are:

(1) good tasting or bad tasting.

(2) breakfast food or dinner food.

(3) eaten hot or cold.

(4) appetizer, main course, or dessert.

(5) cooked or eaten raw.

b) Classify household objects. Use pictures or real objects and have him classify them according to whether they are:

(1) hard to move or easy to move; heavy or light.

(2) for sitting on or lying on.

(3) living room pieces, bedroom pieces, or kitchen pieces.

(4) constructed of metal, wood, or plastic.

(5) rough or smooth in texture.

c) Classify clothing. Show him pictures and have him classify them according to whether they are:

(1) for boys or girls.

(2) for winter or summer wear.

(3) rough or smooth.

(4) heavy or light.

(5) worn above the waist or below the waist.

d) Classify sports equipment. Show him pictures and have him classify them according to whether they are

(1) used indoors, or outdoors, or both.

(2) used in summer or winter.

(3) heavy or light.

(4) thrown, kicked, or batted in some way (for example, a golf ball, a tennis ball, a football).

• 5. Find hidden shapes. Here the child is to learn the concept that large patterns contain collections of identifiable smaller patterns. For example, have him:

a) Find all the hidden circles. Show him pictures of automobiles, household objects, and other things, and have him "find all of the hidden circles"—for example, the *wheels* of an automobile; the *bottom* of a pot. You need not use pictures; real objects will do. Also, this may be extended to hidden squares, triangles, and so on.

b) Find all the hidden numerals in a room—in calendars, clock dials, radio and television dials.

c) Find all the hidden flowers in the house—in carpet and towel designs, hanging paintings, kitchenware.

d) Find the hidden letters—on bookcovers, newspapers, mailboxes, street signs, billboards. (This procedure can be modified to focus the child on specific letters—for example, "Find all the *A*'s you can," or "Find the letters of your name."

- 6. Painting, drawing, and other graphic tasks. The purpose here is to give the child the opportunity to see and reproduce details—and have some fun doing it. This should range from coloring books and follow-the-dots, to weaving and finger painting. As I mentioned earlier, do not be afraid to use coloring books. I do not think it will limit his artistic development. Every creative artist worthy of the designation *artist* knows his craft and the potentials of his media. He knows these things as a result of disciplined training or disciplined self-instruction. Coloring books will not make your child into an artist, but neither will they prevent him from being one.
- 7. Block play and other construction activities. There are a great variety of construction toys on the market. They are all useful, so long as they do not impose unreasonable demands on the child. Start with simple ones; then progress to the more complex ones as he shows that he is able. You need not be limited to commercial toys. Popsicle or paste sticks and straws are all good construction materials that can be glued together. For that matter, so is construction paper that may be cut into various shapes and assembled into a number of designs.

ACTIVITIES TO TEACH AUDITORY PERCEPTUAL SKILLS TO PRESCHOOL CHILDREN

- 1. Matching tasks.
    a) Fill a number of empty tin cans about halfway with various food articles—salt or sand, dried beans and dried cereals. Cover each can with a foil lid so that the contents are not visible. Prepare at least two cans identically. The child is then to sort the cans according to the sounds they produce when shaken.
    b) Tapping patterns. You tap a pattern with your hand on a table. The child is to match the pattern. Start with a simple tap-tap-tap and work into more complex patterns as the child shows progress.

c) Sound effects. You attempt to reproduce the sounds made by an airplane, a carpet sweeper, automobile, railroad train, cat, dog, lion, and so forth. The child tries to copy you.

d) Musical tones. Fill three drinking glasses or soft drink bottles with unequal amounts of water—one almost to its rim; the second about halfway; the third with very little. Each will emit a different tone when tapped with a wooden rod. You tap a tone pattern (high, low, middle); the child then attempts to reproduce your pattern. Start off with simple patterns. Introduce more difficult ones as he shows that he can deal with them. (At first, have him watch you. Then he is to listen only while looking in another direction.)

This can be varied to include loud and quiet tones as well as long and short tones.

- 2. Classifying tasks.

a) Classify nonverbal sounds. Produce sounds for him (either taped sounds or ones that you imitate) and ask him to classify the sounds according to whether they are:

(1) animal or mechanical
(2) loud or quiet
(3) friendly or unfriendly animals

b) Classify spoken words. Name objects and have him classify them according to whether they are:

(1) long words or short words—*astronaut* versus *cat*
(2) long sentences or short sentences

- 3. Talking and listening. The most effective way to teach a child auditory perceptual skills is to foster his language development. Read to him. Talk to him. Teach him new words. If he engages in some of the visual tasks just described—sorting, say—teach him synonyms. Hence, he should not only be sorting "big" and "little" objects, but "huge" ones, and "tremendous" ones, and "tiny" ones, and "long" ones, and "wide" ones, and so forth. The more words he knows, the more likely it is that he will recognize that spoken words are constructed of spoken

288

sounds. Encourage him to speak clearly as well as intelligently. Have him pronounce *all* of the sounds in words; including word endings. Help him avoid confusing the sequence of sounds in words (*pizzhetti* for *spaghetti*). Give him a chance to speak. Help him organize his thoughts, but do not yield to the temptation of "helping" him by saying it for him. And inform his brothers and sisters that they, too, must give him a chance to speak for himself.

ACTIVITIES TO TEACH GENERAL-MOTOR SKILLS TO PRESCHOOL CHILDREN

In addition to the activities already described, the following are appropriate:

- 1. Imitation. This, in effect, is a matching task where the child is asked to imitate a pose. Assume various postures and ask the child to "Do what I am doing" or "Stand the way I am standing."
  - a) Stand on one foot.
  - b) Kneel on hands and knees.
  - c) Show index finger on one hand.
  - d) Place one hand on head, the other on chest.
- 2. Identify body parts. Ask the child to point to his: eyes, ears, nose, mouth, shoulders, elbows, wrists, knees, hips, and toes. Then ask him to name those parts as you touch them.
- 3. Ask him to look surprised, shocked, frightened, sad, happy, tired. The child is to assume a pose that reflects the word.
- 4. Construct clay people showing their eyes, shoulders, arms, and various other major body parts.
- 5. Draw faces, showing eyes, ears, nose, lips, and other details.
- 6. Have him engage in some movement activity; then instruct him to "freeze"—stop all movement—in whatever

position he may be when he hears (or sees) a signal such as a bell, a clap, the interruption of a musical record, or a light.

- 7. Walk with an object (book) balanced on his head.
- 8. Walk, or run, with a small object (a button, a wooden bead) cradled in a spoon held in his hand.
- 9. Sit or stand in various postures and sway to music without losing balance.
- 10. Stretch and reach. Child stands or sits in a designated position and attempts to reach and grasp objects located about him, without losing his balance.
- 11. Leaning tower. Child leans as far as possible in a designated direction (forward, backward, to the left, the right) without losing balance.
- 12. Speak with teeth clenched. Have him start off by saying his own name, the names of friends, relations, and so on. His goal is to speak clearly enough to be understood.
- 13. Lipreading. Have him move his lips in a way that enables others to read them. Can you recognize whose name he has articulated? What numeral he said, and so on? Then change roles.
- 14. Untie simple knots. Make certain that the knots have not been pulled too securely. Start with heavy string.
- 15. Tie simple knots. Start with heavy string or rope.

What about the child who is not high-risk?

That is a very good question and, in answering it, I will try to summarize my attitudes and ideas about manipulating children and their environments.

First of all, the simplest way to answer the question is to say, "Do nothing. Let natural circumstances govern the child's development—his day-to-day experiences will foster the acquisition of the basic skills he will need in school. He will be fine." That is not a bad answer. In most instances it is a correct one. Hundreds of thousands of children enter first grade without any special preschool preparation and learn to read, calculate, spell, and write without much difficulty. Would they have progressed faster and learned more if they had entered school with the basic skills well established? The truth is, we do not know. But it certainly is not unreasonable to argue that this indeed would have been the case. It is only logical to suggest that if the child arrives in first grade already familiar with the coding symbols—and the elements that are to be coded—he will learn better and faster.

"Well," the argument can proceed, "that is what his first-grade teacher is supposed to teach him, isn't it?" And that is correct. However, that first-grade teacher may have to deal with as many as thirty children, and they will differ. Some children will be better prepared—better learners. Some teachers prefer to teach this kind of child, and do not work well with the opposite extreme.

Even if they do not particularly favor the one type of child, the teacher's time is limited. The principal of the school expects all the children to be at certain places in their various books by the end of the year, knowing full well that some will not be there. Those who are not, are seen as slow; some are even labeled failures. Have they failed? No, the school failed them by not making certain that they had achieved the basic skills before imposing more complex and more abstract demands upon them. We do not try to build buildings without foundations—we know they will topple. Yet, we do try to do this in school—teach elaborate skills to children who lack fundamental skills. They will surely topple. The architect who designs a building improperly, and the builder who constructs it, are seen as failures. In most schools, it is the child who fails! Unjustifiable, but true!

Until schools become responsive to the individual differences of their students and are prepared to offer truly individualized education, I strongly recommend that parents teach their children the basic skills before they enter the first grade, even if they do not seem to be high-risk. Yes, the children may do very well without this extra effort, but even then, what is wrong with giving them a little bit of a head start?

291

And that brings me to the final section—some tempering remarks, and perhaps even a warning that too much of a head start may not be such a good thing.

Guide him, teach him, but do not shove him

This book has focused on one aspect of a child's development—the cognitive; how to test and teach some of the skills that underlie a child's ability to code and ultimately to communicate abstract information with symbols. We all know, however, that children develop along more than a cognitive dimension; that they also grow and develop physically and emotionally. We know also that though we label and describe these three aspects of development separately, —physical, cognitive, and emotional—they are inseparable. Affecting one will surely have effects on the other two.

The close ties between cognitive and physical development are apparent in this book. Consider how much stress I placed on the fact that the child's ability to analyze and organize visual and acoustical information will be enhanced if he also explores it physically with his hands; with his speech production mechanism.

What has not been acknowledged, and must be now, is the close relationship between these two aspects of development—physical and cognitive—and the third—emotional.

I make no pretense at extensive knowledge in this field, but one does not have to be a professional anything—except, perhaps, a human being—to recognize that unless a child's emotional development keeps pace with his physical and cognitive development, certain difficulties are likely to arise. In a sense, these areas of development are like three pillars that support a structure. If they are all intact, and equally and adequately developed, they form a sturdy base. Weaken or distort one, and the total supportive power of the three is affected. As the structure they bear becomes weightier, as demands on the pillars increase, the other two, initially intact, must assume some of the burden not carried by the third. As a result, they too are weakened or distorted.

I do not want to belabor the illustration, but the point is important. Do not stimulate growth along one dimension of development at the expense of the other two. Thus, while I have just finished urging all parents to teach their children certain skills, I am at the same time urging them not to honor cognitive development to the extent that the child is placed in situations that he cannot cope with physically and emotionally.

We have all seen children who, for some reason or another, displayed an early facility with language, or numbers, or both. Their exceptional abilities earned them special attention, and probably motivated them to practice and expand that ability even further. This is fine, unless it resulted in their being placed in a classroom with children who were older, more socially mature, more physically adept than they—albeit no "smarter."

Such situations impose stress on children, stress that may very well have negative effects on their total development. Life is more than doing well in school. The child is entitled to fulfill his developmental potential along all three dimensions—physical and emotional as well as cognitive.

The point, then, is simple. Yes, teach him the basic skills he will need to know. Yes, encourage him to be aware of details, to be able to sort them, and organize them, and classify them in a variety of ways. Yes, stimulate his interest in learning. But remember, he is a total child—not a walking brain—and provide him with the conditions he needs to fulfill all of his potentials. Do not stimulate one aspect of his development to the exclusion of the others—to the point where he finds himself in situations that are beyond him.

CONCLUSION

CHILDREN VARY in how well they do in school. Some do very well; some do poorly. Some do well in certain subjects only, and not so well in others. They vary for many reasons, one being their ability to learn under standard school conditions.

Some children are above-average learners. They require relatively little direct instruction. Given adequate conditions, they can figure out a great deal on their own. Some children are below-average learners. They require a great deal of direct, explicit instruction.

Schools best serve the average learner. The above-average learner is served fairly well, especially if he is provided with interesting and instructive materials. The below-average learner—whatever the cause of his problem—is served poorly. Group instruction imposes overwhelming demands on him. He quickly falls behind and remains there. And no one is upset, except the child himself, and his parents. (The idea of rating children on a curve is firmly established; the term *average* requires that there be children both above and below that mid-range level.) He becomes more and more accustomed to being excluded—not physically perhaps, but certainly intellectually. In time, he stops trying.

According to official records, he has failed. The major theme of this book has been that *he* did not fail. The schools failed; the system failed because it did not accommodate his needs.

The time has come for schools to be more responsive to the individual learning needs of *all* its students—not by lowering standards for the slower ones but, rather, by finding more effective ways to teach all of them, and providing the resources that will accomplish the job.

Fortunately, many educational researchers are now working on this problem. Although there remains much to be done, there is little doubt that we are closer than ever before to being able to specify the design and operations of an adaptive educational environment—a school that is responsive to the individual differences of its students.

This book is meant to serve as a source of aid for those children who need adaptive conditions *now*; who do not have time to wait for the researchers to accomplish their mission. I hope it serves its purpose.

APPENDIX
Visual-motor patterns

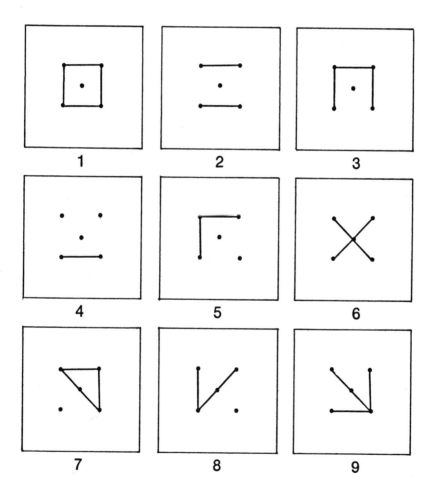

1 2 3

4 5 6

7 8 9

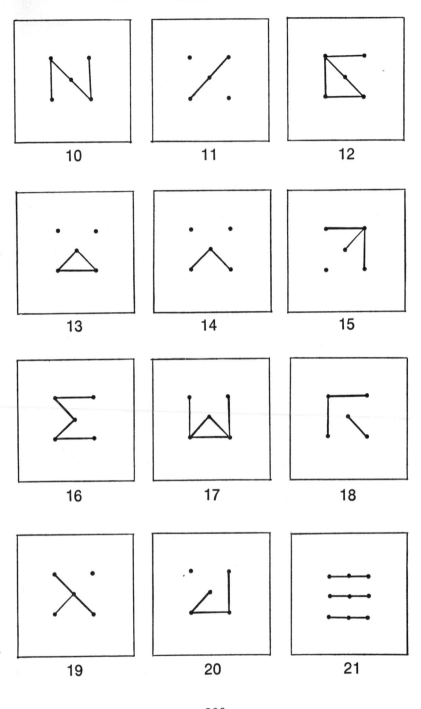

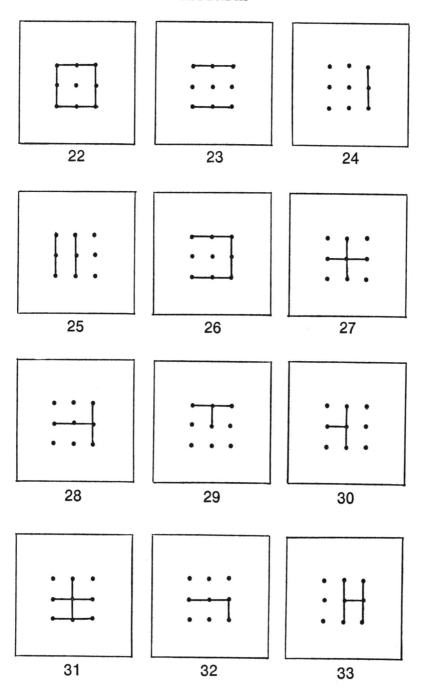

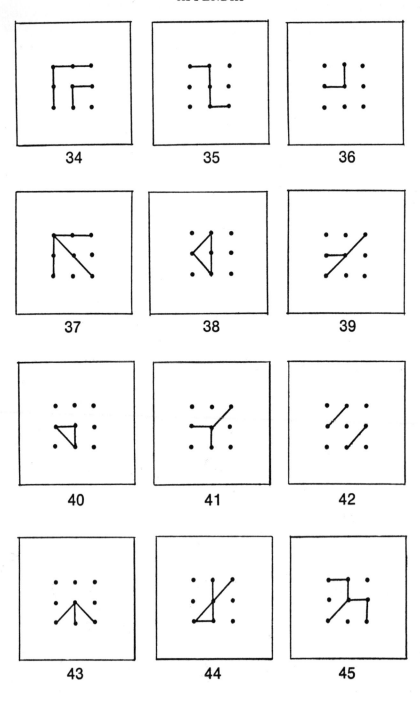

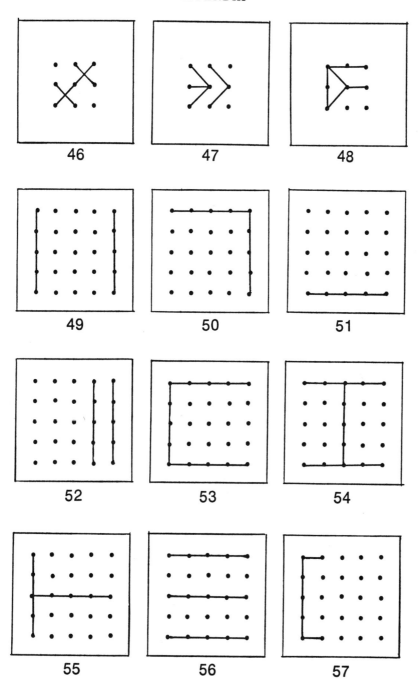

46

47

48

49

50

51

52

53

54

55

56

57

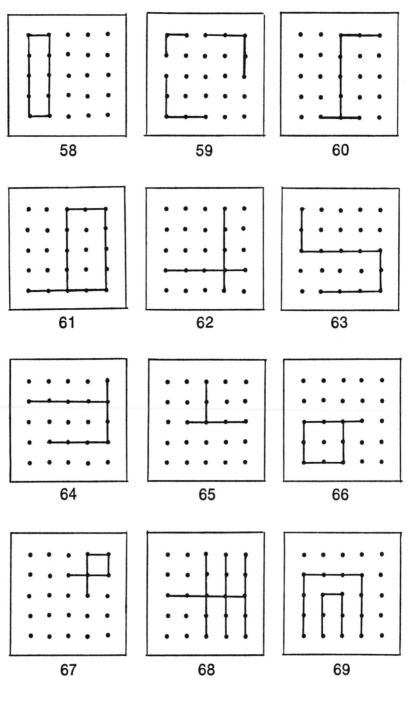

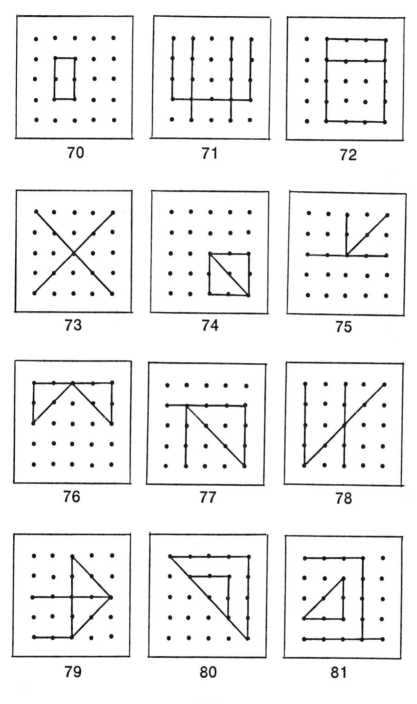

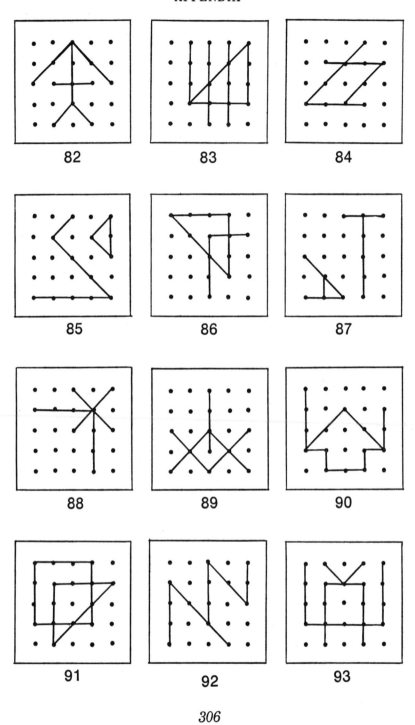

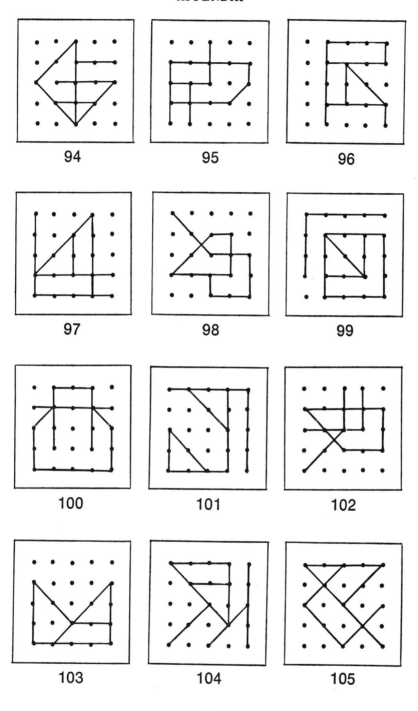

94

95

96

97

98

99

100

101

102

103

104

105

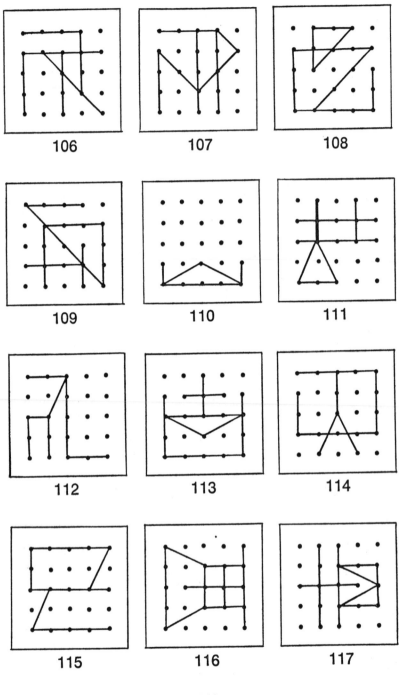

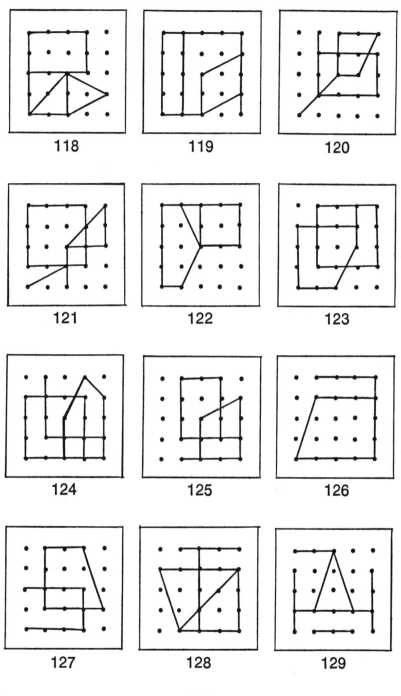

118 119 120

121 122 123

124 125 126

127 128 129

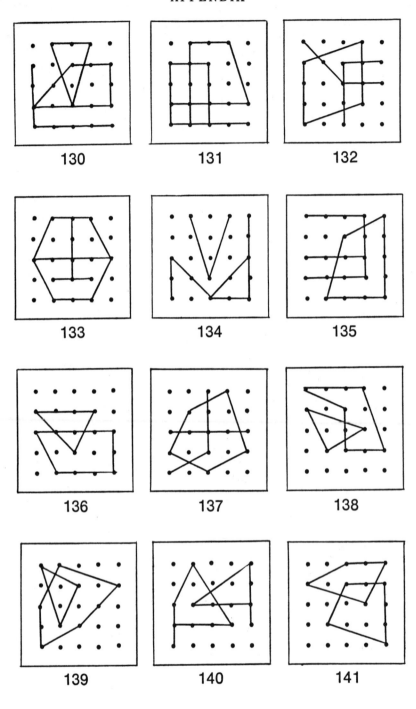

130

131

132

133

134

135

136

137

138

139

140

141

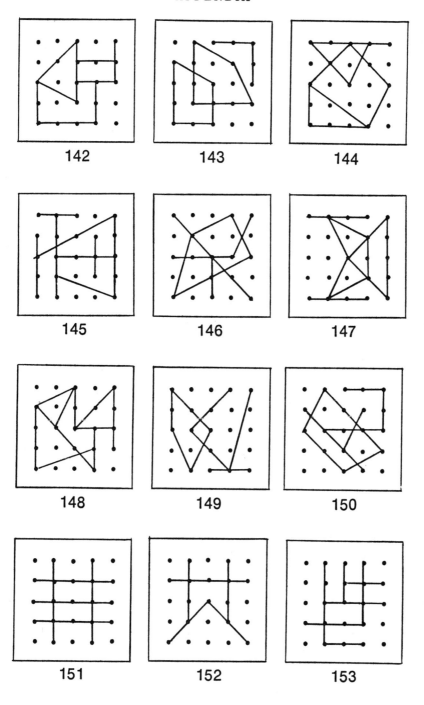

142

143

144

145

146

147

148

149

150

151

152

153

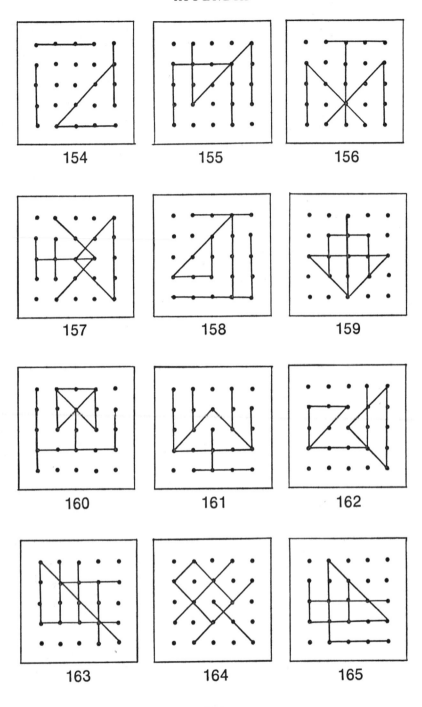

154   155   156

157   158   159

160   161   162

163   164   165

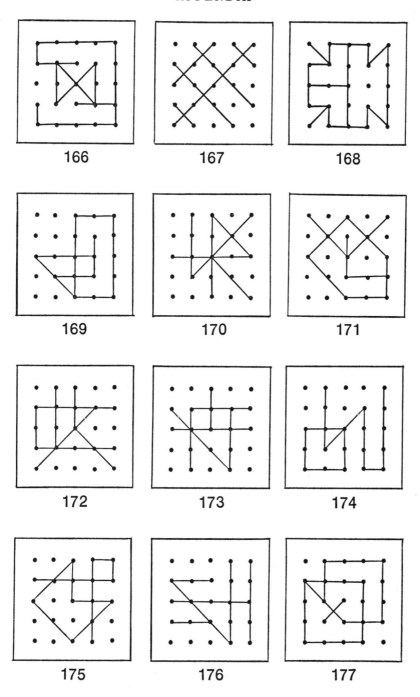

166   167   168

169   170   171

172   173   174

175   176   177

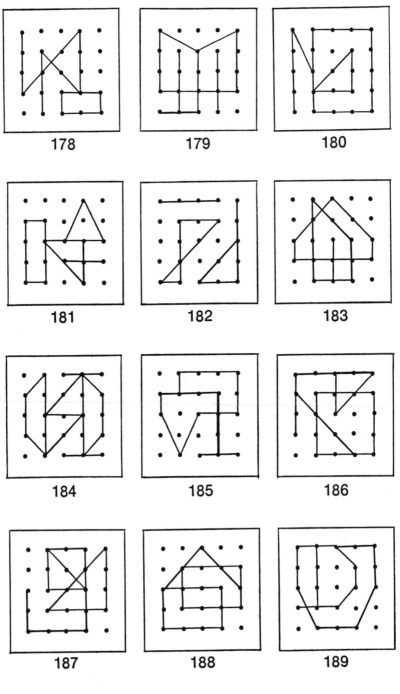

178   179   180

181   182   183

184   185   186

187   188   189

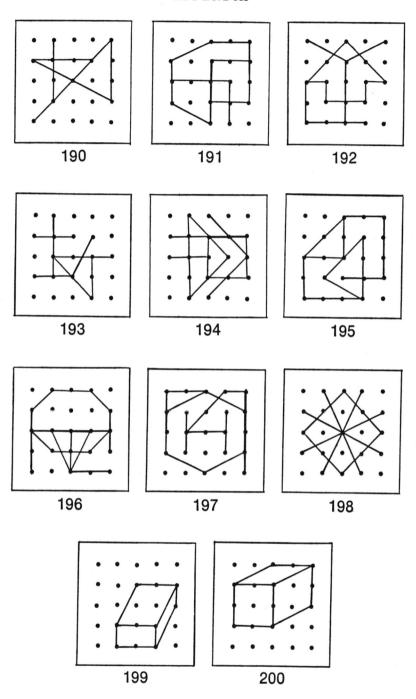

190

191

192

193

194

195

196

197

198

199

200

INDEX